The Origins of the Syrian Conflict

T0373856

Does climate change cause conflict? Did it cause the Syrian uprising? Some policy-makers and academics have made this claim, but is it true? This study presents a new conceptual framework to evaluate this claim. Contributing to scholarship in the fields of critical security, environmental security, human security, and Arab politics, Marwa Daoudy prioritizes non-Western and marginalized perspectives to make sense of Syria's place in this international debate. Designing an innovative multidisciplinary framework and applying it to the Syrian case, Daoudy uses extensive field research and her own personal background as a Syrian scholar to present primary interviews with Syrian government officials and citizens as well as the research of domestic Syrian experts to provide a unique insight into Syria's environmental, economic, and social vulnerabilities leading up to the 2011 uprising.

MARWA DAOUDY is Assistant Professor in the Center for Contemporary Arab Studies at Georgetown University. The co-organizer of a major climate-change conference at Princeton University, she has been a policy adviser and consultant for government agencies including the UNESCO World Water Assessment Program, and she has contributed to the establishment of the Oxford Water Network, a research-led project that focuses on improving water security across the globe. She is the author of *The Water Divide between Syria, Turkey and Iraq: Negotiation, Security and Power Asymmetry* (2005) which was awarded the Ernest Lémonon prize by the Académie Française.

The Origins of the Syrian Conflict

Climate Change and Human Security

MARWA DAOUDY
Georgetown University

CAMBRIDGE
UNIVERSITY PRESS

CAMBRIDGE
UNIVERSITY PRESS

University Printing House, Cambridge CB2 8BS, United Kingdom

One Liberty Plaza, 20th Floor, New York, NY 10006, USA

477 Williamstown Road, Port Melbourne, VIC 3207, Australia

314–321, 3rd Floor, Plot 3, Splendor Forum, Jasola District Centre,
New Delhi – 110025, India

79 Anson Road, #06–04/06, Singapore 079906

Cambridge University Press is part of the University of Cambridge.

It furthers the University's mission by disseminating knowledge in the pursuit of
education, learning, and research at the highest international levels of excellence.

www.cambridge.org
Information on this title: www.cambridge.org/9781108476089
DOI: 10.1017/9781108567053

First published 2020

A catalogue record for this publication is available from the British Library.

Library of Congress Cataloging-in-Publication Data
Names: Daoudy, Marwa, author.
Title: The origins of the Syrian conflict : climate change and human security / Marwa Daoudy.
Description: Cambridge, United Kingdom ; New York, NY : Cambridge University Press,
   2020. | Includes bibliographical references and index.
Identifiers: LCCN 2019043960 (print) | LCCN 2019043961 (ebook) |
   ISBN 9781108476089 (hardback) | ISBN 9781108466820 (paperback) |
   ISBN 9781108567053 (epub)
Subjects: LCSH: Water security–Syria. | Water-supply–Political aspects–Syria. |
   Food security–Political aspects–Syria. | Climatic changes–Syria. | Human security–Syria. |
   Syria–Environmental conditions. | Syria–History–Civil War, 2011--Environmental aspects.
Classification: LCC GE160.S95 D36 2020 (print) | LCC GE160.S95 (ebook) |
   DDC 956.9104/231–dc23
LC record available at https://lccn.loc.gov/2019043960
LC ebook record available at https://lccn.loc.gov/2019043961

ISBN 978-1-108-47608-9 Hardback
ISBN 978-1-108-46682-0 Paperback

Contents

List of Figures   *page* vii

List of Tables   ix

Acknowledgements and Preface   x

Part I   The Context: History, Geography, Security   1

1 Climate Change and the Syrian Revolution   3
    From Climate Change to Climate Security   5
    From Global Climate Security to the Arab Spring and the Syrian
    Revolution   8
    The Book's Approach   12
    Shifting the Paradigm: Human–Environmental–Climate Security   15
    Methodology   21
    Summary   23

2 The Many Faces of Environmental Security   24
    Reexamining and Broadening the Security Agenda   24
    From Traditional to Nontraditional Security: Security Narratives
    and Performance   26
    Securitization and the Politics of Fear   29
    Critical Environmental Security: Water Security, Food Security,
    and Drought   41
    Human Security: An Emerging Framework for the Environment   49
    Interconnectedness in a Globalized World: A Climate,
    Food Insecurity, and Migration Nexus?   56
    Summary   76

3 When Geography Rules History   77
    Water in Middle Eastern History   77
    Syria's International Interactions over the Euphrates and
    Tigris Rivers (1980–2011)   89
    Summary   98

Part II   Human–Environmental–Climate Security (HECS)   101

4   Rules of Ideology and Policy: From Ba'athism to the
    Liberal Age   103
    Of People, Land, Water, and Food   103
    Ideology in Syria: Definitions and Implementation   107
    Ideology and Policy under Ba'athism: A "Green Uprising"   112
    The Securitization of Food Production: Narratives and Practices 117
    Tools and Dilemmas of Food Security: "Strategic" Crops, Intensive
    Irrigation, Dams with Institutional, Environmental, and Social
    Problems   120
    An Arab Encirclement: The Agrarian Revolution and Syrian
    Kurds under Ba'athism   135
    The Move to Decollectivization and Liberalization   138
    Summary   148

5   Vulnerability and Resilience: Human–Environmental–
    Climate Security in Syria   150
    The International Debate   152
    Environmental Vulnerability: Drought, Temperature,
    Precipitation, and Surface and Groundwater Quality and Quantity 162
    Economic Vulnerability: Agricultural Production,
    Food Prices, Poverty, Unemployment, and Urban–Rural Divides   174
    Social Vulnerability: Internal Migration, Mismanagement
    of Drought, and Corruption   197
    Summary   202

6   Syria: A (Hi)story of Vulnerability, Resistance, and
    Resilience   205

References   213
Index   246

Figures

1.1 Syria's Jazira/Hassake Governorate   *page* 13
1.2 The HECS framework   16
1.3 Applying the HECS framework to Syria: vulnerability
    and resilience   20
2.1 The Malthusian model   34
2.2 The neo-Malthusian model   35
2.3 Population predictions   41
2.4 Water crowding indicator   44
3.1 The rise of agriculture and water legislation worldwide
    and in Syria and the Middle East   78
3.2 Phase 1 of Syria and Turkey's water interactions
    (1980–1998)   92
3.3 Phase 2 of Syria and Turkey's water interactions
    (2002–2011)   94
4.1 Timeline of critical domestic policy decisions:
    agriculture, water, and land (1958–2011)   105
4.2 Water projects in Syria   122
4.3 Number of wells (country level)   124
4.4 Irrigated area from wells (country level)   124
4.5 Areas of Syria inhabited by Syrian Kurds   136
5.1 Temperatures (annual average)   163
5.2 Rainfall (annual)   166
5.3 Regional variations: variation of SPI in selected Syrian
    stations   168
5.4 Total wheat production (country level)   178
5.5 Rain-fed and irrigated wheat production in Syria
    (1997–2008)   179
5.6 Peaks in price of soft wheat   184
5.7 Per-capita food-price variability   185
5.8 Value added from agriculture   187

5.9 Employment in agriculture as a percentage of total
employment (country level) 190
5.10 Regional agricultural employment 193
5.11 Regional percentage of employment from
agriculture 193
5.12 Population by rural and urban areas 196
5.13 Corruption index 202

Tables

3.1 Mutual threat perceptions in Syria and Turkey's
    relations (1980–2015)   *page* 92
4.1 Main dams on the Euphrates river   128
4.2 Irrigation networks and surfaces in Euphrates
    Basin (2000)   130
4.3 Delays in irrigation plans on the Euphrates   131
5.1 SPI calculator   167
5.2 Sectoral water allocations (1995–1998)   170
5.3 Sectoral water allocations (2000)   171
5.4 Water resources in Syria (1995–1999)   172
5.5 Available water sources (2000–2005)   173
5.6 Extension of wells in Khabour Basin   174
5.7 Licensed and unlicensed wells in Syria's
    Northeast   175
5.8 Wheat production in Deir ez-Zor and Hassake
    compared to country levels (2007–2011)   183
5.9 Share of agriculture to GDP by percentage   186

Acknowledgements and Preface

The origins of this book date back to the great revolts of 2011 when Syrians from all backgrounds confronted their deepest fears and peacefully demonstrated their dignity in the face of unprecedented adversity. The project took shape when hope was met with arms, betrayal, and chaos. The government's militarized response to the peaceful uprisings propelled Syria's tragic descent into one of the bloodiest conflicts of the early twenty-first century. The "impossible revolution" dreamed by one of Syria's most reputable writers and dissidents, Yassin al Haj-Saleh (2017), is now "orphaned" in the words of Syrian novelist Khaled Khalifa. His latest novel *Death Is Hard Work* (2019) depicts the surreal challenges facing those determined to continue honoring their deceased loved ones in the midst of chaos and indifference. "The only victor in Syria," writes Samar Yazbek, "is death" (2015: 11). In *The Crossing*, she describes her brave, secret, trip back home to Syria during the war. Her book is dedicated to the martyrs of the revolution, betrayed and dead. Banished from her Alawi family and community for siding with the uprising, Yazbek's story exemplifies the deep divisions that continue to tear families apart and the trauma experienced by generations of Syrians burdened by the sheer scope of the conflict, its death toll, the disappearances, the torture and detainees – circumstances and practices absent from the current debate about post-conflict reconciliation and reconstruction plans in Syria.

This book ends in the year 2011. By deliberately adopting a backward-looking perspective, it investigates the origins of the conflict through a reflection on human insecurity. As a scholar and native Syrian, I wanted to add my voice to the ongoing conversation on the calamitous events in Syria and its future. Having extensively researched water and environmental security both in Syria and in other countries, I felt compelled to share my perspective on the alleged climatic causes of the conflict. Climate change matters. Like so many other countries, Syria has suffered devastating consequences of climate change. But these consequences and the seeds of their discontent are not solely due to climatic stress. They can be found in a combination of political, economic, social, and environmental vulnerabilities that impacted Syria's most vulnerable population for decades before the 2011 uprisings. By offering a "human–environmental–climate-security" framework that brings human and environmental insecurity together, my research broadens the concept of climate security and investigates Syria's history and politics through the prism of environmental security.

There have been important milestones and encounters on the way. Of the many people I met on this journey, some are now dead, many others live in increasingly dire conditions. They all embody, one way or another, the book's central focus on the people's need for dignity and human security, notions that are at the heart of my endeavor. My deepest gratitude extends to all those Syrians met in and outside the region, refugees, civil-society activists, and experts, often under conditions of anonymity, for their hospitality, invaluable insights, and lessons in life. From the former Orthodox archbishop of Aleppo, Mar Gregorios Yohanna Ibrahim, who read novels to neutralize the sound of bombs falling on Aleppo to the refugees who encountered more insecurity and vulnerability after fleeing the conflict. A preacher of mutual coexistence, he refused the government's push to arm Christians and other minorities in what proved to be a successful strategy to sectarianize the uprisings. Sadly, the archbishop was kidnapped by extremist groups and is now presumed dead. The many visits I undertook in recent years to visit Syrian refugees in informal camps in Lebanon offered shocking insight to the unspeakable disruption to their daily life, to the layers of vulnerability, their gloomy prospects, and the many destructive ways through which elite decisions can affect many generations. The trash thrown at the entrance of camps by spiteful neighbors, the restricted access to basic heat and clean water services, the unreliable jobs that often remain unpaid, parents living in constant fear for the security of their children. These regrettable conditions depict an actual picture of human, environmental, food, and water insecurity. Oum Adel and Oum Ali, a couple of the many mothers met in these camps, continue to struggle to maintain a semblance of decent life. Many children experience exploitation and child marriage and are cheated out of basic education. Faced today with the looming threat of deportation to Syria, their fate continues to be marred with insecurity and fear. The young Syrian civil-society activists I met in the Bekaa Valley, Beirut, and Istanbul personified a combination of vulnerability and resilience. Many, since we've met, have been forced to leave their host country. Halted in their studies and professional ambitions, often faced with many legalistic hurdles in host countries, they prioritize the needs of the most vulnerable by supporting non-profit organizations, such as Basmeh wa-Zeitooneh and Jusoor, in providing informal schooling structures and work opportunities for the mothers. If getting enrolled in local schools is not hard enough, access to a daily ride is the last insurmountable challenge in remote areas of the Bekaa Valley. When this obstacle is finally overcome, parents sometimes opt to remove their children as they experience discrimination and abuse on the part of staff and other children. The hope for education motivates not only children. When offering language workshops to their children, I was deeply moved to see Oum Adel and other mothers yearn to understand and learn alongside the children.

Several past and current students at Georgetown University have also considerably contributed to this book. Their outstanding research skills, keen interest in my project, and renewed enthusiasm carried the project until its completion. They are all warmly thanked: Ghazi Ben Hamid Al-Sharif, David Balgley, Caris Boegl, Agathe Christien, Ryan Folio, Helen Lunsmann, Laura Pedersen, Jonathan Thrall, and Jacob Uzman, and, in the last crucial stages of completion, Eliza Campbell, Juliette Leader and Bushra Shaikh whose unfailing commitment and rigor have been instrumental. All the students enrolled in my Environmental Security and Conflict and Politics of Water class not only made teaching enjoyable but indirectly contributed to the intellectual process with their insightful comments, critiques, and questions.

I also sincerely thank my colleagues at Georgetown University, the London School of Economics, and the University of Toronto who have supported this project in one way or another. At Georgetown University, my colleagues at the Center for Contemporary Arab Studies, Osama Abi-Marshid, Fida Adely, Rochelle Davis and Judith Tucker, offered their valuable advice and renewed support. Andria Wisler, Director of the Center for Social Justice, reached out spontaneously at a crucial personal time, embodying the true spirit of solidarity. At the School of Foreign Service, Lahra Smith has unfailingly and generously offered her support and guidance on personal and professional levels; Jeffrey Anderson never failed to make himself available for advice; George Shambaugh provided valuable mentorship; Charles King and James Vreeland were amongst the first to reach out and offer guidance when I joined Georgetown; John McNeill took the time to discuss and share with me his deep knowledge of climate and history in the Mediterranean; The Mortara Center for International Affairs extended its support through Carnegie's Bridging the Gap when I was affiliated as Faculty Fellow; Alienor van den Bosch baby sat for me over several months so that I could complete the book; Carole Sargeant provided valuable advice on book proposals and publishing during the scholarly publications workshops she so skillfully puts together for the Faculty; finally, the University and the School of Foreign Service awarded me annual grants that fostered several research trips to the region. At the London School of Economics and Politics, Kirsten Ainley kindly hosted my research and offered a research grant during my sabbatical leave in 2015. Joseph Carens from the University of Toronto offered key advice that allowed me to complete the book in a timely manner.

I also sincerely thank the outstanding editorial team at Cambridge University Press, particularly the commissioning editor Maria Marsh who showed a keen interest and unfailing support for my project from the very beginning, turning an idea into a full-fledged book; Daniel Brown, who took over after Maria's parental leave and made himself available at all times for queries and support. I also warmly thank the editorial and content managers Atifa Jiwa and Thomas Haynes, Saritha Srinivasan who managed the copy-editing and proof-reading process, and the two anonymous reviewers who offered excellent comments and suggestions that considerably improved the manuscript.

My warmest thoughts go to my family and close friends who have accompanied this journey at every turn: in spirit and heart, my late father, Adib Daoudy who would have been truly heartbroken for the country and people he so relentlessly worked and cared for; my mother, Amal Khartabil Daoudy, who was with me intellectually and emotionally every step of the way; Roula, Rania, Joudy, Tyma, Karim, Talia, Tara, and Zeyd, for being there, each one in their own special way, Carla who tirelessly reviewed and commented all stages of writing, displaying her unfailing intellectual support and friendship; Patrizia for the support and friendship she never failed to show since our childhood.

I dedicate this book to Selma, the unexpected ray of life, hope, and peace in a time of despair, and to all the children of Syria, the vulnerable yet resilient heroes of this chronicle.

The Context

History, Geography, Security

1 | *Climate Change and the Syrian Revolution*

Climatic facts are not facts in themselves; they assume importance only in relation to the restructuring of the environment within different systems of production.

(Garcia, 1981)

I just discover as we speak this thesis about our Revolution being climate-induced, and I fail to understand the purpose and context for such a claim. People who voice such explanations are obviously ignorant of our situation and history.

(Yassin al-Haj Saleh, prominent Syrian writer and political dissident, in personal discussion with author, Istanbul, July 18, 2016)

We are who we are today because of past climatic changes. Yves Coppens, the paleoanthropologist who discovered an Australopithecus hominin called "Lucy" in Ethiopia in 1974, argued in his recently published memoirs that our human species emerged as a result of past climate change (Coppens, 2018). Forced to survive under drier climatic conditions, animal species – including humans – developed new physiological adaptations like teeth or better paw shapes, some of which produced the *Homo sapiens* of today. Just as we are physically products of past climate changes, so too are the structures of our contemporary societies. Historian John McNeill (2013) puts forward this argument, using primary sources to track how a region's specific geography and climate helped define the kind of political systems that emerged in Europe, Asia, and North America. For example, McNeill shows that in the Middle East complex and expansive political systems were created early on as a way to handle fluctuations in precipitation, to which the region was more sensitive because of its reliance on rain-fed and irrigated agriculture (McNeill, 2013: 33).

The theory that societies have been shaped by their climates was also popularized for ideological purposes. In the nineteenth century, Social

Darwinists, who sought to justify European colonialism, argued that European societies were naturally superior because of the continent's climate and geography. Imperialists have claimed that the environment determines a country's social and cultural development to create narratives about the inevitable and precocious rise of European civilizations and the alleged delay of societies in Africa and the Middle East (Huntington, 1945; Ratzel, 1897). According to these theories of geographical context, temperate climate and access to the sea made societies stronger, whereas drought and being landlocked paved the way for military, political, and cultural domination. This environmental determinism also obscured imperial responsibilities in managing disasters like famines (Dalby, 2017a: 3). In a compelling book entitled *Late Victorian Holocausts,* Mike Davis (2001) notes that devastating famines in British India, China, Brazil, Ethiopia, Korea, Vietnam, the Philippines, and New Caledonia in late nineteenth century were a result not only of drought but also of bad imperial policies and the international political economy. While drought had created food shortages, it was mismanagement of these shortages that actually lead to widespread famine. Imperial rule had weakened infrastructure and increased corruption while also manipulating the price of crops so that the repercussions of bad harvests due to drought were compounded by fiscal crisis (Davis, 2001: 352, 355).

As much as humans have been shaped by the environment, the environment has also been shaped by humans from the birth of agriculture to the rise of the industrial revolution. (See Chapter 2 for a discussion in the Syrian context.) Although climate is always naturally changing and evolving, human activities have shaped global, regional, and local climates. Starting in about 1800, greenhouse-gas emissions from human activities – primarily related to the combustion of fossil fuels – spurred climate changes, most notably through an average global temperature increase. Since the "Great Acceleration," beginning in the 1950s, these changes have been occurring at an alarming and unprecedented rate. Paul Crutzen coined the term "the Anthropocene" to describe this phenomenon as a new geologic era in which humankind has a central role (Steffen et al., 2007: 614–615). While it has been widely accepted for decades that humans have an impact on the environment, the exact nature and magnitude of this impact remained less certain.

In the 1980s, the World Meteorological Organization and the United Nations Environment Program noticed that there was a lack of comprehensive, accessible, current, and impartial information about climate change. The Intergovernmental Panel on Climate Change (IPCC) was therefore founded in 1988 to assess, synthesize, and share the state of current scientific, technical, and socioeconomic knowledge about climate change by bringing together a diverse community of scientists and policy-makers. Ultimately, the hope was that the knowledge products of the IPCC would trigger global action in the form of clear medium- and long-term carbon-dioxide emissions targets. The IPCC condenses its analysis and recommendations into assessment reports, of which there have been five: AR1 (1992), AR 2 (1995), AR3 (2001), AR4 (2007), AR5 (2014). A sixth report is projected to be released in 2022. AR4 concluded that increasing emissions of greenhouse gases, and in particular carbon dioxide, is the primary cause of climate change and that this is most likely caused by human activities (IPCC, 2007: 871–872). Anthropogenic climate change is a phenomenon of both the present and future: Temperatures have increased on average 0.75 degrees Celsius over the past century and are predicted to increase by a further 1.8–4 degrees Celsius by the end of this century (IPCC, 2018: 6). Temperature increases lead to changing rainfall patterns, rising sea levels, more frequent and intense extreme weather events, melting ice sheets and Arctic sea ice, shrinking glaciers and snow cover extent, and ocean acidification (NASA, 2019). Although the impacts of climate change will be felt globally, the most detrimental impacts will likely be experienced in the developing world and Global South (IPCC, 2007: 4–7).

From Climate Change to Climate Security

Over the past three decades, scholars and policy-makers in the United States and Europe have endlessly debated whether climate change can be linked to violent conflict, developing a climate-conflict discourse similar to that of the "water wars" scenario of the 1990s. Framed within discussions of climate security, climate-conflict narratives focus on the risks posed by climate change to human and ecological life. In particular, threats are perceived to arise from drought and famine in vulnerable areas of the world (Dalby, 2017a: 9). The link is intuitive, as fewer resources generally means more fighting over resources, and this framing has encouraged politicians to make the case for climate action based on a climate-conflict nexus. After all, international and national security discourses have been more effective than concerns about eco-logical security in triggering specific policy responses. The "threats" associated with climate change are therefore legitimized by security actors when they incorporate climate scholars and practitioners into their field (Oels, 2012: 197).

Key to the climate-conflict nexus is the idea that climate change is a "threat multiplier" or "stressor" – a factor that works with others to increase the likelihood of violent conflict. In this line of reasoning, environmental threats compound existing issues to increase the likeli-hood of an armed conflict or war. A briefing report released in 2015 by the Center for Climate and Security makes this case: The authors of the report refer to the multiplied risks of climate change as "exacerbating other threats to security" (Werrell and Femia, 2015). Although the term "threat multiplier" remains unclear and lacking in rigor and precision, it has largely been endorsed by the media.[1]

A wide spectrum of voices, from prominent politicians to media moguls, have relayed the increasingly popular narrative of a climate-conflict nexus.[2] Apocalyptic visions of climate insecurity have made their way into popular culture: For example, scientists expressed hope that blockbuster movies like *The Day after Tomorrow* (2004) would alert the general public to the dramatic consequences of climate change and trigger a more widespread interest in the subject.[3] Climate-wars narratives have also loomed large over popular and scientific publica-tions, with many academic sources still referring to popular author Robert Kaplan's stark predictions on the menacing risks of scarcity and overpopulation (Kaplan, 1994).[4]

[1] For example, Friedman (2019).
[2] Chapter 2 will delve into the academic literature on the climate-conflict nexus.
[3] See interview by Harvard-based paleoclimatologist Dan Shrag in 2004 on the film *The Day after Tomorrow* (Associated Press, 2004).
[4] For example, Scheffran et al. (2012) and Levy and Sidel (2014). See also Hsiang et al. (2013), in which the authors attempt to quantify the influence of climate change on conflict, and Buhaug et al. (2014), in which the authors rebuke Hsiang et al., writing that their meta-analysis "blends all sorts of actors at all sorts of spatial and temporal scales. ... [They] draw sweeping conclusions that, supposedly, are robust and apply across scales and types of violent conflict. Of course that doesn't make sense. But it works if you seek attention." This was followed by a reply by Hsiang (2014) on the G-FEED blog, in which he countered this argument: "Buhaug et al.'s alteration of our meta-analysis misrepresents

These narratives offer dramatic and disastrous predictions of vast societal collapse as a result of climate-induced conflict, spawning a new discourse of "collapsology." This term, coined by French researchers Pablo Servigne and Raphaël Stevens (2015), refers to a general collapse of societies induced by climate change, scarcity of resources, vast extinctions, and natural disasters. "Collapsology" as a movement emerged from Jared Diamond's incredibly popular (2004) book on the subject, which suggested that human degradation of the environment helped precipitate historical collapses in societies such as the Classical Maya, Norse Greenland, and Easter Island. Scientific and popular publications picked up Diamond's conception of the environment as a potentially existential threat, linking current events, such as the wildfires in California, to climate change to imply they signal our impending doom. More recently, the discourse has broadened to show how climate change can result in the breakdown of public services, telecommunications, and trade, especially in more vulnerable poor countries, which could in turn lead to the collapse of systems and states. Narratives of collapse have been used with the aim of incentivizing climate action, given the assumption that fear is a powerful catalyst, though the expected action has largely not taken place.

The response to "collapsology" has been diverse. While it has been embraced by some scholars, others have treated it as an opportunity to question both capitalist modes of production or the distribution and the relationships between humans and their environment. For example, the philosopher and sociologist Bruno Latour has proposed a new form of agency shared by both nature and society in the Anthropocene to replace traditional models where all agency is given to either nature or humans in a binary subject–object divide (Latour, 2014). On the other end of the spectrum, climate optimists argue that human adaptive capacity can match the scale of ecological threats, so we will be able to respond well to climate change. Steven Pinker (2018), a cognitive psychologist and linguist by training, points to the immense progress humanity has made in improving living

---

findings in the literature, makes statistical errors, misclassifies multiple studies, makes coding errors, and suppresses the display of results that are consistent with our original analysis. We correct these mistakes and obtain findings in line with our original results, even when we use the study selection criteria proposed by Buhaug et al. We conclude that there is no evidence in the data supporting the claims raised in Buhaug et al."

standards over the past 250 years as a sign that we can respond effectively to the new threats of climate change.

Nevertheless, the consensus is that climate change is happening and global action is indeed urgently needed. The question, then, becomes: Should we securitize climate change in order to raise awareness and spur action? The answer, to some, is no. Certain scholars posit that public reporting about climate risk constitutes a form of social drama, building upon existing contextual cultural biases to decrease the likelihood of effective policy intervention (Smith, 2015). Moreover, these narratives can be used to justify repressive measures to stop human mobility at the domestic and international levels, feeding perceptions of the responsibility of "environmental migrants" rather than authoritarian regimes in triggering social and political unrest. Employing this climate-conflict nexus narrative also makes autonomous governments, particularly those in the Global South, passive actors and mere victims of nature rather than political actors with the will and power to make their own policy to address climate instability. The conflation of climate change and conflict could also obfuscate the relevant drivers of conflict for the sake of dramatization. This is particularly apparent when governments and their policies are themselves at the root of unrest and conflict, as in the Syrian case (De Châtel, 2014; Selby and Hoffman, 2014).

From Global Climate Security to the Arab Spring and the Syrian Revolution

When little Aylan, who traveled on a boat with his family from Syria, was found dead on a Turkish beach and had his picture widely disseminated, the Canadian *National Observer* proclaimed: "this is what a climate refugee looks like" (Dinshaw, 2015). The idea that the Syrian conflict was a product of climate change was not a new or marginal one. In Leonardo DiCaprio's documentary *Before the Flood* (2016), President Obama links drought to civil unrest in Syria, a thought that was echoed a few months later in an interview with Prince Charles prior to the opening of the COP 21 global climate summit in Paris.[5] The narrative of a climate-induced conflict was applied years earlier to

---

[5] As Prince Charles puts it, "And in fact there's very good evidence indeed that one of the major reasons for this horror in Syria, funnily enough, was a drought that

the conflict in Darfur: A 2007 opinion piece in *The Atlantic* named climate change among the "real" roots of the conflict (Faris, 2007), and this claim was quickly reproduced in a statement by UN Secretary-General Ban Ki-Moon on the "real culprit in Darfur" (Ban, 2007).

In 2011, however, climate change was not at the forefront of the minds of people on the streets in Syria and across the Arab world. Instead, most people were focused on a moral ideal: the end of repression and injustice. The unrest in Egypt and Tunisia in early 2011 triggered brewing discontent of populations in other part of the Arab world, like Syria, and on March 18, 2011, the people of Deraa in southwestern Syria came out in massive numbers to protest the torture of schoolchildren by security services. Sit-ins had already taken place on March 15, 2011, in the capital, Damascus, in solidarity with the Egyptian and Tunisian revolutions, and in the months that followed Syrians who took to the streets broke the barrier of fear and pressed their demands for dignity, freedom, social justice, economic opportunity, and political reform.[6] The country saw popular protests on an unprecedented scale, and the regime opted for a strategy of sheer survival, responding with brutal repression and the threat of chaos and civil war. Activists, intellectuals, and ordinary people turned the initial mobilization into a national uprising, labeled the Syrian Revolution. Quickly, however, dreams of change and hope shifted into tragedy as the country went from peaceful demonstrations and youth activism to armed insurgency, counterinsurgency, civil war, and a regional proxy conflict. The military involvement of foreign powers such as the United States, Russia, Iran, and Turkey, and the financial support of Arab gulf states for Islamist armed groups on the ground, transformed the initial popular mobilizations into an international conflict. Meanwhile, the emergence of the Islamic State of Iraq and

---

lasted for about five or six years, which meant that huge numbers of people in the end had to leave the land but increasingly they came into the cities" (Holden, 2015).

[6] The location and date of the start of Syrian Revolution remains the object of domestic debates. Syrian activists interviewed by the author stated that the mobilizations started in Damascus on March 15, 2011, in front of the Tunisian and Egyptian embassies. They were, however, limited in scale. The real popular mobilization happened a few days later in Deraa on March 18, 2011. The emphasis placed here is on the urban nature of the Revolution in addition to its rural roots.

Levant and its conquest and loss of large sections of territory and infrastructures in Syria from 2014 to 2019 added an additional geostrategic layer to the Syrian conflict.

The Scholarly Debate about the Syrian Conflict

Since 2011, policy-makers and scholars have tried to unravel the causes of the Arab Spring broadly, but in particular in Syria, given the conflict that erupted after the 2011 uprising. Many Arab and Syrian analysts wrote sophisticated and well-informed accounts of the revolution's background and the country's structural weaknesses in the preceding decade (e.g., Arab Center for Research and Policy Studies, 2013; Barout, 2012; Bishara, 2012, 2013). Others took historical, political, or personal approaches, or focused on the role of religious scholars and Islamic networks (e.g., Abboud, 2016; Hashemi and Postel, 2013, 2017; Hinnebusch and Zintl, 2015; Lefevre, 2013; Lesch, 2012; Lynch, 2014; Neep, 2012; Pierret, 2013; Salamandra and Stenberg, 2015; Van Dam, 2011; Yazbek, 2012, 2015).

The role of authoritarianism, and its relationship to business and informal economic networks, has also been explored in the scholarly literature (Haddad, 2012; Heydemann, 1999). This re-entrenchment of economic power and systematic cronyism has been referred to as an "authoritarian upgrading" (Heydemann, 2007) that created "new vulnerabilities" (Hinnebusch and Zintl, 2015: 290). Economic liberalization increased corruption and further concentrated power among key insiders, leading to a loss of support in the traditional rural stronghold of the Ba'athist regime (Hinnebusch and Zintl, 2015: 291). The "losers" of the upgrading were the ones who would propel the 2011 uprising.

The influence of identity politics, or sectarianism, on domestic politics has also been investigated as a potential driver of the conflict. The politics of "sectarianization" has been used both by internal and external actors and featured prominently in Bashar al-Assad's economic, social, and military reforms, as he played on sectarian divides to shore up his regime's base and ensure continued power (Hashemi and Postel, 2017; Hinnebusch and Zintl, 2015: 285). For example, the alliance of minorities and rural populations during the Ba'ath regime saw the steady advancement of Alawite recruitment in the military, which ensured the army remained fairly loyal during the uprising and civil war (Hinnebusch and Zintl, 2015: 302; Phillips, 2015: 364). In charge of the military, Alawites were a check on Sunni officers' power and influence and a way to protect the regime from further coups (Hinnebusch, 1990: 163). Bashar al-Assad's strategies of "authoritarian upgrading" were incredibly effective at exploiting preexisting tensions and fears and framing divides as sectarian in nature. Christopher Phillips (2015) actually attributes the semi-sectarian aspects of the civil war to the fallout from Bashar al-Assad's social and economic reforms which exacerbated sectarian divides. Under Assad, economic opportunities were handed to regime elites – namely Alawites – and key subsidies were cut for many Syrians, particularly the Sunni peasantry; this decrease in the "social reach of the state" encouraged strong substate actors such as tribal, religious, and sect leaders to play roles previously filled by the state (Phillips, 2015: 367). As such, substate actors were able to mobilize identity politics at subnational levels (Heydemann and Leenders, 2013: 149).

Some scholarship sets aside domestic factors such as the economy and identity politics to look at regional structural factors as drivers of conflict (Abboud, 2016; Salloukh, 2017). For example, Salloukh argues that the ongoing conflict between Saudi Arabia and Iran since the 2003 Iraq War directly encouraged sectarian narratives in Syria as another proxy fight (Salloukh, 2017: 39). Abboud also notes that regional alliances across sectarian lines are increasingly common given changing economic interests and geopolitical factors (Abboud, 2016: 130).

Finally, a group of scholars spearheaded by American think tanks have analyzed social unrest in the Arab world and Syria in the context of climate change (Femia and Werrell, 2015; Femia et al., 2013). In a series of scientific and academic journal articles, Syria became a showcase for "climate-induced" displacement and unrest, sparking a debate as to whether climate change contributed to the conflict (Ababsa, 2015; Burke et al., 2014; De Châtel, 2014; Femia and Werrell, 2012; Fröhlich, 2016; Gleick, 2014, 2017; Hendrix, 2017; Hoerling et al., 2012; Kelley et al., 2015, 2017; Selby et al., 2017a).[7]

---

[7] This international debate will be analyzed in detail in Chapter 5 and contrasted with our findings on the climate, political, and economic indicators of human insecurity. Questions relating to sampling biases are addressed in Chapter 2.

While all of these perspectives have great value in understanding the larger question of the causes of Syrian conflict, what is largely missing from these conversations is a more in-depth analysis of the complexities of Syria's history and politics with regards to human and environmental security. This book fills that gap.

The Book's Approach

Would the Syrian uprising have occurred in 2011 without the Arab Spring? Probably not. Political repression, corruption, and the regional upheavals were sufficient to motivate people to take to the streets. However, as argued in this book, policy decisions also mattered. In the context of climate change, the severe stress on water and land resources magnified inequities, producing a ticking bomb waiting to detonate. While these factors might not have been sufficient to produce the Syrian uprising in 2011, the long-term structural seeds of conflict had been planted long before through unsustainable practices pursued by the government, aggravating poverty and food insecurity. Did water scarcity and its consequences trigger the 2011 uprising? Again, probably not. I do not dispute the existence of, or the impact of, climate change. In fact, I start from the premise that more studies linking climate change, environmental stress, and social unrest are necessary. However, I remain skeptical of the current trend that sees climate change as the primary driver of water scarcity and conflict given the significance of human factors and local context.

There are, in my view, three major problems with the existing explanations linking climate-induced water scarcity and the 2011 uprising. First, the revolts did not take place in the rural areas struck by drought. The uprising started in Damascus and Deraa in southwestern Syria, while the drought occurred in the northeastern and eastern provinces, and more significantly in Syria's breadbasket region, the Hassake governorate. Formerly known in official documents as the Jazira region, and often still referred to as such by Syrians, this area lies between the Euphrates and Tigris rivers.[8] Figure 1.1 shows the location of the Jazira. In addition to concentrating the national production of

---

[8] According to engineer Abdullah Droubi, former director of the Department of Water Studies at the Arab Center for the Study of Arid Zones and Dry Lands (ACSAD), in an exchange with the author (July 18, 2019). Syrian official reports divide the country into five main agricultural regions: Southern (Damascus,

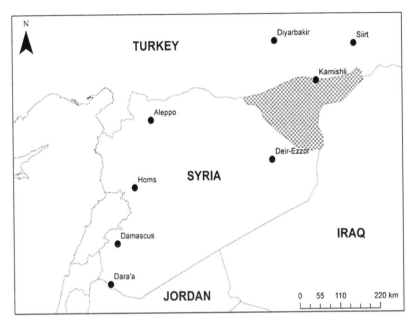

Figure 1.1 Syria's Jazira/Hassake Governorate.
Source: Selby et al., 2017a: 235

cereals and cotton, this region contains more than 80 percent of Syria's oil reserves.

Second, although some of the farmers from these regions had relocated to the suburbs of Damascus and Deraa, there is no evidence that these migrant farmers contributed to the uprising. Based on interviews with civil society members and a few migrant farmers, for the most part the relocated farmers did not take part in the early phases of the popular mobilizations. People took to the streets to denounce political repression and corruption with no explicit reference made to a lack of access to water or food. Third, water scarcity has plagued the country since the 1950s. To the extent that drought caused human suffering that could have fueled further discontent, the drought itself was not only a consequence of climate change but also the result of long-term pressures and official mismanagement of water resources.

Deraa, Suweida, al-Quneitra), Central, Coastal (Lattakia, Tartous), Northern (Aleppo, Idlib), and Eastern (Deir ez-Zor, Hassake, Raqqa) (FAO, 2008: 4).

Therefore, I build on two inferences that contradict prevailing narratives. First, since drought is not an inevitable consequence of climate change, climate change is not a necessary driver of conflict. Second, since water scarcity is not a recent phenomenon in Syria, climate-induced drought cannot fully explain why the Syrian people rebelled in 2011. This study sheds new light on water and agricultural politics by examining Syria's climate–water–food security from a historical, political, and economic perspective. I argue that structural long-term pressures are important in the Syrian case and allow us to make a distinction between triggering and structural factors. Across the Arab world, structural factors included demographic changes, urbanization resulting from drought, price increases, and resentment over rising inequality and reduction in public-service provision. In the Syrian case, water and economic insecurity were additional structural pressures. Syria has suffered from chronic water scarcity for decades, and, while climate change worsened water insecurity, I contend that climate change played an accompanying role to another key variable: ideology.

Long-term pressures on water and food security were playing out in a context of intensive irrigation, increased poverty, low wages, high unemployment, and rising corruption. By the time of the uprising, the ruling elites were increasingly unpopular and perceived to be both corrupt and authoritarian. Triggering short-term factors were the exogenous shock represented by the Arab Spring and the torture of schoolchildren in Deraa, which prompted local mobilization that spread to the rest of the country. Obviously, it is impossible to say if the unrest would have precipitated into uprising had there *not* been the Arab Spring. However, there is a plausible case to be made that the government would eventually have had to confront large-scale protests by people living below subsistence levels. Thus, rather than looking at the short-term causes of the uprising, I analyze water insecurity from a theoretical and historical perspective to reveal the importance of structural long-term pressures. The goal of this book is to answer the question: What were the causes and consequences of water insecurity in Syria in the decades that preceded the historical 2011 uprising?

While I accept that climate change plays a role in creating water scarcity, I argue that the principal cause of water insecurity in Syria was government policy, framed by specific political and water

ideologies.[9] The different ideologies adhered to or implemented by the
Syrian government, from rural Ba'athism in the 1960s to neoliberalism
beginning in the 1970s – including the *Infitah* (Opening) in 1990 and
the shift to the social market economy in 2005 – exerted different kinds
of pressures on different groups within society. Some groups received
privileged access to water, land, or capital, while some communities
became less resilient to climate change. These policies were not climate-
induced: They were government decisions that reflected the ideology
and preferences of ruling elites. Motivated by their own short- or long-
term reasons, elites pursued policies that were not compatible with
long-term water or food security. In explaining water insecurity, food
insecurity, and, more broadly, human insecurity, I treat climate change
as a background factor that amplifies the impact of ideology and
unsustainable water and agricultural policies. In other words, I argue
that the consequences of climate change on water and food resources
in Syria could have been attenuated by sound government policies.
A paradigm shift is required when reflecting on issues of climate
security and water security, particularly in the Syrian case.

Shifting the Paradigm: Human–Environmental–Climate Security

Scholars and policy-makers have applied a variety of explanatory
frameworks and theoretical tools to the intersection of climate insecurity, political instability and conflict. The HECS framework developed
in this book provides a critical new perspective that positions *vulnerability* and *sustainability* at the center of environmental and climate
insecurity and risk.

The HECS framework, shown in Figure 1.2, treats climate, water,
and food security as interrelated concepts, with a focus on the impact
of such insecurities on populations at the subnational levels and the
role played by government structures. This approach to vulnerability
brings to the fore the concepts of environmental, climate, human,
and water security and their theoretical and policy framings over
time. Combining security and development concerns, human security
is a concept used to analyze people's economic, food, health,

---

[9] Refer to Figure 4.1 in Chapter 4 for a detailed timeline of critical policy decisions
on agriculture, water, and land between 1958 and 2011.

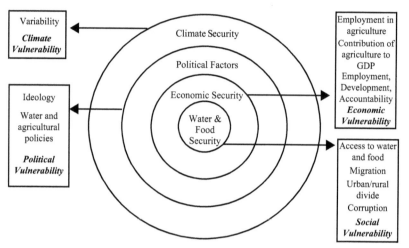

Figure 1.2 The HECS framework.
Source: Author

environmental, personal, community, and political security. I explain water conflict in Syria through the lens of human security because it allows me to examine vulnerability and resilience to disruptions of daily patterns of livelihood, including how elite decisions affect general access to food and land for farmers. By contrast, the broader concept of climate security is not well suited to capture the direct impact of climate change, poverty, political repression, and corruption on individuals and communities. A critical element of the HECS framework is its applicability and utility in analyzing and untangling the structural, political, and economic factors of real cases of human insecurity and conflict. It also seeks to move beyond deterministic narratives and orientalist biases about the risks of population growth and mobility, demand-induced scarcity, resource depletion, and insecurity that fall into patterns of core–periphery and Global North–Global South divides.

At the core of the HECS framework is multidimensionality in analyzing how political, economic, and climate factors contribute to aspects of human vulnerability at all levels. This study therefore examines the vectors of influence together as equally valid and equally critical, showing how water and food security, political, economic, and environmental factors act in tandem with one another to drive population displacement and human insecurity. While not discounting seemingly opposed frameworks of explanation but rather taking a multidisciplinary approach that shows how these factors interact with each other through feedback loop effects, the HECS framework offers a concrete and nuanced picture of the environmental, socioeconomic and political situation in Syria in the decades that preceded the historical 2011 uprising. This framework can be widely applied to other cases of climate (in)security throughout the world, particularly in the Global South. By centering the narrative on the Global South, the HECS framework allows for a discussion of the human security impacts of the environment, including poverty, marginalization, and failure of sustainable development but also calls into question how environmental degradation causes risk to human security more globally.

The Three HECS Factors

The HECS framework is uniquely capable of considering both theoretical situations and real cases of conflict and insecurity that interact with climate instability. The framework engages with definitional debates relating to food and water security; Chapter 2 therefore reviews competing explanations of climate insecurity at the frontier of research in area studies, political economy, critical security studies, and environmental politics. Additionally, the framework draws attention to three main types of factors – structural, vulnerability, and resilience – critical for understanding both the Syrian case and situations of human insecurity more broadly. Each of these three factors will be closely examined in the Syrian case in the following sections and chapters.

The first type are structural factors, including context-specific preconditions for political, social, economic, and climate vulnerability and human insecurity. Chapter 3 will explore the role of water and agriculture in shaping the Middle East, and, by extension Syria, through a historical and regional lens, including the cultural and legal norms surrounding water in Syria and a contemporary view of Syria's transboundary interactions over the shared rivers of the Euphrates and Tigris rivers. The second type are vulnerability factors, which involve development conditions (water, agricultural, employment, poverty), policies (corruption, subsidies), and environmental variables (precipitation, temperature). Chapter 5 applies each of these vulnerability factors to the Syrian context, with a special focus on two periods of major drought since 1990. The third type are resilience factors; Chapters 4 and 5 trace the political, economic, and institutional variables that explain why Syrians were, and at other times were not, prepared to cope with various aspects of insecurity and instability in the decades since 1960.

Sustainability, Vulnerability, and Resilience

Discussions of all three factors, especially in the context of human security, depend on an understanding of the concept of *sustainability*. Major human security thinkers, such as Amartya Sen (2000) and Mahbub Ul-Haq (1995), agree that the most pressing risk to human security is the inability to provide sufficient resources to sustain human and ecological life, which is often compounded by local, regional, and global inequality. The critical human security perspective adopted by the HECS framework places freedom from want and "a life of dignity" at the heart of understanding threats to human life; as such, it sees sustainability not just as a matter of sufficient resources but also as a matter of equitable power relationships (Ul-Haq, 1995: 32).

In the HECS framework, *vulnerability* and *resilience* are parallel concepts that reveal how a lack of sustainability in combination with specific structural factors and inequalities threatens human life through the inability of systems to cope with unexpected change (UNDP, 2010: 20). In the broader sense of the term, vulnerability refers to a community or ecosystem's ability to cope with change or disruption. More specifically, scholars and policy-makers have referred to climate vulnerability as the degree to which a particular system is susceptible to the ecological, economic, sociological, and political effects of climate change. As Simon Dalby argues, vulnerability should be understood as a "complex social and ecological situation" that is related to and works in connection with "social and economic entitlements" of a specific community or context (2013: 128). Vulnerability is a helpful measure for understanding the feedback effects between different types of human insecurity precisely because it forces a focus on specific contexts while also calling to attention the role of larger structural inequalities.

For the purposes of this study, *vulnerability* is defined in terms of disruption to patterns of daily life from the perspective of the marginalized and dispossessed. Such disruptions to patterns of daily life include chronic water insecurity, land degradation, arable land scarcity, food insecurity, and poverty, as well as a combination of inefficient irrigation schemes and relocation plans as a result of irrigation projects. The critical environmental security approach adopted by HECS deliberately centers the narrative on individual human lives, making food and water insecurity a critical component of understanding how macro political, economic and environmental trends drive individual's daily access to sustenance. Working in connection with the concept of vulnerability are a series of *resilience* factors that show how societies and community units respond to and cope with these risks. Wisner et al. (2004: 11) pull these parallel concepts together to define vulnerability as "the characteristics of a person or group and their situation that influence their capacity to anticipate, cope with, resist and recover from the impact of a natural hazard." In this sense, vulnerability and resilience factors show the relationship between political, economic, climate, and food and water insecurity identified by the HECS model.

Applying the HECS Framework to the Syrian Case

Figure 1.3 creates a visual representation of the HECS framework, where climate security, political factors, economic security, and water and food security interact, and includes specific examples of each variable in the Syrian context. The outermost circle represents climate security, or threats related to environmental instability and change, including threats from anthropogenic climate change and natural cyclical climate changes. Environmental threats are sometimes categorized as the main drivers of conflict, but in reality they interact with economic and political factors both concurrently and intertemporally at different levels in a way that puts vulnerable communities at higher risk. Environmental and economic factors therefore compound existing political stressors to human security as political and government actors play upon these threats to make strategic political gains. In Syria, the regime instrumentalized ideologies that focused on certain environmental and economic threats to mitigate growing social instability; for example, Ba'athism prioritized food security to appeal to agrarian communities, and the social market economy championed market-oriented growth to appease urban merchants. This third layer of the HECS model, namely political factors such as policy decisions of key political actors and state institutions, has been less rigorously

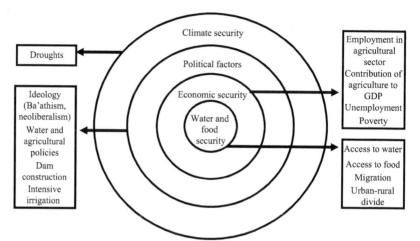

Figure 1.3 Applying the HECS framework to Syria: vulnerability and resilience.
Source: Author

examined in previous conceptions of climate security and human security. The HECS framework therefore plays a key role here in including these political factors in the frame of analysis.

In the Syrian case, the relevant political decisions are changes to key agricultural policies, including less equitable land-sharing policies, more intensive dam construction at the expense of local communities, and the aggressive expansion of irrigated surfaces failing to enhance productivity because of weak institutional and economic frameworks. Chapter 4 shows how the rise to power of a socialist, ruralized Ba'ath Party in 1963 paved the way for a period of land reform and state-led management of water and agricultural resources. Ba'athism identified food security as a national goal in order to maintain legitimacy in the eyes of their rural base, with the government implementing policies of intensive irrigation and dam construction to achieve this goal. The first part of Chapter 4 therefore details water and agricultural policies from the 1960s to the early 2000s, including dam construction, intensive irrigation, modernization of irrigation, and the forced Arabization of Kurdish-inhabited areas, and their combined effect of poor governance, lack of water sustainability, and decreased soil quality. The second part of Chapter 4 traces the transition to a social market economy in 2005 after several decades of gradual liberalization. Pursuing this ideology, the regime cut fuel and water subsidies to the detriment of constituencies in the rural peripheries, while a new class of urban businessmen prospered. Chapter 4 therefore also evaluates the impact of these policies on small rural landowners against the backdrop of the drought of 2006–2010.

This last element of insecurity in the HECS framework, shown at the center of the diagram in Figure 1.2, is water and food (in)security, which is brought about by the interaction of previously discussed environmental, political, and economic drivers. Chapter 5 examines food and water security in Syria, where changes to existing resources in terms of access to water from transboundary rivers and precipitation levels meant reduced output and lowered, disrupted, or altered access to water and food. This, in turn, led to poverty in rural and urban areas, unemployment, especially in the agricultural sector, and mass migration. *Adaptive capacity* can be a critical component of a community's susceptibility to climate insecurity, but in Syria, this was relatively low due to poor governance and institutional weaknesses. A water-related vulnerability analysis demonstrates how specific ideological and policy choices were the guiding principles behind these disruptions and the ensuing vulnerability. By defining the negative outcomes of such policy choices in terms of their vulnerability effects, this analysis shows how the different dimensions of threats measured in the HECS framework can be understood as interlocking and interrelated.

To conclude, the HECS framework crucially acknowledges that interacting environmental, political, economic, and pressures occur in tandem with threats to water and food security and their ensuing migration and poverty, which in turn reinforce the original pressures in a recurring positive feedback loop. By considering multidimensional factors of human insecurity and by analyzing them as interrelated and occurring with mutual feedback effects, the HECS framework is the first of its kind to examine human insecurity and climate vulnerability in a way that avoids common overgeneralizations and missteps in past conceptions of security and attempts to understand the interaction of these factors in a specific case: the Syrian case.

Methodology

In order to make inferences from a single case study, this book includes multiple measures of the dependent variable (human–climate–environmental security) over two periods of major drought in

Syria: 1998–2001 and 2006–2010.[10] It also outlines historically and conceptually the ideological context and policies that were framed by these ideologies. This research is based on public sources from the Central Bureau of Statistics and the Ministry of Agriculture and Agrarian Reform, as well as classified documents of the Ministry of Irrigation and the Ministry of Foreign Affairs on water availability and infrastructures obtained during trips to Damascus carried out in the decade prior to 2011. During this field research, I was able to interview several Syrian policy-makers and water engineers from the Ministry of Foreign Affairs and the Ministry of Irrigation, as well as members of the ruling elite. I contrast and check official sources with debates between officials, economists, and water experts in the Syrian Association of Economic Sciences (SAES) in the years that followed major economic shifts, as well as confidential documents and information obtained under conditions of anonymity from Syrian ministry officials involved in the country's water-development projects, technocrats and nongovernmental representatives. To date, the bulk of these primary sources and interviews remain untapped. I also draw on statistics from the Food and Agricultural Organization, the United Nations Economic and Social Commission on Western Asia and the World Bank to assess subsistence levels and food security.

In 2014–2016, I also undertook extensive fieldwork to Lebanon and Turkey and was able to carry out semi-structured interviews with activists and refugees, some originating from the northeastern parts of Syria, as well as with key economic and political actors, some formerly involved with the State Planning Commission and Ministry of Economic Affairs during the crucial economic shifts of the 2000s. Approximately twenty refugees were interviewed during two separate trips to the Bekaa Valley, Lebanon, in the informal refugee camps (Mahmoud al-Jild, Omariyyeh, Shaher) which were set up after war erupted in Syria. The inhabitants of these camps were primarily from the wider Damascus area but also included some farmers from Homs and Deir Ez-Zor.

I also met and discussed water and agricultural policy with Syrian engineers and civil-society activists in Lebanon, the United Kingdom, and the United States, sometimes under conditions of anonymity to

---

[10] Drawing on the guidelines for conducting robust qualitative research with generalizable findings by King et al. (1994).

better safeguard their security. Moreover, this research greatly benefited from discussions held with long-time analysts and critiques of government policies in Syria, such as Yassin al-Haj-Saleh, whose writings continue to shape current debates about the fate of the country and the future of its citizens. The historical and conceptual sections built on exchanges held during joint panels at international conferences, online or personal interactions, with leading figures in environmental history, policy or security, such as Simon Dalby, Malin Falkenmark, Thomas Homer-Dixon, Richard Matthews, and John McNeill. Other interviews were carried out in Europe and the United States with international experts of water and food security. These various interviews and encounters will be included whenever of relevance into the different chapters of the book. In addition to interviews and primary sources, I analyze speeches, press interviews, and memoirs by policy-makers available through open sources. Secondary sources on Syria's history and development also provide useful background information.

Summary

This chapter has made the case for why a new method of analysis is needed in discussing the climate–conflict nexus generally and with regards to Syria and has proposed the multidisciplinary HECS framework. In applying the HECS framework to the Syrian case, a more substantial engagement with the theoretical foundations of the framework is needed, and Chapter 2 takes up this task.

2 | *The Many Faces of Environmental Security*

We have lost everything: our house, our land, our life. Our children are out of school. And we are unable to go back home. Now you tell me that we, who had to leave our home town first because of the drought and now the conflict, are described as the causes of all this? We are the victims.

(Former inhabitant of Hassake Province, Shaher refugee camp, Bekaa Valley, Lebanon, interviewed by author, December 12, 2015)

Reexamining and Broadening the Security Agenda

Security remains one of the most controversial and contested concepts in international politics (Williams, 2008: 1). Policy analysts, academics, and practitioners have long debated its meaning. What exactly does this term entail? What are the implications of choosing one definition over another? In the context of this project, how does the definition of security impact its application to the environment? At the center of this discussion are two essential and interrelated theoretical challenges: Can a security framework be applied to environmental issues, and, if it can, whose interests are best served by this framing? Answering these questions is a task that will only become more pressing as environmental degradation becomes more acute, but it is also a task that requires a much deeper and more comprehensive theoretical framing than has been addressed in the literature. The goal of this chapter, therefore, is to lay out and justify the theoretical model used by our HECS framework in the context of critical human–environmental security.

The first theoretical challenge involves questioning the degree to which a security framework is appropriate for addressing the threat of environmental degradation and its downstream effects, either in theoretical or practical terms. This challenge requires a thorough understanding of the multitude of definitions of security and how scholars have contested its definitions since the Cold War. The second theoretical challenge works from the assumption that some variant of a security framework is a useful analytical device but then questions whose interests are prioritized by framing environmental instability as a security issue and whose perspectives are excluded; after all, the choice to "securitize" the language of the environment is a clear discursive act with concrete policy implications. This securitization language can either reify or challenge the status quo of power relations not only between states but also between a wider array of actors.

Newer perspectives on security narratives about resource consumption and water security are therefore crucial. Critical-security stances are essential in these debates as they examine structural inequalities of power and distribution of resources while also considering the role of states as providers of insecurity and centering the narrative on individuals and groups that address power gaps. The field of critical security has revealed the need for a more nuanced and diverse definition of the concept of security; this will also require a thorough examination of how actors – including scholars and policy-makers – working from the traditional concept of security have imbued the field with uncontested biases and values that can prioritize the concerns and interests of the Global North and West, especially the United States and Western Europe (Bilgin, 2017: 653). New fields of security studies are attempting to address this imbalance and reframe the traditional security narrative to account for previously ignored sources. These new security perspectives have moved to incorporate broader perspectives in a move that has also been replicated in International Relations. In the field of International Relations theory, scholars are challenging Western theoretical constructs and recognizing that there is a need for plurality and the inclusion of more non-Western voices (Abboud et al., 2018; Acharya, 2014; Bilgin, 2017). In debates relating to environmental and climate security, critical thinkers such as Dalby, Barnett, and Matthews have written eloquently about these "us versus them" binary framings, yet Western perspectives are still privileged and projected onto most of the world while non-Western perspectives are marginalized or silenced. These narratives echo many of the cultural and colonial constructs of the nineteenth century, which were inspired by environmental determinism.

Researchers of climate security can also perpetuate similar conceptual otherizing traps by claiming that increased climate change will encourage human migration, conflict, and grievances against the state.

In response to these security frameworks, I propose a new theoretical framework of security: human–environmental–climate security (HECS). HECS challenges the aforementioned assumptions as overly deterministic and as failing to take into account the economic and sociopolitical factors that interact with resource variation. The theoretical underpinnings of HECS will be discussed in full later in this chapter, but here a broad theoretical overview will demonstrate the ways in which HECS is a natural and needed extension of developments in the field of new and pluralized security studies. In addition, the HECS framework widens human-security approaches, which have also tended to suffer from overly prescriptive and normative modes of inquiry.

This analysis will be informed by a wide range of variables, such as the impact of climate change as an intervening variable over water and food security in Syria, the role of ideology and policy in the agricultural and water sectors, and the government's failure to manage the population's vulnerability and resilience to environmental change. The following sections show how nontraditional approaches to security, including environmental, water, and climate security, have developed over the past several decades and informed the HECS approach of this book.

From Traditional to Nontraditional Security: Security Narratives and Performance

The inclusion of more diverse perspectives in the nontraditional security field was accompanied by a move toward considering a broader set of threats to human life, health, and security, including systemic threats such as those related to environmental and societal concerns. International policy-makers began to better understand climate change in the late twentieth century and therefore also began to increasingly focus on the causes and impacts of environmental instability and the need to develop effective and timely responses. Preexisting literature and discussions of resource-driven conflict paved the way for these new discussions of climate change and instability, and this literature framed environmental concerns in terms of peace and security (Mathews, 1989: 162, 174; Vogler, 2013: 18; Westing, 1986).

At the end of the Cold War, nontraditional security studies started to broaden agendas from traditional threats – military and economic – to include nonmilitary threats – like energy-related and environmental (Romm, 1993: 6; Spector and Wolf, 2000: 410; Ullman, 1983: 133). Environmental factors were first integrated into the concept of security in the early 1980s by two organizations that wanted to investigate the links between environmental degradation, scarcity, and armed conflict: the Stockholm Peace Research Institute (SIPRI) and the Peace Research Institute of Oslo (Gleditsch, 1998).

Environmental security became defined in exclusively realist terms – i.e. managing threats to the integrity of the state – which implied narratives about wars and insurrections that could arise from conflict over diminishing resources (Vogler, 2013: 20). Correspondingly, scholarly work on environmental security flourished within two categories: (1) narratives that questioned how environmental change relates to violent conflict and the integrity of the state and (2) examinations that looked at the broader implications of environmental issues, in which the referent object of security ceases to be the state (Vogler, 2013: 19).

An outline of the major discussions in each of these general categories, especially as they relate to resource management and scarcity, can help us understand the development of the concept of environmental security. First, it is critical to deconstruct the recent conceptual history and terminology of "security." Many have argued that Arnold Wolfers' essay "'National Security' as an Ambiguous Symbol" (1952) marked the beginning of a series of attempts to define and articulate security as a concept. Wolfers presented a "traditional" security concept, grounded in the realist framework, that articulated national security as a field concerned primarily with military statecraft (Baldwin, 1997: 9). A new concept of common security gradually evolved from this perspective during the Cold War: No individual state can obtain its own security without the mutual cooperation and participation of other states (Blackaby, 1986: 395). Later iterations of this theory included comprehensive security, which built upon the common security framework by framing security as the well-being of both states and individuals while also attempting to take into account cooperation and well-being among the globalized world order (Stritzel, 2007: 139). These theories raised questions about what protections they claimed to guarantee: Is a truly "secure" state defined by its ability to act offensively or defensively? The post-realist notion of national security came to be defined as freedom from war and occupation rather than the ability to go to war or occupy, while political security would be defined as freedom from repression, economic security as freedom from want, and cultural security as freedom from ethnic or religious oppression. Post-constructivist ideas of security therefore gradually moved away from states and toward networks of individuals and non-state actors.

Working within this framework, Simon Dalby (2009) and others began to criticize the existing approaches to environmental security. These scholars argued for a new kind of security, one that looked beyond the state to questions of human security and well-being (Dalby, 2009: 19). Other theorists of environmental security were aligned more closely with earlier traditional security scholars; they discussed environmental insecurity in the context of needing to regulate, govern, and "secure" the environment, rather than in the context of analyzing threats to human and environmental well-being in a holistic manner (Dalby, 2009: 13). This was a key inflection point informing different views of environmental and climate security: Some saw the environment as a trigger of conflict and insecurity while others saw the environment as the referent object of security itself.

At this point, it is useful to define terminology around the "environment." In a new security framework, the environment is not a freely existing trove of natural resources to be fought over and monetized but rather encompasses the physical factors that condition human affairs and well-being. Environmental or ecological security, in this definition, is the means and processes that seek to reduce or prevent environmental consequences of war, natural disasters, erosion of the earth's carrying capacity, and war and armed conflict resulting from environmental change (Dalby, 2009: 132). Environmental security, then, represents a critical move in new security, one that attempts to remove hegemonic political domination from the equation by discussing security at its simplest: the desire to prolong and improve life on the planet.

Predictably, however, these moves toward a new security conceptualization were not welcomed by traditionalists such as Stephen Walt and John Mearsheimer, who stood by traditional and neoconservative concepts of security and state (Hough, 2014: 23). Indeed, for traditionalist security scholars such as Andrew Baldwin, these expansions of the concept of security carried the risk of voiding the concept of any meaning (Baldwin et al., 2014). The existence of this reluctance, however, seems to be evidence in and of itself of the fundamental narrowness of the field. The inclusion of environmental concerns in traditional security discourses has forced academics, analysts, and practitioners to broaden not only the consideration of potential threats but also, significantly, the consideration of who or what is being threatened. These conversations widened the lens of security issues by discussing and analyzing the process of securitization, which in turn moved the security literature in a critical and much needed direction.

Securitization and the Politics of Fear

Securitization theory extends the new examinations of threats and security. Threats are at the foundation of security; when particular issues appear to threaten lives, political responses necessarily follow (Hough, 2014: 9). Traditional and realist notions of the "security dilemma" have informed the downward spiral of insecurity between sovereign states based on threats arising from military and economic capabilities. Meanwhile, there is a need to examine more deeply the sociological approach to the construction of security issues, one which requires, by contrast, the conceptualization of "the power of discourses" (Trombetta, 2011: 148–149). Security is essentially about power, whether material or discursive. For sociological perspectives on security, power is the successful (re)framing of discourses and the capacity of the few to mobilize resources necessary for the social and political construction of threats (Floyd, 2007: 330).

The Copenhagen School's definition of security outlines the social and discursive construction of threats through the establishment of "referent objects" – particular activities or sectors beyond the state (Buzan et al., 1998: 22–23). It argues in favor of a more profound extension of security threats to nonmilitary issues – such as the environment – beyond the traditional "objective" materialist threat analysis (Buzan, 2007: 2).

The introduction of discourses is crucial since showing how they are constructed and amplified reveals many assumptions. In this context, discourses refer to "specific ensemble of ideas, concepts and categorizations that are produced and transformed in a particular set of practices and through which meaning is given to physical and social realities" (Hajer, 1995: 42). The Copenhagen School analyzes discourses in terms of both speeches and the identification of the practices that fall within the "logic of war and emergency" (Trombetta, 2011: 136,

148–149). In these circumstances, actors create securitized discourses by arguing that there is a need for "legitimiz[ing] emergency measures" (Buzan et al., 1998: 25) and actively draw attention to the perceived threats by using alarmist language when framing their narratives. The securitizing actors, or "enunciators," consist of individuals or groups that perform the speech act; they represent voices of authority within a society or "someone ... some group, movement, party or elite ... who purports to advocate on behalf of the nation" (Buzan et al., 1998: 41).

The process of securitization therefore means that actors in the field communicate specific discourses about perceived threats that have implications for policy outcomes. In this framework, common patterns emerge: For example, when an actor claims that a referent object is existentially threatened, they next claim the right to resort to emergency measures, and finally they convince their domestic audience that rule-breaking behavior is justified to counter the threat. This process can be referred to as a "security speech act" and is at the root of discourse creation in the security framework. When elites articulate this "security speech act," they present the threat as "urgent" and "existential," so the public audience is inclined to accept the "utterance itself." As such, a "securitizing move" takes place (McDonald, 2008: 24–26). This "securitizing move" goes on to become securitization because the domestic audience continues to give consent as long as the actor portrays the threat as existential and urgent.

In this way, enunciators can legitimize exceptional measures; they have permission to defend emergency measures on the pretext of defending national survival. The "existential" nature of the threat moves it from the normal domain of politics to the security domain, where it is more likely to gain material support even if citizens are unaware of the issue. This creates the pretext for future exceptionalist measures that require no public support or knowledge. Such "politics of exceptionalism" successfully places issues on the regional and international agenda of "high politics," in that the general public need not be involved (Huysman, 2004: 332). Scholars have noted that these processes can lead to security risks from depoliticization and de-democratization; when security issues are removed from the political realm, they can create further potential security dilemmas (Floyd, 2013: 24; Trombetta, 2011: 136).

In contrast to the Copenhagen School, the Paris School emphasizes the role of power politics in "practices and context" and their impact on "the construction of threat images" (Balzacq, 2011: 1). Although securitization theory broadens the security agenda to nonmilitary issues and the object of security lies beyond the state, the main actor and referent object remain, in most cases, the state itself (Buzan et al., 1998: 23–24, 29). Research from the Paris School questions this focus on the state's security, moving the focus to its interactions with communities and individuals. In moving away from this state-centered approach, new perspectives focus the discussion on non-state actors and provide alternative definitions of securitization by looking at the daily practices of "insecuritization" of bureaucratic bodies (Balzacq, 2011).

What constitutes successful securitization differs across geographical and theoretical perspectives. For example, India and Nepal used environmental narratives to successfully securitize their interactions over the Tanakpur barrage in the Ganges river basin (Mirumachi, 2013), while Israeli and Palestinian environmental narratives – of territory, resources, and population – that used climate change as a security threat reinforced Israel's military-political domination in the Jordan basin (Alatout, 2006; Mason and Mimi, 2014). Security relates to mutual perceptions, and who or what is being secured is always implicit but often left unstated. These mutual perceptions are of critical importance in understanding the securitization of the environment.

Securitization of the Environment: Pessimists (Neo-Malthusians) vs. Optimists (Cornucopians)

An ontological debate is taking place over security more broadly, and the inclusion of environmental considerations is characterized by a theoretical schism: mainstream concerns, which maintain the state as the referent object, compared to "critical" and "human security" movements, which recenter the focus on human beings. Traditional proponents of security, seeing the state as the unit of analysis, frame environmental challenges in terms of inter- or intrastate conflict, whereas human security considers the environment's relation to human health, hunger, and well-being. This shift in referent object inherently redefines security since the referent object determines the nature of threats and consequently the nature of insecurity (Vogler, 2013: 19).

This consideration sparks critical questions about how concepts of the environment and environmental risk have been impacted and how securitization narratives around these issues have developed. Dalby discusses how security reorders social relations into security relations, although the processes through which these are constituted often obscure power dynamics (Dalby, 2002: 12). Since security as a concept is both a signifier and a transmitter of content, it has a performative function in addition to its descriptive one: It establishes the security situation while it reports on it (Dalby, 2002: 12).

A thorough understanding of the dissemination of environmental security narratives is required to understand how environmental challenges act as stressors to preexisting social systems. The development of scholarly literature on environmental security – especially in relation to natural resources and scarcity – provides a vital understanding of how these issues were initially framed and how their framing has evolved and responded to changes in both international relations and security studies.

As environmental security became more widely acknowledged as a concept, theories that encouraged a securitization of the environment began to emerge. Buzan and others have shown how treating the environment as an object to be protected in a security framework constitutes one of the "securitization moves" by actors who use the threat of insecurity to justify their own political or foreign policy agendas (Buzan et al., 1998: 29). In this framework, actors would be inclined to treat environmental problems as national security threats or matters of high political urgency (Hough, 2014: 21). At its most extreme, the logical conclusion of this process could even be the weaponization of the environment, as in a military use of violence against environmental resources as a means of waging war (Hough, 2014: 11).

Different securitization theories of the environment have functioned along different theoretical assumptions; some actors operate as environmental pessimists who view ecological resources as finite and scarce (neo-Malthusians), and others operate from a framework of cooperation and abundance (cornucopians). Below, we explain how these frameworks have influenced theories of resource conflict in international relations.

Broadly stated, there are five main views on the role of environmental factors in conflict and cooperation in the international system.

Neo-Malthusianism suggests that resource scarcity will inevitably lead to conflict and posits itself as an "environmental security" framework – the environment itself is a scarce resource in need of state protection and regulation. Political-ecology discourses are interested instead in distribution of resources and in analyzing how political aims influence the use and management of such natural resources. Cornucopians have the more liberal view that resource scarcity is not inherent or inevitable but can be managed and mitigated by an administration of resources through markets and trade. At the same time, institutionalists see cooperation through regime formation as a way to overcome resource scarcity. Finally, resource curse theorists see overabundance of strategic resources as a negative factor that encourages conflict and competition over scarce natural resources and the wealth they can provide.

Interestingly, the field of environmental and water security has followed similar debates as those in development studies with relation to the analysis of poverty and hunger. Traditional theories of development have drawn on Malthus' *Essay on the Principle of Population* (1798; see Malthus, 1996) to establish the inevitable risk of global poverty and hunger posed by unchecked population growth. Figure 2.1 provides a basic outline of this Malthusian perspective, and the ensuing discussion explains how neo-Malthusianism can be applied to water scarcity and water insecurity.

Neo-Malthusianism: Green Wars or Water Wars
Neo-Malthusian perspectives have been applied to discussions of resource scarcity and abundance in security, especially in regard to water. The two prevailing perspectives on water resources are resource optimists, who argue that cooperation and strategic sharing of water resources can mitigate potential threats of water instability, and resource pessimists, who see conflict as inevitable because of scarce resources and institutional weaknesses surrounding their governance. Resource pessimists also see demographic growth, water scarcity, and violent conflict as inevitable and interchangeable.

A variety of scholars, from political scientists to geographers to environmental scientists, left their mark on conversations about environmental security in the 1980s and 1990s by focusing on water scarcity. The Toronto School and the Bern-Zürich Group developed the notion of "environmental scarcity" during the 1990s, which paved the way for alarmist predictions of high risks of resource wars because

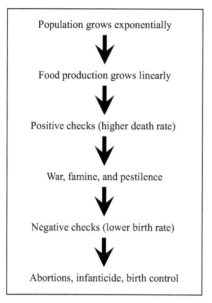

Figure 2.1 The Malthusian model.
Source: Malthus, 1996

of decreased supplies of environmental resources induced by population growth, water depletion, and the socially inequitable distribution of resources (Bachler et al., 1996; Homer-Dixon, 1994: 18–20). Because of their focus on the impacts of population growth on resource depletion, many of these perspectives have been labeled as "neo-Malthusian."[1] An outline of the supply-induced type of environmental scarcity can be seen in Figure 2.2.

---

[1] In a personal communication with the author, Homer-Dixon distances himself from the neo-Malthusian "unidirectional, linear causal sequence" by outlining the fact that his research has identified since the 1990s the "many causal mechanisms that link environmental scarcity and conflict in feedback loops." He further argues that his research shows that "the most important and powerful causal mechanisms linking environmental scarcity/stress and violence are highly indirect, with scarcity operating through a series of intermediate causal stages." While "taking population seriously," he outlines "the precursor social factors that drive population size and growth," and discusses "why population is only one of a host of factors contributing to scarcity" (July 11 and 17, 2019). Homer-Dixon's book (1999) on scarcity and violence is examined in another section of this chapter.

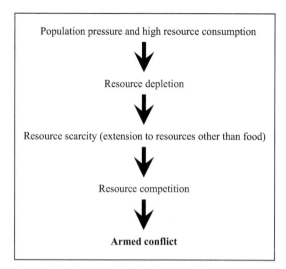

Figure 2.2 The neo-Malthusian model.

Resource curse theorists, who emerged in discussions about both strategic and nonstrategic resources (i.e. scarce resources such as oil or diamonds and life-sustaining resources like water and food), have proposed that abundance rather than scarcity of natural resources leads to low economic growth, corruption, poor governance, and resource capture. In this framework, low economic growth results from mismanagement of resources and concentration in one industry, as in rentier states, while corruption naturally ensues from capture of rents and price inflation related to these resources. Poor governance emerges because states have low incentives to develop functional or socially equitable institutions, while resource capture and looting follow as a result of poor governance. Greed and grievances theory establishes a powerful connection between the abundance of primary commodity exports like diamonds, oil, and other strategic resources and the likelihood of disputes over the control of such resources (Collier and Hoeffler, 2004, 2005; Fearon, 2005). These models predict the emergence of civil conflicts on the basis of state strength, poverty, and resource abundance (Koubi et al., 2014: 238). However, resource curse theory, along with neo-Malthusianism, have key theoretical weaknesses that leave room for new approaches.

These theories developed about nonrenewable resources have suffered from patterns of oversimplification and weak theoretical framing. The evidence shows that states rich in resources experience a wide variety of economic outcomes, which suggests that institutions are key to explaining the lack of conflict (Mehlum et al., 2006). The resource curse paradigm also suggests that resource-wealthy countries tend to be rent-seeking, dysfunctional, and experience more civil strife, especially as states with resource wealth are more vulnerable to poor governance from low taxes, political strife from domination of resources by one group, or negative externalities of natural resources – such as in migration or pollution (Collier and Hoeffler, 2004; Karl, 1997; Koubi et al., 2014: 232). However, more nuanced views suggest that there is variance within these assumptions. There is evidence that the specific conflict location within a state, as well as the type and duration of conflict, impact the determination of any potential link between conflict and resource scarcity (Fearon, 2005).

From a normative perspective, the securitization of the environment on the basis of scarcity is a double-edged sword. As a linguistic and rhetorical tool in the hands of elites, these discourses can raise awareness and mobilize collective action around environmental degradation and climate change. Less useful, however, is the tendency of these narratives to favor doom-and-gloom scenarios that rely upon "collapsology" theories or self-enforcing forecasts regarding the inevitability of the demise of our natural and human systems, as explained in Chapter 1. This language perceives threats as stemming from unchecked population growth in other parts of the world, inter- and intrastate conflicts over resources, the permeation of national borders, and international migration flows due to resource depletion. This approach therefore tends to regard threats through a Western lens and has been put forward primarily by scholars from North America and Europe. The discourses surrounding overpopulation further highlight the politically problematic nature of creating and validating causal linkages between environmental degradation and conflict as they are inextricably linked to the economic relationships that privilege the Global North at the expense of the Global South; for example, focusing on birth rates in Global South communities moves the responsibility for the environmental damage caused by resource-intensive lifestyles of citizens in the Global North to citizens of the Global South (Barnett, 2001: 58–60). Dalby establishes an interesting analogy between Malthusian conceptions of overpopulation and the weaponized deployment of population control by colonial administrators to control local communities; in both cases, the onus is placed on the less powerful state with fewer resources as a more direct threat to environmental degradation while hegemonic forces remain unchallenged (Dalby, 2009: 17–18).

There is also a way in which this hegemonic approach to environmental degradation as a "political construction" allows security to become "a powerful producer of endangered identities" (Dalby, 2002: xxii). The issue can continue to be exploited to mobilize electorates in the Global North against what is perceived to be unchecked danger from the Global South. The question, then, is how these theories have been instrumentalized in the hands of actors seeking to force a particular narrative of resource management, including water security. The reality is that institutionally weak and developing countries face a "double insecurity" threat: They are faced by both discrepancies in their responsibility for and their vulnerability to environmental problems (Barnett, 2001: 20).

However, as mentioned previously, interstate conflict over resources and environmental problems has rarely occurred (Dalby, 2002: 47). Barnett draws upon the work of Lipschutz and Holdren (1990) to argue that military conflict over resources is unlikely due to alternative means of resolving resource scarcities, such as trade and the development of new technologies (Barnett, 2001: 52–53). In fact, it is the fear itself and the *perception* of scarcity through securitization narratives that creates the very insecurity that drives unsafe and violent behavior, both on the part of states and individuals. Thus, even though the electorates in the Global North may not be facing a real threat of resource scarcity, it is the perception of scarcity that motivates otherizing and violent actions (Matthews, 1989). Additionally, and ironically, increased militarization in response to environmental degradation can pose a significant risk through escalation (Barnett, 2001: 19).

Many perceptions of a scarcity and conflict nexus have been driven by self-confirming and largely baseless studies perpetuated by the persistent, more than 200-year-old Malthusian narrative about population spikes and scarcity, which has been largely found to be without conclusive evidence (Dalby, 2009: 15). Neo-Malthusian narratives about fears surrounding food scarcity have remained unusually persistent in global discourse and, paradoxically, have even informed moves that have actually aggravated food crises (Jarvis et al., 2005: 49). Security scholars' tendency to conflate "resources" (whether renewable or nonrenewable) with the environment as a concept have acted to enforce the idea of resource wars, thereby acting as discursive tools of the Global North more broadly and the security establishment more specifically (Barnett, 2001: 52).

An increasing number of analyses have started to show that the neo-Malthusian assumptions about environmental stressors and the link between conflict and environmental scarcity, especially along the axis of renewable resources, are fraught with oversimplification, a lack of accurate data, and theoretical weakness (Koubi et al., 2014). Homer-Dixon famously delineated three types of environmental scarcity – supply, demand-induced and structural – leading to a series of intermediate causal stages, namely social effects such as migration and constrained economic productivity that weaken state institutions and their capacity to absorb these shocks, which, in turn, lead to violence in the form of group-identity conflict, coups d'état, and insurgency. Kahl also points out that elites in a given state have the potential to manipulate their power over access to resources during times of scarcity, suggesting that systemic and sociopolitical factors are often left out of the discussion (Homer-Dixon, 1999: 80; Kahl, 2008: 50).

Contrary to popular forecasts of looming water wars, recent empirical work predicts that countries are more likely to cooperate than to fight over internationally shared waters. Empirical studies at Oregon University and the Pacific Institute have revealed the surprising result that there have hardly been any "water wars" in human history (Wolf, 1998; Wolf et al., 2003). An analysis based on a total of 1,831 events connected to transboundary "basins at risk," shows that riparian states tend to cooperate rather than enter into conflict (Giordano et al., 2002). In the past fifty years, there are only thirty-seven recorded acute conflicts over international water resources (MacQuarrie and Wolf, 2013: 177). Although the detailed chronology of disputes over water since 3000 BC shows that water has been used as a military tool and target, water wars have for the most part not taken place, even in highly water-insecure regions such as the Middle East (Pacific Institute, 2015). Scarcity and degradation reduce the probability for conflict by providing the impetus for negotiation and coordination between and across states as well as the desire for increased equity and environmental justice (Deudney and Matthew, 1999; Diehl and Gleditsch,

2001: 3). More broadly, environmental cooperation has a positive impact on the reduction of tensions, demilitarization, and peace-making between states and different groups (Conca and Dabelko, 2002).

The key remaining issue is the sustainable use of natural resources in coordination with poverty reduction and the mitigation of potential conflict. Although explicit water wars have not yet taken place, social conflicts over water are increasingly common and important (Conca, 2006). Weak water management and governance contribute to emerging social conflicts over water – rather than military confrontations – by adversely affecting poor and rural communities. The potential for cooperation, therefore, lies in alternative institutional forms and the consolidation of global environmental governance (Conca, 2006). For example, liberal institutionalist perspectives on resource management have refuted the neo-Malthusian model of resource scarcity.

Cornucopian-Liberal Perspectives: Water Cooperation as the New Mantra

In their framing of solutions to environmental insecurity, cornucopian theories have adopted assumptions from institutional liberal perspectives in international relations. In particular, cornucopians share liberal assumptions that the presence of democracy, economic interdependence, and international institutions will necessarily reduce the likelihood and impact of military conflict (Rousseau and Walker, 2010: 26–28). Others outline the importance of regime design in international water management (Bernauer, 2002; Giordano et al., 2005; McLaughlin Mitchell and Zawahri, 2015). Cornucopians, or "resource optimists," share the view that resources are scarce but that their scarcity is a matter of mismanagement and the lack of market regulation for price and distribution of key resources. They concede that scarcity of water resources may put human security at risk but emphasize the ability of states and international systems to adapt through market mechanisms, technology, social institutions for resource allocation, and other market-based mechanisms for cooperation (Lomborg, 2001). In this framework, neo-Malthusian perspectives are criticized as overly deterministic and mired in the same theoretical weaknesses as securitization narratives (Gleditsch, 1998). In addition, cornucopians argue that if environmental insecurity is related to conflict, it will exist along a spectrum of other factors, including domestic, geopolitical, and economic factors that tend to drive conflict alongside environmental risk (Gartzke, 2012). Other criticisms of the link between environmental insecurity and conflict suggest that studies have relied upon insufficient data, made assumptions about time lags that may not hold true, and have ignored the risk of endogeneity in constructing causal arguments (Koubi et al., 2014: 227). These criticisms suggest that, in the absence of strong evidence to the contrary, cornucopians may be correct in considering a variety of factors beyond environmental risk when explaining conflict (Koubi et al., 2014: 229).

Cornucopians posit a number of methodological and theoretical objections to neo-Malthusian views of resource management and security. Methodological objections to neo-Malthusianism include criticisms about the low number of systematic studies to support resource scarcity models, as well as the tendency to limit such studies to states or cases that are also mired in economic insecurity and poverty; such studies raise issues of endogeneity and fail to address the separate question of the relationship between resource scarcity, poverty, and conflict. Other Cornucopian objections to the neo-Malthusian paradigm are economic in nature and focus on the substitutability of key resources as well as the potential for technological innovation and market pricing strategies to prevent resource-related conflict – for example, alternatives to fossil fuels may alleviate conflict associated with those resources.

There are also political objections to neo-Malthusianism. For example, moves toward democracy are sometimes seen as leading to environmental reform, and greater levels of democracy are seen as discouraging conflict and boosting the likelihood of cooperation in the environmental arena (i.e. cooperation trumps conflict). Liberal political objections to neo-Malthusianism also argue that greater freedom of information encourages better economic outcomes and that pluralism, pragmatism, and more market-focused environmental orientations have the capacity to mitigate potential conflict. Finally, other political objections claim that democratic and international institutions encourage greater respect for human life and well-being, and, accordingly, address threats brought about by resource insecurity with cooperative and peaceful means rather than with conflict.

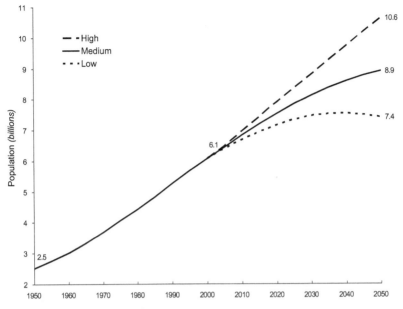

Figure 2.3 Population predictions.

Source: United Nations Population Division, 2004; reprinted with the permission of the United Nations

Critically, cornucopians have also articulated key demographic concerns and objections against neo-Malthusianism, revealing some of the scientific and data-based limitations of the type of population-based theories that had allowed resource scarcity arguments to flourish in the security sphere. First, the three types of population pressure – density, growth, and youth bulges – do not have a clear impact; second, population pressure is not always necessarily harmful to societies. Additionally, as Figure 2.3 shows, our current predictions of future population growth do not match the very high predictions of previous generations, with slowdowns in population growth in certain areas.

Critical Environmental Security: Water Security, Food Security, and Drought

The divide between cornucopians and neo-Malthusians that exists in discussions of resource scarcity also exists in the conceptualization of water security, with resource optimists and resource pessimists following similar patterns of theoretical divides around a scarcity–conflict and scarcity–cooperation nexus. In this framing, cornucopians identify a more cooperative version of water interactions, while neo-Malthusians are more likely to view water as a national security issue linked to conflict (Zala, 2013: 169–170).

Defining Water Security

This ongoing debate has critical implications for academic research and policy, and, more directly, for our HECS framework with regards to Syria. Some of these implications are linked to the sheer theoretical difficulty of defining and articulating the concept of water security, especially in its current iteration. There is a consistent amount of theoretical opacity and lack of consistency across disciplines, making a coherent discussion difficult. A review of the concept of water security in academic and policy literature shows that although the term has become much more popular in recent years, studies across different scientific and social-science disciplines tend to utilize very different scales, making meta-analysis much more difficult. Current literature also shows that the use of the term varies greatly based on the study's particular field. For example, the legal field frames the issue as a matter of instance allocation rules to secure entitlements, while the agricultural field looks at the issue in the context of flood protection and drought risk (Cook and Bakker, 2012: 95–97). Despite these divergent trends, three common themes and issues in water security emerge across the literature – water-related hazards, human need (which is often tied to food security), and sustainability, which incorporates perspectives on protecting and maintaining the natural environment) – while water availability and quantity are assessed to quantify water security.

Water availability and quantity are sometimes used as a proxy for water security, especially in policy and environmental science spheres, because they allow for a measurable definition of water security that can be compared across contexts. Water availability is generally defined as the presence or absence of sufficient freshwater supply for humans, in both domestic and commercial uses (i.e. agriculture), and is employed as the primary indicator of water security in the majority of existing literature. However, different disciplines have focused on different scales and contexts for water availability, such as the national, communal, or watershed scale. Scales and methodologies used to measure water availability tend to vary greatly across different disciplines, even though some supply-side indicators have been broadly accepted. In the 1980s, Swedish hydrologist Malin Falkenmark designated the following standard definitions for water insecurity, later coined as "the Falkenmark indicator": Greater than 1,700 cubic meters per person per year is defined as relative water sufficiency, between 1,700 and 1,000 cubic meters as a state of water stress, between 1,000 and 500 cubic meters per year as meeting the water scarcity line, and absolute water scarcity starts at less than 500 cubic meters per person per year (Falkenmark, 1986; Falkenmark et al., 2007; Falkenmark and Molden, 2008; Rijsberman, 2006). International organizations, such as the World Health Organization, the United Nations Environment Program (UNEP), the United Nations Commission on Sustainable Development and the World Bank, endorsed the thresholds. Meanwhile, the concept of annual water available per capita is a standard measure of availability, with sustainable water availability being 1,000 cubic meters per person per year, or 50 liters per person per day without accounting for food production and a minimum of 2,300 liters per person per year with food production (MacQuarrie and Wolf, 2013: 172). The "Falkenmark indicator" has, since then, evolved into a new standard, referred to as *water crowding* (see Figure 2.4).[2] The diagram distinguishes between *demand-driven* (water stress) and *population driven* (water crowding) water scarcity. The countries that appear in the brown upper-right-hand corner of the box are the ones experiencing high climate vulnerability with severe population and demand-driven water shortages.

Humans need water to survive. Three concepts – human need, sustainability, and vulnerability to water-related hazards – enrich the debate about the definition of water security as it relates to sustaining life. Scott G. Witter and Scott Whiteford define water security as "a condition where there is a sufficient quantity of water at a quality necessary, at an affordable price, to meet both the short-term and long-term needs to protect the health, safety, welfare and productive capacity of position (households, communities, or nation)" (1999: 2).

---

[2] In an exchange with the author, Malin Falkenmark notes: "The version of the Falkenmark indicator from the 1980s tends to live a life of its own rather far away from a more up-to-date view on respectively water stress, water scarcity and water shortage" (July 30, 2019).

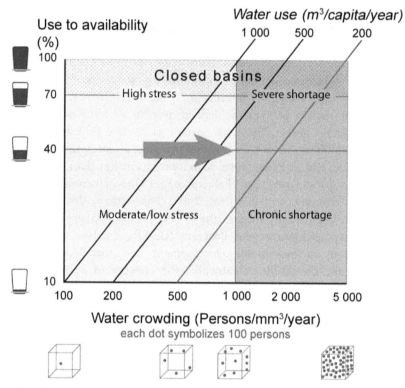

Figure 2.4 Water crowding indicator.
Source: Falkenmark, 2018

Water security inherently involves the protection of vulnerable water systems and sources and also includes the protection against water-related hazards such as floods and droughts, as well as sustainable development of water resources and safeguarding access to water. Although there is no universal definition of drought (Von Uexkull 2014: 20), definitions contain social, ecological, and biological components.

While drought is generally defined as a natural reduction in the amount of precipitation over an extended period of time as a result of climatic factors, there are three generally accepted types of droughts. First, meteorological drought occurs when there is a prolonged period with lower than average precipitation. Second, agricultural drought occurs when a climate experiences "insufficient moisture" for crop production; this can occur during periods of sufficient precipitation if soil conditions or other agricultural factors are limiting crop production (Erian, 2011: 3). Finally, hydrologic drought occurs when water reserves fall below their average supply, which can also occur during periods of sufficient precipitation with overuse of water reserves (Erian, 2011: 3). Beyond these three definitions, socioeconomic drought can also occur when water demand exceeds supply because of human use, such as during excessive irrigation (Wolchover, 2018).

Drought is a key component of water security, a term that also has many competing definitions. In 2000, Global Water Partnership (GWP) offered a more comprehensive definition, combining access, affordability, human needs, and ecological health. As they put it, in an ideal water secure world, "every person has access to enough safe water at affordable cost to lead a clean, healthy and productive life" (GWP, 2000: 12). In this sense, GWP has perceived water security as "a complex concept of holistic water management and the balance between resource protection and resource use" at local, national and regional levels (GWP, 2000: 12).

Framings of Water Security

The framing of water issues greatly impacts the response to the perceived threat. Unfortunately, no one definition can account for all of the social and political nuances that shape water access and distribution, which are arguably the two determining factors of water security. Since no universal definition of water security exists and its implementation at the policy level depends on its framing, stronger actors with "greater influence" tend to have a better chance at convincing public audiences about the "importance and acuteness" of this securitized issue (Fischhendler, 2015). In the field of international relations, realists have endlessly predicted conflict between riparian states since states sharing a river would strive to gain a maximum share of the finite (albeit fugitive) resource (Frey, 1993; Waterbury, 1997). Generally, in such a situation, one party intentionally or unintentionally frustrates another's objectives, but open conflict only occurs when it is in the hegemon's interest (Lowi, 1993). Environmental instability in water resource allocation thus becomes a threat to state security, without being a central reason for armed conflict (Lowi and Shaw, 2000: 149). Another proposed route from demographic and environmental stress to conflict is in the context of weak states, where a process of state disintegration leads to civil violence. Several major studies, however, have refuted this theory, as in the case of Mali (see Kahl, 2006).

The traditionalist understanding of water security also shapes policy-making in the defense and security sectors of countries such as the United Kingdom and the United States, which creates "overly militarized responses" to water resources (Zala, 2013: 280). At the same time, neo-Malthusian policies are applied to the "impoverished South," which is perceived as "both a natural phenomenon and a threat to American affluence" (Dalby, 1999, 2002: 165). For example, in 1991, the George H. W. Bush administration included issues relating to environmental security with a focus on threats emerging from developing countries in the "National Security Strategy of the United States" (Deudney and Matthew, 1999: 2). Neo-Malthusian theories also inspired foreign-aid policies adopted in 1993 by the Clinton administration in favor of population control in sensitive areas around the world. As a result of his approach, the Middle East and Africa were soon regarded as potential hotspots for future "water wars" (Hough, 2013: 22–23).

Definitions of water security also have political dimensions, which focus on its ability to provoke conflict. Some theorists argue that resource scarcity has historically been the single most critical issue in armed conflict, especially if the conflict is a territorial dispute, as territory can be a proxy for other scarce resources (including minerals, energy sources, food, and water). At the same time, the sharing of water resources, such as an intra-border river, can contribute to inter-national conflict, and resource scarcity stressors have historically led to external and internal fighting and even societal collapse. Finally, cli-mate change has been shown to be a definite stressor of conflict, since increased variation of water flows and more frequent extreme weather events can trigger conflict and resource allocation issues (MacQuarrie and Wolf, 2013: 175).

The impact of internal and external politics on perceived water security or insecurity can be explored using this political orientation. Gleick's (2006) study of water conflict chronology argues that in numerous cases political forces interact with water resources, leading to conflict. Although he found no cases in which water access or supplies were themselves the root of an armed conflict, there were ninety-one cases of conflict in which water resources or systems were used as weapons or as targets during armed conflict. In addition, he finds 173 cases in which water resources or systems were used by a nation, state or non-state actor for a political goal, or by non-state actors as a tool of terrorism, and fifty-five cases in which water resources or systems were shown to be a major source of contention in the context of economic or social development. These classifications show clearly how definitions of water security can become enmeshed with discussions of political stability. Often, it is the mixing of real resource scarcity with political aims, goals, or motivations that results in the wide variety of water security definitions.

Water Security as Cooperation

In the past decade, the debate over water security has shifted toward finding incentives and benefits for cooperation over natural resources (Vogler, 2013: 12) and the promotion of an integrative approach to water security as both quantity and quality. This can be accomplished through institutional management and international policy tools, including, for example, the policy tool of integrated water resource management (IWRM) for equity, efficiency, and sustainability purposes (Cook and Bakker, 2012). Endorsed by key international institutions, IWRM addresses the challenge of working with sometimes opposed interests (ecosystems vs. human needs, surface water vs, groundwater resources, upstream vs. downstream interests, different uses, etc.). Where water wars were once regarded as the next great security threat, cooperation is increasingly seen to be favored because of technological innovation, human progress, market pricing, and resource substitution mutual regimes, international agreements, and political economy (Allan, 2000, 2001; Gleditsch, 1998: 381; Wolf, 1998; Wolf et al., 2003). In this new framework, resource scarcity can be overcome through a variety of institutional and political tools, including treaties on navigation, pollution, and water use (Dinar, 2011). Other potential tools for addressing greater water security include the establishment of international water law and river authorities, along with increased emphasis on a climate of cooperation and trust among actors, which could be accomplished through "peace-promoting institutions" such as international legal and cooperation bodies (Hensel et al., 2006).

Liberal institutionalist approaches contend that international conflicts over resources are not simply issues of supply and demand but rather function according to three measures of political effectiveness. Resource conflict is more likely to occur where: (1) resource sovereignty is ill defined; (2) presiding regimes are weakened by political change; or (3) the change in resource availability outpaces the government's institutional capacity to adapt (Jarvis et al., 2005: 47–48). Such holistic approaches to conflict analysis de-emphasize the significance of the resource itself in favor of the social and political systems in which the resource is situated and distributed. Conflict thus occurs when institutions (defined here as the formal or informal structures that facilitate coordination between people) fail to manage the resource or resources in question (Jarvis et al., 2005: 53).

Both of the prevailing approaches – the scarcity–conflict and scarcity–cooperation nexus – can be seen as overly deterministic, as they imply predetermined outcomes rather than adequately accounting for local realities. Complex interactions over water cannot fall neatly into "conflict" or "cooperation"; rather, such engagements can be defined as transboundary water interactions, which are inevitably mixed. An overly normative approach that sees cooperation as "good" and conflict as "bad" fails to consider local forces and political context on the ground in each case, as in the Jordan River example (Zeitoun and Mirumachi, 2008: 305, 309). It is therefore critical to shift away from this sort of strict delineation, while also shifting the unit of analysis to water as a source of intrastate, rather than interstate, conflict. This approach looks outside state-centric models and measurements such as gross domestic product (GDP) by examining more localized case studies with individual and local-level data, as well as by analyzing other modes of conflict like demonstrations, communal violence, and so forth (Koubi et al., 2014: 238; MacQuarrie and Wolf, 2013: 180). Such approaches will be better equipped to untangle the complex knot of human and environmental factors that drive interactions over shared water resources.

Overall, there are several gaps in the current literature on environmental security, many of which will be aided by the HECS theoretical framework developed in this study. This HECS framework integrates climate, water, and food security as interrelated concepts, with a focus on the impact of such insecurities on populations at the subnational levels, while considering the role played by government structures and policy choices. This multidimensional approach to climate vulnerability that emphasizes the importance of policy choices brings to the fore a notion precisely developed within international policy circles: the concept of human security.

Human Security: An Emerging Framework for the Environment

In 2012, the United Nations General Assembly (UNGA) adopted Resolution 66/290, recognizing that human security synergizes the three pillars of the UN (i.e. development, human rights, and peace and security) in "an interlinked and mutually reinforcing manner" (UNGA, 2012). Human security as a concept was first developed by two prominent non-Western economists – Nobel Prize winner Amartya Sen and special adviser to the United Nations Development Program (UNDP) Habib Ul-Haq – in a 1994 report for the UNDP Human Development program. Combining security and development concerns, human security was framed in terms of the principles of social justice, mutual cooperation, and equity. In recent years, the discussion around human security expanded to include environmental security experts like Jon Barnett, Simon Dalby, Ken Conca, Rita Floyd, Richard Matthew, and Erika Weinthal, who advocate for considering climate change in human security terms (Barnett, 2001; Barnett and Adger, 2007; Dalby, 2009, 2013; Floyd and Matthew, 2013; Matthew, 2014a; Weinthal et al., 2015). By adopting a human-security lens, these scholars are shifting the focus in security studies away from military-based national-security concerns and are urging scholars to consider vulnerable groups within societies; this development has brought new meaning to policy and academic debates on climate change and its human impacts.

Recent developments of human-security literature have offered a number of definitions. Dalby outlines four essential characteristics of human security:

1. Human security is a universal concern relevant to people everywhere.
2. The components of human security are interdependent.
3. Human security is easier to ensure through early prevention.
4. The referent object of human security is shifted away from states to people.

(Dalby, 2013: 122)

In this framework, human security focuses on issues relating to individual human life and well-being rather than the state-level, militarized concepts that have traditionally dominated the national-security dis-course. At the same time, policy-driven approaches tend to focus on human security as "freedom from" harm, danger, and suffering, rather than the more traditional "freedom to" conception of civil and polit-ical liberties. The Fifth Assessment Report issued by the IPCC in 2014 provides a wide definition of human security as "a condition that exists when the vital core of human lives is protected, and when people have the freedom and capacity to live with dignity" (IPCC, 2014: 759). Human security therefore has to be actively pursued; it is not innate but must be sought after and protected. Still other concepts of human security focus on the need to protect lives from potential risks and dangers – in this approach, human security "is about preven-tion – anticipating dangers and acting to head them off before the downward spirals happen" (Dalby, 2013: 135). All these approaches to human security can help us identify the risks posed by climate change, especially as it interacts with various sociological, economic, and geological factors.

An examination of the discourses around human security sheds light on how this framework is useful for understanding the link between environmental issues and human well-being. It is crucial, therefore, to review and disaggregate the various definitions of the term, since development and human-rights scholars have proposed some new and critical conceptions of human security.

Definitions of Human Security

Human security has often been defined as the framework by which practitioners can seek to protect humans from economic, political, or environmental suffering. The state has traditionally been the referent object of security, but Ul-Haq (1995: 103–104) and Sen (2000) place human beings as the reference objects of security and development by arguing that improving human lives should be an explicit development objective. They focus on vulnerability as an underlying premise of human security and tie the enhancement of human development and security to environmental and ecological concerns. A 2003 report from the Commission on Human Security – established by the Japanese government – builds on this by defining human security as "the neces-sity to protect vital freedoms by building on people's strengths and aspirations ... and protecting them from critical and pervasive threats and situations" (Ogata and Sen, 2003). This approach emphasizes "freedom from want," "freedom from fear," and "a life of dignity" (Ul-Haq, 1995: 32). In other words, in this framework, human security is based on the understanding that every human innately deserves the right to live free from risks and threats, including climate insecurity.

On the other hand, other definitions of human security make explicit reference to addressing the unequal relationship between the Global South and North, which has been the source of much human insecurity. As Ul-Haq puts it: "Human security is a means to instituting a new partnership between the North and the South based on justice, not on charity; on an equitable sharing of global market opportunities, not on aid; on two-way compacts, not one-way transfers: on mutual cooperation, not on unilateral conditionally or confrontation" (Ul-Haq, 1998: 5). This vision of human security is based on equity and can be widely and universally applied – it "should be universal, global, and indivisible" (Ul-Haq, 1995: 39). This framework seeks not only to protect but also to undo unequal power structures that have caused or encourage human suffering. This definition also has significant implications for climate insecurity – as the latter is also linked to unequal power relations between the Global North and South – and for how societies can improve the safety, well-being, and livelihood of their citizens, all of which are made more difficult in an insecure climate. An equity-based human-security definition therefore brings in the notion of human development.

Human Security and Development

When considering human security through a lens of human development, the focus is placed on how promoting human safety and stability is linked to respecting and harnessing the power of human life, with the ultimate goal of facilitating opportunities for people to work toward better lives. Human security is therefore the ability to not only live without harm but also to actively improve one's safety, quality of life, and well-being. Ul-Haq and Sen see people, and not economic growth, as both the means and ends of development. As Ul-Haq writes, "New models of human development will treat GNP [gross national product] growth as a means, not as an end; enhance human life, not marginalize it; replenish natural resources, not run them down; and encourage grass-roots participation of people in the events and processes that shape their lives" (Ul-Haq, 1995: 40). This understanding of human security also emphasizes human well-being and preservation of limited resources – both environmental and human – as the end goal of development, as well as the diversity of human needs. These needs are linked to individual human need and resource use, including in work and daily life (Tadjbakhsh and Chenoy, 2007: 39). Human security can therefore be seen as a framework that encourages the improvement of human well-being in the form of economic, food, health, environmental, personal, community, and political security – all of which are contingent upon a habitable climate and safe access to environmental resources.

Human Security and the Environment

The intersection of human security and the environment provides a framework for exploring questions of resource use, human development, and political and economic freedom. For human-rights practitioners, human development seeks to widen people's economic, social, and political choices and freedoms (Tadjbakhsh and Chenoy, 2007: 107). Therefore, climate instability presents a critical risk to human well-being inasmuch as it limits the ability to pursue development goals. Human security and development can be considered in tandem, since individual human security also enhances human capabilities and quality of life (Sen, 2000: 28). Furthermore, if development goals leave some groups vulnerable to risk, either from natural disasters or conflict over scarce resources, the human-security framework addresses this by pointing to the need for protections for the most vulnerable (Tadjbakhsh and Chenoy, 2007: 105). Sen further argues that human development can be defined as "growth with equity," whereas human security is "downturn with security" (Sen, 1999: 28). Human security enables people to make choices safely and freely; therefore, it is a useful framework to understand resource use and environmental risk (Tadjbakhsh and Chenoy, 2007: 107).

Bringing together human security and the environment, this framework has implications for how policy-makers address present risks to human life in order to prevent future threats and how these risks are related to resources sustainability. Current conceptions of human security in policy-making do not account for the fact that market economies focus on overall growth rather than long-term stability, making them inherently risky to human life, especially as they relate to energy and resource use. In addition, the most rampant overuse of resources and ensuing environmental destruction is attributable to states and communities, often in the Global North, who are much less likely to suffer its risks and consequences (Sen, 2000: 5). Greater democratic participation with the goal of reducing the hegemony of the Global North, therefore, can address some of these threats to human security that arise from environmental risks (Sen, 2000: 4). Education is also key, as there is a significant linkage between education and ecological responsibility, which suggests that greater and more widespread human access to information about climate instability can promote more secure outcomes for individuals (Sen, 2000: 5).

Finally, the human-security framework can be useful in forming an understanding of how to build policy that is centered on the most pressing human priority: sustainability of resources to facilitate the continuation of human and ecological life. A human-security framework shows how environmental damage and "territorial neglect" can constitute one of the most severe risks to human life through the deterioration of resources needed to sustain society (Sen, 2000: 5). Policy-making must therefore put sustainability at the core of all politics – not necessarily just by preserving natural resources but also by preserving human and natural capital (Ul-Haq, 1995: 18). Overuse of natural resources can therefore be seen as incurring an "ecological debt," which, along with economic and social debt, has the effect of severely threatening the sustainability of life (Ul-Haq, 1995: 76). In response, policies are needed to correctly price natural resources based on their contribution to the safety of future human life rather than treating them as free and unlimited (Ul-Haq, 1995: 85). The human-security framework for the environment allows for an understanding of security that considers the deterioration of natural resources as a clear and present threat to human security; it also encourages countries to find regional and national policy solutions to environmental threats (Ul-Haq, 1995: 8–9). Dalby builds on this perspective by reinforcing the environmental facets of human insecurity in terms of a population's vulnerability to daily problems rather than traditional security concerns (2013: 127).

Critiques of Human Security

Advocates of human security view the concept as a "holistic" reflection of "new forces" (Acharya, 2004: 355) and therefore "useful" but at risk of "losing its political salience" (McFarlane, 2004: 368), as a "challenge to power over knowledge of traditional security studies" (Grayson, 2004: 357), and as a "vital core" of security (Alkire, 2004: 359). Critics, however, deem human security, in general, to be "uncritical" (Oels, 2012: 194), a "reductionist notion that adds little analytical value" (Buzan, 2004: 369), a "normatively attractive but analytically weak" and an "unsophisticated" concept (Newman, 2004: 358, 2010: 81). The ethical reorientation implied by human security involves a shift that is more complex than a mere focus away from states to humans. For example, human-security advocate Simon Dalby (2013) also emphasizes state or interstate responsibility in the realization of human security in the context of contemporary globalization and environmental dangers.

Narrow applications of human security can fail to address the ways that environmental factors interact with political, social, and institutional risks to foster conflict. Many of these discourses fail to recognize that environmental processes are fundamentally inseparable from humanity's actions; humanity and the environment are not separate entities. The concept of human security can also fail to address the relationship between wealth and environmental threats. In general, the literature places the onus for most of the causes and threats on the Global South, while requiring the intervention of "actors from outside, who inform, protect, and establish economic growth and good governance" (Hardt, 2012: 217). Therefore, the "central paradox" of human security is that "although structures and norms that produce human insecurity are challenged, the remaining and reinforcing effects of the traditional power structures on the vulnerable may achieve the opposite effects to the emancipatory aims, disempowering the vulnerable even more" (Hardt, 2012: 217). Dalby elaborates on this when he argues proponents of human security must also acknowledge the feedback loops between international capitalism and control of environmental resources. As a result, environmental hazards, such as hurricanes or droughts, must be considered in light of growing international inequalities (Dalby, 2013: 128). This is particularly relevant for our understanding of the Syrian case at a time when drought intertwined with neoliberal policies resulted in drastic regional inequalities and human insecurity.

Moreover, the very framework of human security and its corresponding policy tools can sometimes undermine the goals it seeks to profess. This approach falls within a neoliberal type of governance, one "which regards those governed responsible for their own fate," and often materializes these communities in the form of overwrought and unexamined development aid, which is highly variable and may leave "many of the most vulnerable ... unprepared and unable to cope" (Oels, 2012: 200).

Indeed, development aid has become a business in and of itself, and it can paradoxically perpetuate human insecurity in order to profit from it (Trombetta, 2008: 590). Moreover, much of the research and evidence in this field reveals that human security has not facilitated substantial action on climate change but, rather, that "environmental security is not about the environment, it is about security; as a concept, it is at its most meaningless and malign ... one cannot expect that an appeal to a human centered security will provide different outcomes ... from the appeals to environmental security" (Trombetta, 2011: 139–140).

In addition, without the mechanisms to hold actors in security and development aid accountable for their actions, a human-security understanding of climate risk can make Western-driven assumptions about which humans deserve security and how they should go about getting it. On the policy front, the notion of human security expanded in recent years to include the threats of unchecked population growth, excessive international migration, environmental degradation, drug trafficking, international terrorism, and, more recently, global warming (Dalby, 2013). Hence, rather than breaking away from polarizing divides, human-security framings of climate change by elites in the Global North may potentially reproduce "us versus them" discourses when threats to human security in the Global South are framed as national-security concerns by elites in the North. Ethnocentric policies originating from the Global North may refer to unrest in the Global South due to scarcity, climate change, and human mobility (Barnett, 2001: 53). Such policies encourage repressive measures against human mobility at the domestic and international level, feeding narratives that place the responsibility on "environmental migrants" rather than authoritarian regimes that have triggered social and political unrest. The broad narrative has been that climate-induced drought in the Global South depletes food supplies, which increases the chances for intrastate conflict, which then results in major migrations toward the North; we will now evaluate this narrative and the ways it has been countered to better assess its applicability to the Syrian case.

Interconnectedness in a Globalized World: A Climate, Food Insecurity, and Migration Nexus?

The amalgamation into a "climate–conflict nexus" is characterized by similar theoretical shortcomings and deterministic patterns as the literature on environmental security, through a focus on vulnerability, lack of adaptation, and population growth or displacement as drivers of insecurity. Similarly to the water-security debate, liberal institutionalists draw on the theoretical literature relating to international environmental cooperation (e.g., Haas et al., 1993) to argue in favor of climate adaptation and cooperation through international institutions in the short to medium run (Tir and Stinnett, 2012). Other discourses of climate security outline the link to conflict. In both cases, at the heart of each term are competing conceptions of who needs to be secured, from what threat, by what actors, and through what means (Dalby, 2013: 165–166; Matthew, 2014b). These narratives also tend to perpetuate similar conceptual traps, wherein researchers posit that increased climate change will encourage human migration from vulnerable areas of the world, and increase grievances against the state and conflict, resulting in insecurity everywhere. Critical thinkers of environmental security have written eloquently about these "us versus them" binary framings. Analysts in this arena differ widely with respect to the referent objects of security (state, international community, communities and individuals, or ecosystems), the actors responsible for addressing the threats (military/security apparatus, multilateral organizations, communities, or individuals), and the types of threats (drought/scarcity, rising sea levels, climate variability, or conflict). In other words, making assumptions about "security" without identifying or making the case for a certain referent object of the security policy leads to misunderstandings over the nature of climate insecurity and how it actually operates on political, social, and ecological levels. This consideration sparks crucial questions about how concepts of the environment and climatic risks are conceptualized and how securitization narratives around climate security have developed.

The Lexicon of Climate: Climate Change and Variability, Vulnerability, and Adaptation

Researchers and policy-makers sometimes confuse the concepts of climate change and climate variability, often using the terms interchangeably (Seter, 2016: 2). The confusion regarding the definitions of these terms has implications for empirical research and policy-making relating to these phenomena. The IPCC's fourth Assessment Report (AR4) defines climate change as "changes in mean climate at a location over long periods," whereas climate variability describes short-term changes in climate (such as standard deviations, the occurrence of extremes, etc.) (IPCC, 2007: 871–872).

More broadly, the reports identify the primary goal of stabilizing atmospheric carbon-dioxide concentrations below the 450 parts per million (ppm) global target threshold. To achieve this target of 450 ppm, the IPCC notes the differentiated responsibilities of industrialized and industrializing countries: Industrialized countries must reduce their greenhouse gas emissions to 25–40 percent below 1990 levels by 2020 (IPCC, 2014: 28). The IPCC reports focus on mitigation and adaptation as the two primary responses to climate change. Mitigation aims to reduce the overall impact of climate change, by reducing emissions released by the agricultural, energy, industry, forestry, and transport sectors, among others. On the other hand, adaptation focuses instead on improving the human response to climate change. Adaptation is context-specific and a function of two features: a system's vulnerability and its adaptive capacity to climate change.

In his comparative perspective on the environmental history of the Middle East and North Africa and other parts of the world, John McNeill outlines the region's "high sensitivity to climate change" with regards to rainfall, whereas countries in Europe like Scotland and Finland have historically been impacted by changes in temperature (McNeill, 2013: 33). In other words, both geographical areas are climate vulnerable, albeit through different impacts. Climate vulnerability is a term that broadly refers to the degree to which a system is susceptible to versus able to cope with the ecological, economic, sociological, and political effects of climate change. A review of the literature addressing climate vulnerability reveals varying emphases placed on sociological, geographic, and economic dimensions.

When considering the sociological components of climate vulnerability, the policy world tends to focus on individual societal susceptibility to danger and the resilience factors that allow these societies to cope with climate risks. The IPCC adopts such an approach, defining climate vulnerability as the "sensitivity or susceptibility to harm and lack of capacity to cope and adapt" (IPCC, 2014: 5). The UNDP refines this definition by identifying three core components of climate vulnerability: (1) exposure to hazards and perturbation; (2) sensitivity of the affected environment to these perturbations, which is context-specific; and (3) adaptive capacity of a society depending on various social factors such as class, gender, age, etc. In this context, adaptive capacity refers to the "capability of a system to adjust its characteristics or behavior to anticipate, cope with and respond to climate variability and change" (UNDP, 2010: 20). In the policy world, climate vulnerability – and, by extension, climate security – is primarily concerned with a system's ability to modulate potential damage from climate change and/or to cope with the long-term consequences of this damage.

The academic debate goes a step further by looking at both individual societies and individual humans as the unit of analysis. For instance, Wisner et al. (2004: 11) refer to vulnerability as "the characteristics of a person or group and their situation that influence their capacity to anticipate, cope with, resist and recover from the impact of a natural hazard." In their framework, therefore, climate vulnerability is measured in both humans' and societies' ability to adapt to, and cope with, climate change.

Climate vulnerability is also shaped by economics. Greater economic vulnerability usually implies greater climate vulnerability. As climate risk inherently depends on the relative strength of a given geographical unit, economically underdeveloped areas tend to have less developed infrastructures. As a result, some populations are less adaptive and more vulnerable than others; slums found in Southern megacities tend to lack basic infrastructures that could protect against floods and natural hazards, for example (Dalby, 2009, 2013). Additionally, poverty, disease, lack of access to water, and food insecurity exacerbate climate vulnerability (Ahmed et al., 2009). A variety of studies have also conflated food insecurity with climate insecurity or have attempted to show how the relationship between food insecurity and climate insecurity drives human conflict and migration.

There are also additional sociogeographic components to climate vulnerability. Geographic features such as landscape type, average yearly precipitation, and agricultural patterns play a significant role. These geographic features can help play a role in the vulnerability to drought in terms of the degree of dependence on rainfall for food and income (Von Uexkull, 2014: 18). Of course, a panoply of other factors can play a role in climate vulnerability; as Raleigh (2010) notes, conflict in itself can actually also increase vulnerability.

Ultimately, concepts of climate vulnerability are multidimensional and reflect the multifaceted interactions between climate and human and ecological life. As Dalby argues: "Vulnerability has to be understood as a complex social and ecological situation that is entwined with the social and economic entitlements available to particular people in specific circumstances" (2013: 128). No one working definition of climate vulnerability is enough; the multidimensional approach is required to understand the nuance of how climate vulnerability impacts individuals, societies, and states, and, most importantly, how to begin addressing associated risks on water and food.

Climate, Water and Food Security, and Self-Sufficiency

The Food and Agriculture Organization (FAO) of the United Nations actually links the concepts of water and food security by defining water security as the ability to provide adequate and reliable water supplies for populations living in the world's more arid areas to meet agricultural needs (Clarke, 1993). In 2016, the organization went one step further and released a brief with the UN Trust Fund for Human Security that stated "the relationship between human security and food security is predicated on the idea of the full realization of the human right to adequate food, as a fundamental human right" (FAO, 2016a).

Notions of food security and food self-sufficiency are key to evaluating water security and better understanding the drought period in Syria, even though they have varied widely. The 1996 World Food Summit delineated the most widely accepted definition of food security as "a state in which all people, at all times, have physical and economic access to sufficient, safe and nutritious food" (Coates, 2013; Minot and Pelijor, 2010). However, recent decades have seen the food-security concept evolve from a narrow focus on food availability to a more multidimensional approach (Burchi and De Muro, 2015; Coates, 2013; Dilley and Boudreau, 2001). For example, Burchi and De Muro (2015) identify five main approaches to food security: (1) food availability, (2) income-based, (3) basic needs, (4) entitlement, and (5) sustainable livelihoods.

The Malthusian food-availability approach focuses on the global imbalance between population and food, making food security "merely a matter of aggregate (per capita) food availability" (Burchi and De Muro, 2015: 11). Meanwhile, the income-based approach incorporates macro- and micro-economic variables, such as GDP and economic growth. The basic needs or food-first approach focuses on the capacity to satisfy basic food consumption needs for a healthy life (Burchi and De Muro, 2015: 12). Drawing on Amartya Sen (1981), the entitlement approach challenges Malthusian approaches by shifting the focus from scarcity to socioeconomic dimensions of access to food (Burchi and De Muro, 2015: 12; Dilley and Boudreau, 2001: 233). Finally, the sustainable-livelihoods approach incorporates vulnerability, sustainability, and coping strategies into concepts of food security (Burchi and De Muro, 2015: 14). In this same vein, Dilley and Boudreau offer a critique of the tendency of these terms to focus on outcomes (i.e. famine, hunger), advocating instead for a disaster-management approach, which is defined in relation to hazards, threats, or shocks (Dilley and Boudreau, 2001: 230).

Food self-sufficiency, as opposed to food security, is the "ability of a country, region or household to meet food consumption needs (particularly for staple food crops) from its own production rather than by buying or importing" (Minot and Pelijor, 2010: 1). The FAO defines food self-sufficiency as the ability of a country to produce "a proportion of its own food needs that approaches or exceeds 100% of its food consumption" (FAO, 2015: 2). In this sense, food self-sufficiency focuses more on domestic or community capacity to supply the resources needed to produce food in sufficient quantities to sustain life (FAO, 2015: 3). Food self-sufficiency may be a more a helpful framework for analyzing food security than other approaches, because approaches that place responsibility for meeting food needs on the open market makes consumers vulnerable to volatile prices and supply chains. However, others argue that food self-sufficiency is too "costly" for most households and countries, who would do better to produce food as needed, while purchasing other items (Minot and Pelijor, 2010: xiii). Key to understanding these terms, therefore, are the social and economic variables to resource access.

Climate, Food Insecurity, and Conflict?

A variety of studies have conflated food insecurity with climate insecurity or have attempted to show how the relationship between food insecurity and climate insecurity is a driver of human conflict and migration. In the larger context of the global economic forces of the early twenty-first century, the impact of globalization and neoliberal economic policies in the developing world have certainly led to widespread inequality and the squandering of finite resources, and this inequality has led to further risks that increase food-production interdependencies and food insecurity across the world, particularly in the Global South (Dalby, 2009, 2017b; Swain and Jägerskog, 2016). However, these relationships and definitional debates need to be examined more carefully.

The global economic instability and ensuing food-price crises of 2007–2008 and 2010–2011 led to riots and protests worldwide, threatening governments and social stability and capturing global attention. This unrest affected a diverse group of twenty countries, including Burkina Faso, Haiti, and Mexico (United Nations, 2011). In fact, the World Bank estimated that these events pushed nearly 105 million people into extreme poverty (World Bank, 2012: 29). Global unrest attributed to food prices encouraged researchers to explore the relationship between food insecurity and civil unrest and conflict, and some evidence emerged that unrest tends to begin after global food prices hit certain thresholds or after prices are distorted as a result of food subsidies. In Haiti, food protests helped hasten a change of government in 2008, while increases in food prices occurred concurrently with protests during the Arab Uprising of 2011 (Brinkman and Hendrix, 2011). But does food instability effectively trigger civil or political unrest?

Empirical research focused on Africa shows that climate could indirectly impact conflict through an increase in food prices but that in these instances the effects are purely local (Raleigh et al., 2015). Other scholars have attempted to make the case for broadening this linkage, arguing that there is a definite causal relationship between instability in food production and ensuing social and political upheaval. Sternberg (2012), for example, brings together the cases of China and Egypt in 2010, attempting to show a potential link between drought, decreased food production, and Chinese and Egyptian political instability. He claims that lack of domestic production in Egypt and inelastic demand, coupled with that year's decreased global supply and competing buyers – namely, China – led to shifting subsidies and the rise of bread prices in Egypt that stimulated, or at least contributed to, political instability (Sternberg, 2012: 520–522). He argues that the nature of an interconnected and globalized world food economy allowed a regional case of food insecurity in China to drive bread riots in Egypt, and, ultimately, act as one of the reasons for the downfall of Hosni Mubarak in 2011. The forces of global climate insecurity and drought drive physical change, like reduced rice production, but also social and political change, since, as prices rise, citizens revolt and regimes change. According to Sternberg, the Middle East as a whole is highly food insecure due to a lack of domestic production of basic food staples, as evidenced by the fact that nine out of ten of the top wheat importers worldwide are located in the region (Sternberg, 2012: 523).

Although this case is compelling, there are major weaknesses in the argument, as the author himself notes, which make the overall claim about the link between food insecurity and political unrest worthy of further examination. Indeed, the evidence cited by Sternberg does not find a relationship between bread prices and political upheaval in the Egyptian case, and the analysis merely assumes that "[the bread protests'] resonance with the wider public as an expression of dissatisfaction merged with demonstrations calling for the government to be replaced" (Sternberg, 2012: 520). His depiction of many of the Middle Eastern countries that experienced unrest in 2011 as major wheat importers is correct. However, two of the countries where upheavals took place at large scale during the same period – namely Syria and Bahrain – are absent from his list (Sternberg, 2012: 523). Alternate narratives that have more critically examined the relationship between climate, food insecurity, and human conflict therefore remain crucial.

Mitchell (2002) offers a counter-narrative to the assumptions about food insecurity in Egypt by more specifically accounting for the socio-economic and political changes that transformed the country's environment and agricultural sector. Importantly, Mitchell explicitly challenges the widespread assumption that Egypt does not have enough food for its growing population. He examines rates of Egyptian population growth and agricultural production from the 1960s to the 1990s to show that rates of production largely kept pace with population growth, refuting the commonly held claim that Egypt is growing in size beyond its production means. At the same time, Egypt was importing larger and larger amounts of food, especially grains, making the country dependent on grain imports after 1974. What accounts for this contradiction? Mitchell argues that specific structural and policy choices – including Egypt's shift toward more meat consumption in wealthier parts of the population – and economic liberalization supported by considerable American loans and land reforms explain the country's food and inequality problem. In fact, as he shows, by 1981, the "richest 25% consumed more than three times as much chicken and beef as the poorest 26%" (Mitchell, 2002: 173). In other words, Egypt suffers from food shortages not because it cannot produce enough food to sustain itself but because state elites intentionally prevent it from doing so through their consumption preferences and agricultural practices.

Discourses about Egypt's supposed food and water scarcity (i.e. that Egypt is inherently drought-ridden and overpopulated) were widely disseminated and accepted by researchers, the aid community, and policy-makers, and conveniently informed the Egyptian government's choice to heavily tax the production of staples by farmers and subsidize the production of meat, poultry, and dairy products. Growing inequality in food purchasing power came at the explicit expense of Egypt's poorest while allowing the narrative of food insecurity as a matter of overpopulation and drought to continue to spread. In a similar fashion, the inequality of government policies regarding land distribution also contributed to triggering Egypt's food insecurity. As Mitchell writes, Egypt's food problem was not a matter of "too many people occupying too little land," (2002: 175) but rather one in which land management was privatized, shifting ownership away from agricultural workers and the state and toward the private sector. Claims were made about the need to turn to "managerial and technical" solutions to solve Egypt's land problem, in particular by making existing natural resources "more productive" through this privatization (Mitchell, 2002: 179). In this sense, Egypt's food insecurity was not an issue of too little land but of the deliberate dispossession of the many by the few – a problem confirmed by Barnes when she argues that Egypt's expansion of agricultural land through land reclamation occurred through a process of dispossession of rural people by the state and international "experts" (Barnes, 2014: 125, 130–133). In the context of this book, this resonates with many of the drivers of insecurity and the challenges facing the more vulnerable farming communities in Syria following land reforms and privatization measures under the auspices of international institutions.

It may be the case that food insecurity is actually an extension of previously existing societal inequality made possible by the strategic privilege wielded by elites. As discussed during the delineation of food security earlier in this chapter, Amartya Sen's entitlement approach attempts to challenge the prevailing Malthusian narrative of development by shifting the focus from scarcity of resources to the socio-economic dimensions of access to food. Food shortages, he writes, tend to reveal underlying and preexisting food entitlements, which Sen defines as "the ability of different sections of the populations to establish command over food using the entitlement relations in that society" (Sen, 1981: 459). In other words, food scarcity usually adversely affects those who were already at risk of hunger, and the problem is not one of scarcity but of structural inequality and distribution. This principle of food entitlements holds true in the case of Syria, where food shortages in the mid-2000s were triggered by elites' focus on wheat production instead of barley as a strategic crop and ensuing government policies in the agricultural sector that exacerbated this choice. This case example provides the basis for further analysis of the complex and interrelated variables food insecurity and civil unrest.

A key challenge to determining the link between food security and conflict is finding ways to clarify and operationalize the causal relationship between the two. Intuitively, it can be argued that conflict and violence disrupt food production and supply. Further, conflict may cause sociopolitical instability through reduced market confidence leading to higher food prices or through disrupted food supply also raising prices. However, a lack of rigorous empirical evidence and theoretical grounding makes it difficult to confidently make the argument for this relationship. To this end, some scholars have attempted to analyze intervening variables between food insecurity and socio-economic conflict. Using economic analysis, Barrett explores the link between sociopolitical stability and food security, citing Syria as a case in which disruption in food supply was a "primary trigger" to instability, although he does not discount the population's outrage at a corrupt regime as another significant factor (Barrett, 2013: 342). Chapters 4 and 5 of this book analyze the disruptions in food and water supplies in the decades preceding the uprising, which serves to nuance this assertion. Brinkman and Hendrix (2011) support Barrett's arguments in their World Food Programme report on the same topic. Although they find that food insecurity can itself be a cause of conflict, they present a more nuanced version of this argument, conceding that insecurity can be considered both a cause and consequence of conflict, and that the causal direction is not clear (Brinkman and Hendrix, 2011: 4, 20). However, in the case of the relationship between food insecurity and interstate war, they suggest that evidence is weak, while there is a strong correlation between low caloric intake and local civil conflict, protests and rioting, and some evidence for communal violence. This suggests that there is value in looking at specific contextual factors within individual cases of conflict.

Finally, another critical dimension of the existing work on the link between food insecurity and conflict, and one with special salience for the case study of this book, is the relationship between food insecurity and the state's structural vulnerability (Jones et al., 2017: 340). State vulnerability can be defined as a state's capacity and susceptibility, where susceptibility refers to the share of agriculture in GDP. This concept of susceptibility is especially important in the case of Syria, and a deeper examination of this variable and the evolution of the share of agriculture in GDP and employment in the agriculture sector will be examined further in Chapter 5. Jones et al. show in particular how low state vulnerability proves a more important linkage to conflict than climate insecurity or food prices, suggesting that socioeconomic unrest is the product of both food insecurity and underlying state vulnerability (2017: 342). In conclusion, a closer examination of food insecurity and the economic and political structures of Syria, which made the state and communities more vulnerable to climate variability during periods of drought, will set the stage for our research. As a result, large-scale migration occurred in the regions hit by water and food insecurity during the 2006–2010 drought; against this backdrop, we will see how migration becomes intertwined with food and climate security in climate-conflict debates.

Climate Change, Conflict, and Security: Weakness and Sampling Bias

Generally, research on climate change and its impact on socioeconomic variables has been inconclusive. An overall weak theoretical framing has plagued the literature, leading to poorly defined variables and variation in definitions of key terminologies that make finding patterns difficult (Gemenne et al., 2014). Studies also define the dependent variable (e.g., interstate or intrastate conflict) and independent variable (e.g., rainfall patterns) variables differently. For example, climate events such as droughts come with a multiplicity of social and economic intermediate variables that often go understudied, such as the tendency of droughts to push labor markets and institutions in adverse directions or change patterns of natural resource use (Von Uexkull, 2014).

The relationship between climate change and conflict may be more broadly influenced by sampling bias in the datasets. Methodological challenges have plagued both quantitative and qualitative studies (Dalby, 2017b). In the past decade, many large-N quantitative studies provided differing statistical methodologies to examine the correlation between climate change and violent conflict, hoping to generalize research findings drawn mainly from sub-Saharan Africa and other centers of drought in an attempt to establish causality (e.g., Adger et al., 2014; Gemenne et al., 2014; Seter, 2016). Many of these studies fail to recognize that correlations are not transitive unless they are very high (Gleditsch and Nordås, 2014: 85). In other words, if risk factors associated with climate change can induce conflict, this does not imply that climate change induces conflict – the adage that correlation does not equal causation applies here. Other studies have paradoxically shown cases in which climate variability has reduced or lessened the impact of conflict (Bernauer et al., 2012; Hendrix and Glaser, 2007; Slettebak and Gleditsch, 2012). More importantly, these studies may also be selecting along the dependent variable with countries embroiled in conflict being "mentioned almost three times as often as countries with a lower death toll" (Adams et al., 2018: 200). The result of this methodological choice may be that the relationship between climate change and violent conflict appears stronger than it actually is and that scholars miss opportunities to identify factors that allow communities to weather significant environmental change peacefully (Adams et al., 2018: 202).

Sub-Saharan Africa tends to be overrepresented in studies on the relationship between conflict and climate change while Asia, South America, and Oceania do not feature as prominently despite being similarly vulnerable to global warming (Adams et al., 2018: 200–201). Former British colonies and countries with English as the official language are also overrepresented (Adams et al., 2018: 202; Hendrix, 2017: 252) likely for reasons of convenience, such as better record keeping in former British colonies or the researchers lack of non-English language skills (Hendrix, 2018). Such criticism seems particularly relevant to the Syrian case, especially where the conflict narrative is deployed by policy-makers and the media to warn of the potential consequences of climate change (Selby et al., 2017b: 255). Concerns about the relative weakness of the Syrian conflict's linkage with climate change has led some scholars to warn that using Syria as an example of the climate-conflict thesis risks undermining consensus on the security and economic implications of climate change (Hendrix, 2017: 251–252) and may fuel skepticism of climate change (Selby et al., 2017b: 255).

In addition, a variety of mitigating variables and human impacts makes disaggregating causation in these studies quite difficult and suggests that only the combination of climate change and "structural factors" can consistently be correlated with conflict (Adger et al., 2014; Ide, 2015). Although climate change does not lead directly to violence, its manifestation through drought can challenge local coping mechanisms and add fuel to conflict. Hence, some argue that areas dependent on rain-fed agriculture that do experience sustained droughts are more prone to civil conflict, as economic desperation from drought triggers support for rebel groups or violent movements (Von Uexkull, 2014: 1, 18, 24). As such, it is possible that conflict is only connected with climate instability when other intervening variables, including a lack of "adaptive capacity" on the part of local or state institutions, are in effect (Feitelson and Tubi, 2017: 39).

Although limited in terms of generalizability, pure qualitative analysis drawing on case studies or a mix of both methodologies through qualitative comparative analysis has enriched the conversation by introducing local contextualization while providing more in-depth data that counters the climate-conflict narrative. For example, a study of rainfall patterns in Kenya in relation to patterns of violence has shown that below-average rainfall was associated with peace in the years that followed the drought and that violence was more likely in years following abundant rain (Theisen, 2012: 81). In another empirical analysis of several African countries, the authors discuss the northern Ethiopia famine of 1984–1985, finding that drought turned to famine as a result of government policies and the responses to those policies, thereby showing there was not a direct link between the climate process (drought) and conflict (Theisen et al., 2011: 88). The Sudanese case, on the other hand, shows that abundance, rather than scarcity, has fueled conflict (Selby and Hoffmann, 2014). In general, only approaches that look at climate change itself as an intermediate variable related to other main drivers of conflict (institutional and sociopolitical variables) have demonstrated a substantive and useful link between climate change and conflict.

At the global level, the IPCC'S AR5 provides a more balanced account of the relationship between climate change and conflict than those of previous IPCC reports. The report largely shows contemporary scientific skepticism of the climate-conflict narrative, but internal inconsistencies and rampant ambiguity in the use of terminology make the report's conclusions open to interpretation (Gleditsch and Nordås, 2014: 89). It was the first report of its kind to dedicate a significant portion of its research to the "human security dimensions" of climate change in the context of growing debates about climate change and conflict. The report embraces uncertainty with the use of "probability terms" such as "may" or "has potential to" appearing throughout. However, this stated uncertainty is often later translated into definitive assertions in academia and the media, leading to misunderstandings (Gleditsch and Nordås, 2014: 87, 88). This is exacerbated by contradicting conclusions; in particular, several chapters contradict the chapter on "Human Security" in which the report reaches the conclusion that climate change leads to conflict based on little evidence (Gleditsch and Nordås, 2014: 86).

The limited conclusiveness of past research findings underlines the importance of social context and the relevance of local politics and institutions in explaining climate vulnerability. In order to untangle the causal relationship between climate insecurity and human conflict, it is critical to analyze a third intermediary variable: food insecurity. The role of migration has also often been debated with respect to climate change and conflict.

Climate Change, Migration, and Conflict: Syria and Beyond

Myths and disinformation about migration crises are widespread, and the same is true for climate change. The bulk of human mobility is internal or across the border of a neighboring country for the purpose of seeking short-term safety from extreme climate events (Biermann and Boas, 2010: 8; Null and Risi, 2016: 7). With regard to migration crises, large groups of displaced persons moving from Syria to Europe have fed many recent controversies, political debates, and misinterpretations. Both political rhetoric and policy-making now successfully securitize migration as a global and regional threat (Trombetta, 2014).

On September 7, 2015, *Time* magazine featured an article with the title: "How Climate Change Was Behind the Surge of Migrants to Europe" (Baker, 2015). In response to condemnations of Hungary's migration policies, the foreign minister simply stated that "migration has become a 'security threat'" (Al-Jazeera, 2016). According to such discourses, migrants and displaced persons appear as threats to the integrity and well-being of the nations to which they flee.

Today, climate change and disaster-based human displacement are presumed to have a strong causal link (IPCC, 2014). The multicausality of migration also explains why the large body of empirical support for climate-induced migration – at least in terms of the causal link between drought, shocks to livelihood, and migration – is not conclusive, despite drawing from many methodologies, including case studies. An ethnographic survey of three agricultural villages in Tanzania, for example, found higher incidences of outmigration in those affected by frequent drought, with residents citing the inability to maintain a livelihood as the cause of their migration (Afifi et al., 2014: 53–60). Regression models have also shown that in low-income regions, drought-susceptible production systems tend to induce more net migration than areas that are less susceptible to drought but have similar economic conditions (De Sherbinin et al., 2012). However, Fröhlich (2016), Simonelli (2016) and Tertrais (2011) have also effectively argued that multiple social, economic, and political factors lead individuals to migrate, and it is difficult to isolate the environment from other drivers of migration. Black et al. (2011) also supported these claims by proposing a comprehensive conceptual framework that analyzes the multiple drivers (social, demographic, economic, political, and environmental) and factors (obstacles, facilitators, personal characteristics) that all affect the decision to migrate.

Migration due to climate change is mostly an internal phenomenon, and populations are therefore considered to be migrants or internally displaced persons and not refugees (Boas, 2015: 8; Tertrais, 2011: 24). The reality of internal displacement reduces predictions of mass migration to Europe or other areas in the Global North (Goff et al., 2012). At the same time, many studies have also attempted to show the causal relationship between forced migration and conflict (Greenhill, 2010; Martin and Tirman, 2009; Newman and van Selm, 2003). The link, however, between climate change, migration, and conflict remains difficult to examine or prove empirically (Boas, 2015: 9). Frequently, theories that attempt to draw a causal relationship between these phenomena rely upon inconsistent data or are based on widely accepted assumptions rather than facts. Understanding the way in which discourses surrounding migration have gone unquestioned and been allowed to shape policy is therefore critical. Indeed, the nature of supposed causal linkages between climate change and conflict are deeply limited and highly problematic, at best. For example, scholars and policy-makers continue to speculate about the overall number of climate migrants, which is the foundation of these causality studies. "Maximalists" cast alarming numbers about future climate refugees, while "minimalists," who tend to be more prominent in academia, dispute quantitative reasoning by highlighting the complexity of the issue and the difficulty of collecting trustworthy data (Baldwin et al., 2014: 122). This debate echoes the arguments surrounding narratives in the 1990s, when scholars such as Homer-Dixon and Norman Myers emphasized the role that water scarcity and population pressures played in creating social upheavals that could overwhelm institutional and social structures, leading to conflict and forced migration (Homer-Dixon, 1994; Myers, 1997). This narrative on the looming invasion of millions of environmental refugees is perhaps best captured by the opening paragraph of Norman Myers' article on "Environmental Refugees":

There are fast-growing numbers of people who can no longer gain a secure livelihood in their homelands because of drought, soil erosion, desertification, deforestation and other environmental problems. In their desperation, these "environmental refugees" ... feel they have no alternative but to seek sanctuary elsewhere, however hazardous the attempt. ... There are at least

25 million environmental refugees today, a total to be compared with 22 million refugees of traditional kind. ... The total may well double by the year 2010 if not before. (Myers, 1997: 167)

These two hypothesized causal relationships are exceptionally important in the case of Syria because of its high levels of internally and externally displaced people after 2011. There are significant regional trends for migration overall in the Middle East; the region currently hosts 45 percent of all global refugees, including those registered with the United Nations Relief and Works Agency (International Organization for Migration [IOM], 2017: 65). There were also 2.8 million people in the region by the end of 2016 seeking international protection and awaiting status determination (IOM, 2017: 32). The number of refugees from Syria has also increased dramatically because of the ongoing conflict. By March 2019, there were an estimated 6.2 million displaced Syrians within the country and an additional 5.6 registered refugees outside its borders, making the country one of the largest producers of refugees in the world (UNHCR, 2019).

Following the dramatic drought of 2006–2010 and before the war started in 2011, approximately 80,000–100,000 families from northeastern and eastern Syria – equivalent to approximately 370,000 to 460,000 individuals – were forced to leave their homes to seek better livelihoods in other parts of the country.[3] Forced to move to slums in Deraa and Damascus, to flee insecurity and seek work, these displaced populations (referred to in Syria as "the displaced" or *al-nazihin*) faced utter neglect on the part of their government and were not able to positively adapt to their new home. In past years, the populations that were flooded ("the flooded" or *al-maghmureen*) after the completion of the Tabqa Dam (1973) on the Euphrates River had been permanently displaced and only partially resettled. The displacement of the late 2000s was partially a result of the government's failure to provide an effective economic and political infrastructure for displaced civilians, and in particular for the most vulnerable.

Although much has been made of the migration–climate nexus, a lack of consistent evidence and theoretical grounding makes it difficult to trace the causal mechanisms that might drive this relationship. According to the IOM, there are no reliable estimates of climate-induced

---

[3] See Chapter 5 for a discussion of post-2006 migration flows.

migration, but it is clear that gradual climate trends have already resulted in significant displacement as a result of climate events. In 2008, for example, 20 million persons were displaced by extreme weather events, compared with 4.6 million displaced for conflict-related reasons over the same period. In 2018, the IOM assessed the number of total new displacements at 18.8 million, of which 1.3 million migrated because of droughts. Furthermore, current estimates show the potential for 25 million to 1 billion environmental migrants by the year 2050 (IOM, 2019a).

From Semantics to Policy over Migration

There are also significant definitional issues with the term "climate migrant." As the IOM has shown, people migrating for climate-related reasons do not fall within one particular category of asylum-seeker within the current international legal framework, and, as such, this term has no basis in international law and should be used with care (IOM, 2019b). The IOM broadly defines environmental migrants as "persons or groups of persons, who for compelling reasons of sudden or progressive changes in the environment that adversely affect their lives or living conditions, are obliged to leave their habitual homes, or choose to do so, either temporarily or permanently, and who move either within their country or abroad" (IOM, 2007). Such language is useful in explaining the fact that climate displacement is an increasing global issue, but it also instrumentalizes security rhetoric against the human needs of such people. Rather than examining larger systems of climate change and global inequality, this discourse places the onus on displaced persons as the object of their own insecurity. Climate-induced migration is a subcategory of environmental migration that first emerged in a 1985 study led by the UNEP. El-Hinnawi, the author of the report, refers to environmental migration as temporary or permanent displacement due to natural disasters, drought, crop failure, and human-made changes to habitat (Simonelli, 2016: 41). However, there is no larger consensus on what constitutes an environmental or climate refugee, and this term has yet to be addressed in international legal terms on a more defined, functional level. The ensuing lack of institutionalization, which would have otherwise guaranteed climate refugees' rights and protection, weakens and delegitimizes state obligations toward the displaced (Biermann and Boas, 2010; Keane, 2004; Weinthal et al., 2015: 295–296).

The definitions and terminologies that make use of this rhetoric, such as "environmental refugees" or "distressed migrants," potentially also foster negative "othering" and xenophobia in the public discourse (Ransan-Cooper et al., 2015). They relate more to "western fears of 'barbarians at the gates' than ... the foreseeable reality of the consequences of climate change" (Tertrais, 2011: 25). Such perceptions encourage repressive and punitive measures against displaced persons at the domestic and international level, feeding narratives that place the responsibility on "migrants" themselves rather than attempting to address their needs under international law and the underlying structures of inequality or authoritarian political systems that are the actual triggers of unrest. Furthermore, these terminologies have revealed themselves to be racially and ethnically coded; it is rare that European or North American immigrants to other countries are included in this framework.[4]

As such, perceptions and framings of environmental migrants have the power to affect and determine policy. It is possible to identify four distinct framings or typologies of environmental refugees, which are based on whether these migrants are perceived as victims, threats, adaptive agents, or political subjects (Ransan-Cooper et al., 2015: 106). However, these framings present some critical theoretical limitations that make them less helpful in discussing the links between displacement and conflict. For example, none of these categories are mutually exclusive, since an individually displaced person or community can fall in one or all of these categories at once. These framings also fail to account for the unique contextual conditions that prompted these populations to migrate away from their countries or communities of origin. Another limitation of this framework is that the "victim" and "security threat" labels were developed in countries in the Global North and tend to bear implicit geographical and racial bias or assumptions. The "victim" frame, for example, is problematic in its tendency to frame victims of conflict and war as weak or lacking in agency, while simultaneously framing the Global North as the implicit source of stability and political neutrality (Ransan-Cooper et al., 2015: 109–110).

---

[4] For an example, see coverage surrounding citizens of the UK who have decided to leave the country in the wake of Brexit (O'Neill, 2019).

In these first two categories, agency almost entirely resides with Northern policy-makers, and, unsurprisingly, this approach has been adopted by the work of environmental security theorists. The choice of these theorists to frame climate migrants as "threats" is predicated on a neo-Malthusian logic of scarcity and conflict. This approach relies on debunked and oversimplified notions of resources and population mobility and has crucial theoretical limitations, as outlined in previous sections on the neo-Malthusian approach. With this in mind, a more holistic and meaningful approach may lie in seeing people displaced by climate variability as political subjects first and foremost rather than security threats. It is also critical to engage with a contextual background and the structural reasons for displacement: How did they originate? What structural and political factors stress already vulnerable populations? In this way, the "adaptive agent" framing views environmental migration as constituting a key form of adaptation to climate change. The climate-migration narrative alternatively posits the claim that migrants constitute a benefit to their host communities in the form of adaptive and developmental capacity. This argument is frequently raised in the context of development as a means to both neutralize the potential political tension refugees might pose to their host communities, as well as to depoliticize these populations by framing them as units of economic benefit. This adaptation builds resilience through actions such as upskilling and sending remittances but requires these migrants to be "model neoliberal subjects" that assimilate and require little external help, without taking into consideration the limited reach of these benefits outside of the migrant's family or immediate community (Ransan-Cooper et al., 2015: 111). The next chapters show that the farmers displaced in Syria at the time of the 2006–2010 drought primarily constituted nonadaptive agents.

Ultimately, the most useful frame is that of "political subjects," which focuses on the root causes and historical context of inequality, resource scarcity, self-determination, and social injustice that affects many environmental migrants. However, this framing takes a bottom-up approach, which creates a false comparison with policy solutions rooted in the Global North by failing to consider different local traditions or alternate understandings of good governance outside of the Global North framework.

Climate-induced migration, therefore, remains largely a speculative phenomenon, based on misperceptions rather than actual facts. It is some sort of "futurology," in which climate-induced migration is "a theoretical possibility, but not an actually existing clearly defined group of people" (Baldwin et al., 2014: 122). The result of these myths and misperceptions is that policies regarding displaced persons in their country of asylum are based on misinformation. Moreover, human-security views of climate change held by elites in the Global North perpetuate "us versus them" discourses rather than breaking away from polarizing divides, especially when threats to human security in the Global South are framed as national-security concerns by elites in the North. In addition, the lack of migrant and refugee voices in these discussions creates a devastating lack of agency. Although some ethnographic and creative approaches to documenting these policy discussions have been able to include more migrant and refugee speakers, a lack of dialogue between disciplines on this topic continues to exclude Syrian refugees and other key voiceless groups, who are often spoken of but less often allowed to speak (Di Giovanni, 2016; Pearlman, 2017).

Is Syria, as a case study of climate change and mass migration, therefore an example of how displacement has triggered conflict and political instability? Was their movement triggered solely by drought-induced water and food insecurity, as is frequently posited? What was the political and social context of the drought that led to their sudden and massive migration? Moreover, why did a previous drought of the same size, such as the drought of 1998–2001, not trigger the same levels of displacement? The HECS framework offers an explanation as to why drought was not the only factor causing displacement of rural and farming communities. They were not the instigators of the uprising in Deraa and Damascus and thus do not fit the category of security threats, as was frequently suggested. Rather than bringing insecurity in the form of a direct threat, these displaced persons constitute one feedback loop of insecurity as a result of specific government policies, as the HECS framework seeks to capture. This framework is therefore uniquely positioned to examine the impact of migration as a factor of other types of human insecurity, rather than a threat in and of itself. The HECS approach outlines the role of ideology and policy (Chapter 4) on the key factors of climate, social, economic, political *vulnerability* and *resilience* (Chapter 5), and attempts to do so from the perspective of the marginal and dispossessed in Syria during two key drought periods, as will be shown in the following chapters.

Summary

This chapter has investigated the theoretical underpinnings of the HECS framework in terms of discourses of security, critical environmental security, and human security. Critically, this chapter also explored the climate–food insecurity–migration nexus put forward by some scholars, which will be revisited in Chapter 5 in the Syrian context. First, however, there must be an understanding of the historical and regional context of Syria's quest for water and food security. Chapter 3, therefore, delves into the history of water in Syria, including its cultural and legal importance over the past several millennia, and fast forward to the contemporary issue of transboundary interactions with Turkey over the Euphrates and Tigris rivers.

3 | *When Geography Rules History*

When the Prophet saw Sa'd performing *wudu* he said: "What is this? You are wasting water." Sa'd replied: "Can there be waste while performing ablution?" The Prophet replied: "Yes even if you perform it in a flowing river."

> (From the Sunna, traditional practices and customs of the Islamic community, Musnad of Imam Ahmed)

This chapter provides the broader historical and regional context of the case under study. It traces the role of water in Syrian society throughout history, first by reviewing water legislation from a domestic lens and then by examining Syria's international riparian relations. Water resources contributed to major early historical developments throughout the Middle East, which led to early regulation of the resource. Rules of conduct over water-sharing were codified in Mesopotamian times and later under Islamic law, which emphasized the principles of social justice and environmental protection that were included in modern Syrian legislation centuries later. The historical assessment of water policy gives us insight into the cultural and institutional norms surrounding water in Syria in place prior to our study period. A regional analysis further broadens the scope to understand how the management of Syria's main transboundary rivers has been impacted by its relations with upstream Turkey. Figure 3.1 summarizes the main milestones outlined in this chapter from the birth of agriculture to the emergence of water legislation both worldwide and in Syria and the Middle East.

Water in Middle Eastern History

Human history has always been shaped by water. This is exceptionally true of the Middle East – and, by extension, of Syria – where water resources have played a key role in the development and decline of civilizations that attempted to harness water resources for millennia.

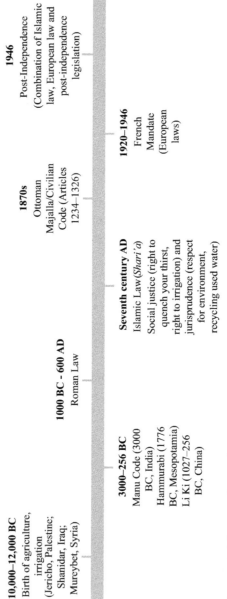

Figure 3.1 The rise of agriculture and water legislation worldwide and in Syria and the Middle East.

In fact, the oldest dams in the world, which were built for irrigation purposes, are found in the Middle East: In the seventh century BC, the Shalalar dam was built on a tributary of Tigris in Iraq; the three gravity dams near Persepolis in Iran date back to the Achaemenid era (558–331 BC); and the Romans built the Habarga dam in Syria in 132 AD (Furon, 1963: 80; Wolf, 1994: 9).[1]

Over the past three millennia, the region has experienced periods of rapid and large-scale construction of water projects and periods of decline, and the region still bears the marks of large-scale water constructions from the Achaemids to the Abbasids to the French and British Mandates. In fact, some of these ancient water projects are still in use today: Water canals and underground aqueducts constructed by the Romans for irrigation were restored by Syrian farmers in the beginning of the nineteenth century.[2] Large-scale irrigation projects gained prominence under the Achaemenids in the fifth century BC and the Sassanids in the third century AD, though they were only sporadically maintained in the centuries until the expansion of Islam in the Mediterranean. These projects were once again restored under Abbasid rule, and water distribution to the people increased (Hourani, 2002: 103). The use of irrigation then faded away until the Mongol invasion in the mid-thirteenth century, during which already deteriorating canals were completely destroyed. Attempts to control the major rivers of the region – the Tigris and Euphrates – then ceased. Carefully planned human-made irrigation canals were replaced by unpredictable flooding until after World War I, when the French and British mandates introduced modern water-control techniques. These techniques were notably implemented in the construction of the Hindiya Dam (1911–1914), Diyala Dam (1927–1928) and Kut Dam (1934–1943), as well as of the large modern dams in the 1950s.

"When Geology Ruled History"[3]

Water is at the crossroads of history and geography. Humanity's agricultural, cultural, and political developments are inextricably

---

[1] Discovered by the German archeologist Bergner in 1936.
[2] Based on author's interview with Ronald Jaubert from the Graduate Institute of International and Development Studies, 2000. According to Jaubert's analysis of soil surveys, these canals have been dry since the 1960–1970s.
[3] According to H. G. Termier, quoted in Furon (1963: 70).

entwined with water, as controlling water resources has been tantamount to societies from the pre-ancient period to today.

Some of the largest and most famous ancient civilizations have been founded on the basis of reliable water resources. Mesopotamia, for instance, grew to prominence because of its ability to manage water in order to better capitalize on the advent of agriculture through the use of fire for deforestation and later irrigation. These agricultural practices are generally traced back to southwest Asia about 10,000–12,000 years ago (McNeill, 1992: 70–71; Steffen et al., 2007: 614–615), and the early evidence of grain domestication suggests that it was in this area that irrigation techniques were first used. Traces of grain collection from 10,800 BC were found in the Shanidar Cave region of Iraq, and while there is evidence that people from the city of Mureybet, on the West Bank of the Euphrates in Syria, used to grill barley some 10,000 years ago (Bakour and Kolars, 1994: 125). These types of grains do not naturally grow at such low altitudes so it is likely that they were imported, potentially from the plains of Jericho, where people were already using simple irrigation techniques. Although the exact birthplace of agriculture remains disputed, it quickly spread through Mesopotamia and the rest of the region.[4]

Why did agriculture flourish first there and not elsewhere? For some, the explanation lies in the fact that these regions were suitable for a "flood-retreat" type of agriculture that grows crops with minimal labor (Scott, 2011: 191). Other scholars have linked the development of more sophisticated practices of irrigation and water control with the rise of the great imperial city-states of Sumer and Akkad in the fourth millennium BC. At this point, the hydrological landscape was radically different than today though still carefully developed: The Arab-Persian Gulf extended all the way inland to the sea port of the city of Ur and was used as a flood-control mechanism, and the Tigris and Euphrates were major sources of water for intensive irrigation (Furon, 1963: 71). In 1958, archeologists Jacobsen and Adams tracked the management of water resources by the Sumerian

---

[4] Personal communication with Prof. John R. McNeill, Georgetown University, November 20, 2018. Interestingly, McNeill writes with his coauthors Steffen and Crutzen that the agriculture practiced in the mid-Holocene by means of "clearing of forests through fire about 8000 years ago and irrigation for rice about 5000 years ago led to increases in releases of atmospheric carbon dioxide" and "prevented the onset of the next ice age" (Steffen et al., 2007: 615).

civilization and noted it was closely associated with the rise and decline of its empire. They identified the pivotal date of about 1700 BC, at which point Sumerian wheat harvests were declining, irrigation abruptly stopped, and Sumer was conquered by Babylon (Furon, 1963: 70).

Karl Wittfogel (1957) and others clarified this mechanism by arguing that the development of big hydraulic projects was a product of the first complex agrarian societies. Wittfogel put forth the claim that the arid environment of the Middle East required careful control of water resources and large-scale hydraulic projects, which in turn required a strong centralized state. He labeled this specific political entity the "despotism of the Oriental State" (Wittfogel, 1957). While, according to Wittfogel's theory, one would expect to see big hydraulic projects constructed during the rise of Sumerian city-states, the discoveries of the archeologist Robert Adams showed the opposite. In fact, there were no big hydraulic projects during the period of the Sumerian civilization, as they appeared later as part of a "hydraulic bureaucracy" (Adams, 1981; Curtin, 1984: 63).

For almost as long as they have been using water, humans have been fighting over water and have used water to fight. Hydraulic resources have been utilized in both offensive and defensive strategies. For example, the Chinese Zhou dynasty built dams to submerge the aggressor in the fifth century BC, and Europeans mastered rivers to spread colonial rule to the Americas through the Amazon, Mississippi, and Saint Lawrence rivers, Africa through the Nile, and Asia through the Yangzi Jiang. On the other hand, at the beginning of the fourth century BC, Babylon defended itself using flooded trenches from the Tigris and Euphrates (Lacoste, 1993: 11–12).

Early conflicts over water also saw early attempts to legislate water usage. About 5,100 years ago, the Sumerian cities of Umma and Lagash, both users of the Euphrates river, fought over shared water resources. The conflict was settled with the world's first treaty, and the victorious city of Lagash took action to prevent future conflict by digging a diversion canal for the Euphrates that would ensure Lagash's exclusive access to the water resources (McCaffrey, 1997: 43). Unfortunately, the surplus of water caused by this canal and its dilution with brackish waters led shortly after diversion to waterlogging and the salinization of soils, and Lagash's land became unsuitable for growing plants. However, the historical settlement of this conflict illustrates the way in which water rights were appropriated and codified after fighting a battle over shared resources.

Religion also played a role in defining early water-rights legislation globally, from the first Egyptian dynasties and the Hammurabi Code in ancient Mesopotamia to the Manu Code in the Indus valley and the Zhou dynasty in ancient China (Caponera, 1992: 11).[5] Early interactions between humans and water in the Middle East trace how hydrological resources were closely associated with the rise and fall of civilizations, whether through irrigation practices or water treaties. These historical developments also establish a baseline for conferring water rights.

Establishing Water Rights

Before the introduction of Islam, there were already water-rights systems in place in the Middle East. The first Egyptian dynasties centralized the administration of water (3400–2650 BC) to better manage shared water usage, and successive dynasties maintained this centralization (2650–2300 BC). Similarly, Mesopotamian civilization was organized around irrigation and navigation of rivers, though, in this instance, the issue of water distribution led to written sources of water laws. The most famous of these water legislations is the Code of the Babylonian King Hammurabi (1776 BC), which consisted of a series of instructions to local governors about the maintenance of hydraulic projects and canals, with the ultimate goal of enabling people to benefit from "well irrigated land" (Caponera, 1992: 16; Glassner, 2002: 168).[6] Articles 53 to 56 of the code discussed individual water rights and responsibilities; prohibited certain actions which would negatively impact water distribution, like flooding a neighbor's crops; and mandated compensation of a flooded neighbor with replacement crops or a share of the profit. These articles also specified

---

[5] Caponera defines the Egyptian civilization as that of the Nile, the Assyro-Babylonian or Mesopotamian civilization as that of the Tigris and Euphrates, the Hindu civilization as that of the Indus, and the Chinese civilization as that of the Huang-He or Yellow river. See Caponera (1992: 11–62), for a detailed historic analysis of early water regulations in these regions.

[6] King Hammurabi is also known for creating the calendar and names of months used in most Arab countries today (except Algeria, Egypt, and Tunisia), after implementing a reform that unified the multiple calendars of the cities of Sumer and Akkad.

punishment for the violation of these regulations. Some five centuries later in the same region, Hittite laws established the payment of fines for any illegal diversion of water (Caponera, 1992: 18).

In the Indus Valley, the Manu Code of 3000 BC enshrined the notion of water as a public good and prohibited water diversion and obstruction; punishments ranged from the death penalty to the payment of a very high fine for water losses. The legal Chinese system, or Li Ki, established by the Zhou dynasty (1027–256 BC), also institutionalized the importance of hydraulic infrastructures and the punishment of offenders of water laws (McCaffrey, 2001: 138). Similarly, Roman law from the tenth century BC to the sixth century AD outlined water property and existing user rights as well as protection against torrential rains and the control of hydraulic infrastructures by a central authority (Caponera, 1992: 29–53). These existing systems of water rights were later incorporated into Islamic societies.

Water Management in Islam: Incorporating Social Justice

Religion has always played a major role in the political, judicial, and economic systems of most countries in the region, especially in Syria, where the constitution notes that the state follows Islamic doctrine (Faruqui, 2001a: xv). This section seeks to demonstrate that before postcolonial legislation of the late 1940s, Islamic law already governed water use.[7] Moreover, the notion of water as a universally accessible public good was already present in Islamic principles and was later codified in Ottoman legislation. The Islamic principles of universal access, specified property rights, non-waste, and proportionate legislation regarding irrigation created a solid foundation for modern legislation regarding equitable use of shared resources. These principles have been enshrined in contemporary international resource law under the United Nations, which focuses on issues of equitable use and prohibition of causing significant harm. Islamic law was an early advocate of the social-justice aspects of water use and access, and, as such, many of the earliest Islamic principles regarding water are highly relevant to water-management debates today.

[7] Issues of irrigation, priority given to upstream over downstream users (Shia doctrine), priority to upstream users only in case of water scarcity (Sunni doctrine), and the obligation to not damage groundwater resources are universally relevant.

From the advent of Islam in the Middle East until the fall of the Ottoman Empire after World War I, Islamic law was at the core of the Syrian legal system. Existing Islamic legal principles were codified during the 1870s by the Ottoman Empire in the Civilian – or Majalla – Code in the late nineteenth and early twentieth century. This code and its ninety-two articles relating to water use (Articles 1234–1326) regulated water management in all the countries of the empire until the complete disintegration of the Ottoman Empire in 1923 (Mallat, 1995: 130). In ex-Ottoman Syria, the Majalla Code was replaced by new European-based legislations during the French Mandate (1920–1946).[8] After 1946, the new independent Syrian government once again established new water laws. Today, local systems of water management in Syria are still a combination of Islamic law, imported laws from Europe, and post-1946 independence legislations (Mallat, 1995: 130).[9]

Islamic law and local water-management customs (*'urf*) are still at the heart of water management in Syria. In a society where Islam regulates all aspects of both individual and communal life, an understanding of this Islamic law is key to understanding the way water is used and valued in Syria, even in the twenty-first century. This section therefore explores Islamic values related to water and their diverse origins in the seventh century.

The primary source of Islamic water-management practices is *Shari'a*, which is an Arabic word meaning Islamic law. In fact, this term may have initially referred to the law or path to water, which demonstrates the foundational role of water in Islam (Mallat, 1995: 128).[10] Another major source of guidance regarding water usage is the teachings of the Prophet, which established some of the first water laws in the Arabian Peninsula. Prior to his leadership, wells belonged to an entire tribe or to individuals whose ancestors had built their foundations, and any foreigner who wanted to drink from these wells had to

---

[8] See Chapter 4 for details about the current legislation in Syria.

[9] Mallat (1995) differentiates between a unitary consolidation of legislation under the Water Code in countries under French influence like Lebanon (Water Code 1926/1930) and the fragmented approach in non-colonized countries (Turkey) or countries under British influence.

[10] Mallat (1995) refers to the writings of the famous lexicographer Ibn Manzur (fourteenth century) as well as the dictionary of Al-Zubaydi (eighteenth century).

pay a fee (Caponera, 2001: 94). This limited access to water sparked many conflicts between nomads and sedentary populations. However, in the Quran, water was recognized as the most important divine creation after human creation, and universal access to water resources was established (Faruqui, 2001b: 1). Water is essential for the daily practice of Islam because of the necessity of purification, or ablution, before the prayer (*wudu*). At the same time, the concept of equitable and universal access to resources is established in the basic Islamic principle of *zakat*, or charity, which ensures resource availability for all members of the community. The principle of charity also indicated larger principles of equity and social justice inherent in the teachings of Prophet Muhammad (Faruqui, 2001b: 2). As such, sharing and access to water for all became a legal obligation under the Quran.

Another major source of Islamic norms regarding water are documented commentaries about the life of the Prophet (*hadiths*). In these hadiths, the Prophet prohibited the accumulation of a water surplus if others were in need and established punishment for those who had accumulated unnecessary amounts of water and those who had deprived travelers of its use.[11] Additionally, the Prophet prohibited the sale of water in order to prevent its stockpiling and misuse, and because it was a gift from God.[12] Water was therefore largely seen as seen as a good with a public (*mubah*) and social value, with a few exceptions (Caponera, 2001: 95; Faruqui, 2001b: 2; Mallat, 1995: 131).[13] Sunni doctrine established three categories of hydraulic resources: (1) private goods (water held in private tanks and containers); (2) restricted public goods (lakes, streams and springs located on private land); and (3) public goods (rivers, lakes, glacier aquifers, seas, and precipitation) (Kadouri et al., 2001: 89–90). Certain hadiths acknowledge the existence of private and public spheres of water when they reference the Prophet encouraging future caliph Othman to buy the well of Ruma to distribute its water to the neediest (Faruqui, 2001b: 12). In that instance, the private purchase of water was justified to help those in need.

Based on the principles of shared access and using resources for social justice, two fundamental water rights were established in the

---

[11] According to the famous commentator Al-Bukhari, quoted in Faruqui (2001b).
[12] According to Yahya ibn Adam (1896), mentioned in Caponera (2001: 95).
[13] Similarly to grass and fire according to the famous commentator Abu-Daoud.

earliest days of Islam: the right to quench your thirst (*shafa*) and the right to irrigation (*shirb*).

The Right to Quench Your Thirst

The first right established that any person, Muslim or not, had the right to drink in order to quench their thirst or that of their livestock or domestic animals (Caponera, 2001: 96).[14] According to Sunni doctrine, this privilege also included the use of underground resources when they did not flow through private property. Similarly, nomads had the right to dig a well and to drink from it exclusively during their stay, though they were still obliged to offer the surplus to anyone who was thirsty. Following their departure, the well became public property again to serve newcomers (Caponera, 1992: 70).

The Right to Irrigation

Ownership of water could only be gained through its transportation in containers or its distribution for irrigation purposes. This property right allowed for the irrigation of land, trees, and plants, and the selling of water in containers (Mallat, 1995: 129–130). However, surface and groundwater resources were also regulated to ensure one person was not overusing the resource. The Prophet acknowledged that regulations were needed because these resources were finite and shared: Ownership of a canal, well, or any other source of water implied some degree of involvement in neighboring land parcels to ensure water quality and quantity. Other landowners were therefore prohibited to dig nearby existing water infrastructure.

Regulations surrounding water sources and infrastructures differed between Sunni and Shia schools of thought. Shia doctrine gave exclusive discretion of usage for irrigation to the owner of the water source. In the case of shared property, water was distributed based on the proportional size of fields and amount of funds invested into the construction of the canals, though upstream irrigation was prioritized. Shia doctrine recognized upstream priority only in situations of water scarcity, or when upstream water levels did not reach above the ankles.[15]

---

[14] The Sunni doctrine expanded this right to all categories of water, while the Shia doctrine limited this right to public resources as this privilege fell under the exclusive right of the owner when it was considered as a private good.

[15] According to Khalil Ibn Ishak (1878) quoted in Caponera (2001: 96).

On the other hand, Sunni doctrine differentiated between irrigation based on the source of the water: lakes, rivers, or rainfall precipitation. The fields nearest the source of water had priority, and if several fields were concerned, the one whose crops were in most need of irrigation had priority. Those who built irrigation canals had the exclusive right of use, though others could use them given mutual consent. Similarly, the construction of wells on one's own land or on an uninhabited parcel gave the right of immediate property and irrigation to its builder.[16] According to the Prophet, the owner of a well benefited from an exclusive portion of adjacent land on which he could prohibit the construction of any additional well.[17] This visionary sustainability measure, followed by all schools of legal doctrine, sought to protect the quantity and quality of groundwater resources by preventing infiltration and overpumping – an environmental protection measure that today's Syrians will fail to pursue, as will be seen in Chapters 4 and 5.

Contemporary Interpretations: Respecting the Environment, Recycling Used Water, and Implementing Water Prices

The water laws established by Islamic jurisprudence were in many ways very modern and therefore adaptable to the needs of modern societies. Recent analyses have demonstrated that these laws are still relevant in contemporary Islamic societies and in the face of the development of international water laws (Faruqui, 2001b: 5–22; Hussein and Al-Jayyousi, 2001: 128–135). For example, the respect for nature and conservation of the environment are explicitly advocated in the Quran, but similar values are articulated in contemporary environmental laws around the world (Amery, 2001: 41–42).[18] Some scholars have challenged the adaptability of Islamic water law to modern management situations, citing many differences regarding the pricing and taxing of water (Schiffler, 2001: 455–456). Other scholars respond that while modern Western legal systems have not incorporated that many Islamic water laws, the former could certainly benefit from the latter (Wilkinson, 1990: 71).

---

[16] According to Al Mawardi (eleventh century) quoted in Caponera (1992: 70).
[17] According to Yahya ibn Adam (1896) quoted in Caponera (2001: 95).
[18] See the analysis of *fassad* prohibition or land, sea, wind, water degradation.

Syrian legislation still regards water as public or state property, based on Shari'a law, the Majalla Code, and the French Waters Code.[19] Individual property rights are marginal, and private construction of wells or bottling is subject to approval by a central authority. As water is a public good, the issue of pricing is highly sensitive. Islam prohibits the taxation of water as a good, though it is possible to tax the distribution of water and associated services.[20] A recent trend of bottling water created the perception that a price can be set on drinking water, even though Islamic practice has prevented the pricing of drinking water according to the right to quench thirst (Mallat, 1995: 132). If a price could be set for drinking water, it was assumed that this pricing was merely a matter of choosing a "just" price that could enable a more equitable redistribution within society; some in Syria advocated for increasing the price of water for those with higher incomes while simultaneously offering free water to the poorest (Faruqui, 2001b: 13). These legal experts also established that only user rights, and not actual ownership of water, could be transferred between people, and only with the authorization of the hydraulic administration.

Wastewater recycling is another point of contention in Islamic water norms and modern management needs. Islamic principles advocated for the preservation, or non-waste, of this vital resource, and in response some suggested demand-management measures like wastewater recycling. However, many religious experts argues that wastewater recycling was *haram* or impure, but in 1978 the Saudi religious authority issued a *fatwa* (authoritative legal opinion) that the reuse of wastewater was not prohibited as long as it did not cause health problems (Faruqui, 2001b: 7).

We can therefore trace the application of Islamic legal principles, such as access for all, property rights, non-waste, specific and proportionate irrigation regulation, and reasonable pricing, to contemporary water-management practices, including fair water use, the prohibition

---

[19] According to Mallat, the notion of state property has evolved under the French influence into a "public domain" dimension that includes rivers and lakes, seas and oceans, as well as underground resources (1995: 131).

[20] See the example of Prophet Muhammad, quoted in the previous page, during the buying of a water well. Chapter 4 discusses the reform of the water and agricultural sectors in recent years in Syria and the debated question of water pricing.

of causing harm, the need for compensation, and environmental conservation.

On Water in History and Geography

This historical overview of the role of water in Syria has established the domestic norms in place prior to the rise of Ba'athism in the 1960s, discussed in Chapter 4. To fully understand the context of water management in Syria, we must also examine the regional context in the years that preceded the Syrian uprising. An analysis of Syria's interactions over the international rivers of the Euphrates and Tigris, shared with upstream Turkey, therefore adds another dimension to the understanding of domestic water security, as Syria derives most of its surface waters from the Euphrates river.[21]

Syria's International Interactions over the Euphrates and Tigris Rivers (1980–2011)

The majority of Syria's usable water comes from its major river, the Euphrates, and, to a lesser extent, from the Tigris. As these rivers originate in Turkey, Syria's water supply is highly dependent on its relationship with its upstream riparian neighbor. This section therefore examines that relationship in the context of upstream and downstream interactions from the 1980s to the 2000s, tracing it through more adversarial periods in the 1980s and 1990s to a more cooperative stance on the eve of the uprising.

Phase 1: 1980–1998

In 1980, Turkey launched the GAP (Great Anatolian Project or Güneydogu Anadolu Projesi) mega-development project consisting of twenty-two dams and nineteen HEPPs (hydroelectric power plants) on the Euphrates and Tigris rivers. The GAP spans nine provinces in the Euphrates and Tigris basins, now referred to as the "GAP region" (Republic of Turkey, 2002), while the complementary Eastern

---

[21] Another major international issue lies with Israel's occupation of the Syrian Golan Heights after the 1967 War, which deprived Syria from accessing Lake Tiberias and a major tributary of the Jordan river, the Yarmuk river. This international interaction falls beyond the scope of this book. See Daoudy (2008).

Anatolia Project includes eleven provinces in eastern and southern Turkey (Durutan, 2000: 113). The GAP was scheduled for completion in 2014, but the deadline was pushed to 2050 because of financial constraints.

Although Turkey considers this project to be a "domestic" enterprise, the consequences reach far beyond its national borders. According to international experts, a full implementation of the GAP will ultimately withdraw a maximum of 70 percent of the Euphrates' natural flow, about 40–50 percent of its observed flow, and 50 percent of the Tigris' flow (Kliot, 1994; Kolars and Mitchell, 1991; Ozis, 1993). Syrian projects on the Euphrates also have the potential, if completed, to withdraw 35 percent of the flow (Daoudy, 2005: 210–211). As such, upstream projects in Turkey and Syria place Iraq as the lowest downstream riparian state in the most vulnerable position though midstream Syria is still threatened by the GAP because of its high dependence on external water sources (80 percent) and the centrality of the Euphrates Basin for the overall water supply (65 percent of total water resources).

However, since the GAP is far from complete, the impact has so far been more an issue of the quality of water than its quantity. One of the main concerns of downstream states was the issue of return flows from irrigation, which are not only highly polluted but also increase the risk of water flood and waterlogging for downstream riparians. The first GAP Master Plan of 1989 did not consider how to handle the drainage of return flows from irrigation, and, as a result, it was estimated that 40 percent of the water from the Tigris reaching Syria and 25 percent of the water reaching Iraq from Turkey would have been polluted return flows. At the same time, return flows would also pollute water from the Euphrates reaching Iraq at a rate of about 50 percent of the total water by 2050 (Kliot, 1994: 149). Turkish experts, however, point to the second "Regional Development Plan" – a revision to the master plan issued in 2002 – which did provide for return flows. Regional authorities further claim that in Turkey drains have not been discharging in the Euphrates and also note that return flows are being used in Turkey for irrigation when water is scarce. As a response to the revised master plan, Turkey and Syria began backchannel meetings in the early 2000s over the pollution of the Balikh waters (Kolars, 2000: 259). The Balikh and Khabour rivers are the main recipients of upstream pollution, and a Greenpeace report issued in the 1990s showed that overpumping of the Ras-el-Ayn aquifer by Turkish and Syrian farmers and Syrian had led to the pollution of groundwater feeding these rivers (Al-Hayat, 1996). The GAP's plans to irrigate 60,000 hectares in the Mardin-Ceylanpinar plains would have also negatively impacted the groundwater feeding the upper Khabour in Syria. In fact, the Khabour river is now entirely dried up in Syria because of upstream extractions and local groundwater overpumping (see Chapters 4 and 5).

The negotiations in the early 2000s were not the first of their kind, however: the Joint Technical Committee, founded in 1982, established trilateral meetings between Syria, Turkey, and Iraq. Although the riparian states discussed mutual development projects on the Euphrates and Tigris rivers, Turkey resisted the signing of a basin-wide agreement allocating the shared waters on the basis of sovereignty concerns (Daoudy, 2009). As of 1984, Syrian elites linked the issue of water-sharing to Turkey's domestic security by providing military support to its Kurdish insurgency, the Kurdistan Workers' Party (Partiya Karkaren Kurdistan, PKK) (see Figure 3.2).

Competition between the two riparians continued throughout the Cold War and post-Cold War era. Until the rise of the Justice and Development Party (Adalet ve Kalkinma Partisi or AKP), Turkey's pro-Western Kemalist military establishment and Syria's pan-Arab/Ba'athist identity balanced against perceived threats from the other country and sought support from their respective allies in Washington and Moscow (Ehteshami and Elik, 2011: 645). During the conflict, Syria supported the PKK, which Turkey saw as a threat to the integrity of the Turkish state (see Table 3.1). Syria considered this option as an opportunity to force an agreement on the shared waters of the Euphrates and Tigris (Daoudy, 2005).[22] At the same time, Turkey cut off the Euphrates river when filling the Atatürk Dam, which Syria interpreted as a threat to its core interests (water and food security). Because the elites of these countries perceived each other as sources of threats, they limited their interactions in mutual exclusion and conflict over the shared water resources and the Kurdish issue.

---

[22] The analysis of water and agricultural policies under Chapter 4 will also show food-security objectives drove massive irrigation plans that were also framed to strengthen Syria's claims over the Euphrates waters.

Table 3.1 *Mutual threat perceptions in Syria and Turkey's relations (1980–2015).*

	(1980–1998) Perceived threats	(2002–2011) Perceived threats
Syria	1. Water security 2. Food security	1. Regional security: National security: US hegemony in Middle East (2003 Iraq War); elite/regime survival
Turkey	1. National security: Kurdish insurgency in Turkey (PKK)	1. Regional and national security: Kurdish autonomy in Iraq (KRG)

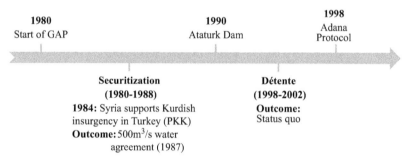

Figure 3.2 Phase 1 of Syria and Turkey's water interactions (1980–1998).

Syria's strategy ultimately worked, with Turkey and Syria reaching a temporary agreement over the shared Euphrates waters in 1987. Syria extracted this commitment through the successful securitization of allocations of the Euphrates waters; Turkey had long refused committing to volumetric allocations in the several meetings held in the Joint Technical Committee. The agreement guaranteed a minimal flow of 500 cubic meters per second (m^3/s) for Syria and was signed in the framework of an economic cooperation protocol with Syria that also covered the oil, gas, trade, electricity, and telecommunications sectors. The water clause specified that

during the filling-up period of the Atatürk Dam reservoir and until the final allocation of the waters of the Euphrates among the three riparian countries, the Turkish side undertook to release a yearly average of more than 500 m^3/s at the Turkish–Syrian borders, and in cases where the monthly flow fell below the level of 500 m³/s, the Turkish side agreed to make up the difference during the following month.

(Syrian Arab Republic, 1987)

This agreement was historic: It was the first bilateral agreement over water between the two countries.

However, Turkey did not always adhere to the 500 m³/s delivery volume (Zawahri, 2006: 1047–1048).[23] The Joint Technical Committee's weak monitoring capacity and lack of conflict-resolution mechanisms meant that Syria was not able to hold Turkey accountable and force compliance. Noncompliance persisted in 1989–1992 and during the 1999–2001 droughts, with volumes ranging from 795 m³/s in 1999 to 450 m³/s in 2000–2001, when the Iraqi and Syrian irrigation ministers voiced official protests (Daoudy, 2004, 2005; Syrian Arab Republic, 2001; *Tishrin*, 2001). Flow cuts were most significant in 1990, 1994, and 1995 during the construction of the Atatürk and Birecik dams and the Sanliurfa canals (Kolars, 2000: 253). In January 1990, Turkey started filling the Atatürk Dam reservoir, unilaterally cutting the flow of the Euphrates and leaving "a trickle" of water to downstream countries (Morris, 1997: 10). Since 1995, Turkey has more or less fulfilled its commitment to an average flow of 500 m³/s crossing the border with Syria (Mualla and Salman, 2002; Zawahri, 2006). However, the water coming from Syria became increasingly unusable for downstream farmers in Syria because of decreasing water quality from upstream drainage.[24] In response, the downstream riparian maintained the link between the Kurdish issue and water-sharing, triggering several peaks of conflict in the 1990s.

The Adana Security Protocol of 1998 induced shifts in mutual threat perceptions: Syria committed to cease support of the PKK and expelled its leader, Abdullah Öcalan, from its territory, who was captured by Turkish authorities in February 1999 (Altunisik and Tür, 2006: 238; Daoudy, 2009: 380). In the immediate aftermath, the PKK stopped

---

[23] In an exchange with the author (May 23, 2019), Syrian water engineer Abdullah Droubi, former director of the Department of Water Studies at the Arab Center for the Study of Arid Zones and Dry Lands (ACSAD), referred to Turkey's hegemony over the shared waters of the Euphrates as a source of water insecurity for Syrians during these years.

[24] Based on personal communication under conditions of anonymity with Syrian water expert residing outside of the country, London, May 11, 2015.

claiming an independent Kurdish state but called for the recognition of Kurdish identity, as well as political and human rights. The PKK revived these claims after the deterioration of Syria and Turkey's bilateral relationship after the 2011 Syrian uprising. The 1998 protocol represented a turning point after years of tense interactions over the Euphrates and Tigris waters (see Figure 3.1). The protocol saw a *détente*, an easing of hostility, thus paving the way for *rapprochement* between new state elites within Syria and Turkey.

Phase 2: 2002–2011

As shown in Figure 3.3, in the early 2000s, regional developments linked to 9/11 and the US-led War in Iraq propelled a change in the regional context and the location of threat eruption, initiating a convergence of strategic interests between Syria and Turkey and precipitating normalization. Scholars in Turkey argue that domestic factors, relating to the accession to the European Union and the change of political climate after the AKP's rise to power in 2002, also favored a change in Turkey's position toward Syria and Iran (Aras and Polat, 2008: 495). At the same time, the emergence of new leadership in Syria under Bashar al-Assad in 2000 reinforced the trend toward *rapprochement*.

New state elites in both Syria and Turkey therefore initiated a crucial shift in Turkey's foreign policy toward active cooperation with regional partners (Dohrmann and Hatem, 2014: 580). Ahmet Davutoğlu, who was then an adviser to Prime Minister Erdogan and later minister of foreign affairs, formulated new foreign-policy goals, which brought Turkey in close trade and political partnerships with

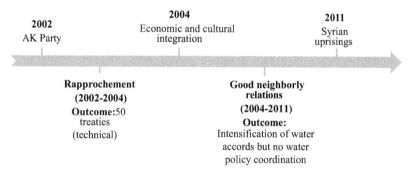

Figure 3.3 Phase 2 of Syria and Turkey's water interactions (2002–2011).

neighbors. Turkey promoted a Middle Eastern identity, as well as a "civilizational self-perception," as per Davutoğlu's own words in 1997 (as quoted in Parlar Dal, 2012: 251). A new language of cooperation shaped his "zero-problem policy" with Turkey's neighbors (Davutoğlu, 2008). His foreign-policy objectives consisted of stability, security, and soft power in the region (Davutoğlu, 2008). Turkey, therefore, projected itself as one of the region's main powers, actively engaged in regional and economic integration as well as mediation (Davutoğlu, 2013). To Turkey, Syria became the entry point to the wider Arab world, which enhanced good relations between the two countries.

The months of anti-regime protests in Syria starting in March 2011 and the subsequent repression by the Assad regime dealt a major setback to the relationship between Syria and Turkey (Daoudy, 2016). The Assad regime withdrew its forces from the Kurdish populated northeastern parts of the country, giving PKK's Syrian affiliate, the Democratic Union Party (Partiya Yekîtiya Demokrat; PYD), a free hand locally. This trend continued with the proclamation in November 2013 of Western Kurdistan (Rojava) in northern and northeastern Syria, the capture of the Tabqa Dam in Syria by extremists from the Islamic State of Iraq and Syria in early February 2013, its public proclamation as the Islamic State in June 2014, and conquest of large parts of territory in Syria and Iraq until its gradual expulsion by the US-led international coalition in 2016–2019. Currently, therefore, relations between Syria and Turkey are once again strained. The next sections will outline the mutual threat perceptions and interactions over water resources between the two countries.

Syria's Hierarchy of Threat Perceptions: From Water, Food, and National Security to Regional Security

In the two phases outlined above, mutual threat perceptions between Syria and Turkey shifted from conflict to cooperation. Table 3.1 outlines threat perceptions between state elites across the Euphrates and Tigris. It shows that Syria perceived Turkey's water projects to pose threats to its water and food security objectives, whereas Turkey's concerns lay in the rise of Syrian-backed Kurdish insurgency and its impacts on national security.

Changes in the mutually perceived threats propelled the move away from mere *détente* toward joint balancing against a shared threat, the US's Iraq War and the rise of Kurdish autonomy. Therefore, in the

1980–1990s, Turkey considered Syrian support for the PKK as a main threat to its national security, which precipitated an alliance with Israel against Syria and Iran. At the same time, another major threat for Turkey came from US and Israeli support for the Kurdistan Regional Government (KRG) in northern Iraq because it meant the possibility of a breakup of Iraq with Kurdish succession, which could have inspired similar separatism in Turkey's Kurdish regions.

In the 2000s, the Euphrates and Tigris waters were no longer a security issue but part of technical and political exchanges. This transformation enabled Syria and Turkey to deepen their strategic and economic relations, with flourishing tourism, positive media images, and even soap operas replacing negative ones. Turkey shifted its focus over transboundary water management from sovereignty to benefit-sharing and technical management (Oktav, 2009; Unver, 2005). Despite the signing of more than fifty technical cooperation treaties and the exchange of information, however, no mutual policy coordination occurred regarding transboundary water management in this period (Daoudy, 2013).

In January 2008, for the first time since the start of trilateral negotiations in 1982, Syria agreed to discuss and sign a memorandum of understanding with Turkey and Iraq on the Tigris waters; the agreement stipulated that Syria could extract up to 1.250 billion cubic meters per year from the Tigris river (Daoudy, 2013: 141). The Syrian–Turkish High Level Strategic Cooperation Council met in October and December 2010 (Republic of Turkey, 2010), and the Joint Technical Committee had three meetings between 2008 and 2009 (Dinar, 2013: 123; Kibaroglu, 2013: 148; Kibaroglu and Scheumann, 2013: 294–295). The meetings paved the way for improved mutual relations and perceptions without impacting upstream patterns of water development. However, local communities – including Kurdish populations in Turkey and Syrian and Iraqi farmers – continued to suffer from water and economic insecurities. Severely impacted during the historical drought in 2006–2010, Syrian officials requested an increase in the cumulative Euphrates flow coming from Turkey that had been set in the 1987 protocol, and in the fall of 2009, Turkey agreed to a minimal flow of 550 m³/s (Kibaroglu, 2013: 152).

In general, however, political elites in Syria acted so as to not jeopardize the special relationship developed with their powerful Turkish partner. Following the Syrian regime's withdrawal from Lebanon in 2005, it sought to secure its survival by sacrificing water security to domestic and national security concerns, even as upstream patterns of exploitation continued unabated (see Table 3.1). Syrian analysts outline, however, the negative impacts of the intensification of trade with Turkey on the Syrian economy (al-Taqi and Hinnebusch, 2013). Unable to compete with massive imports from Turkey, two of Syria's core economic sectors – textiles and furniture – collapsed.[25]

Turkish state elites satisfied their societal, border, and national-security interests with the rapprochement while incurring reputational and financial costs. Turkey received international criticism and withdrawal of foreign investment because of its massive projects in controversial areas (Dohrmann and Hatem, 2014). For example, the Ilisu Dam on the Tigris river continues to mobilize international human-rights groups concerned by the displacement of populations and the flooding of cultural sites, such as the historical city of Hansankeyf (CounterCurrent, 2011; Human Rights Watch, 2002). Turkey's willingness to incur these costs suggests that it saw the GAP water project as an issue of national security.

Turkey also managed to extract a de-facto recognition of its 1939 annexation of the formerly Syrian Sanjak of Iskandaroun (Alexandretta), currently Hatay province, by bringing Syria to recognize Turkey's rights over the waters of the Orontes (Asi) river, which flow in the disputed area. Following the Syrian president's first historical visit to Turkey in 2004, and the trip made to the province, Syria appeared to have informally given up its historical claims on this disputed territory without issuing an official statement on the issue.[26] While annexation of the Sanjak by Turkey was not formally recognized by Syria, the signing of the water agreement over the Orontes waters informally ended the territorial dispute. Both parties agreed to build a "Friendship" dam on the part of the Orontes river in Turkey, paving the way for mutual cooperation over flood prevention, energy, and the irrigation of 20,000 hectares of agricultural land in Turkey and 10,000 hectares in Syria. Both sides officially inaugurated the construction of the dam in February 2011, but the project never got past the level of studies. The Orontes Dam raised issues of human insecurity

---

[25] Based on a personal communication with a Syrian water expert on condition of anonymity, London, May 11, 2015.

[26] Figure 4.2 shows how the province still appeared in official Syrian maps dating back to 2000 as part of the country.

within Syria as the dam was scheduled to entirely flood the city of Darkush in the Idlib governorate in northern Syria, which not coincidentally became a bastion of anti-regime resistance after 2011.[27]

As such, at the eve of the Syrian uprising in 2011, Turkish–Syrian relations were relatively strong. Syria's support for the PKK was no longer an issue of contention, and agreements over shared water resources were in place. New, more mutualistic, patterns of interaction had been initiated, though the downstream riparian continued to be affected by upstream projects as the two riparians failed to coordinate policies for the management of their shared waters.

The 2011 Syrian uprising propelled a return to conflict with Turkey as the relationship between Turkey's Prime Minister Erdogan and Syrian President Bashar al-Assad gradually collapsed (Daoudy, 2016). This signified the end of trade and cultural integration between the two countries and a return of transboundary water management and the Kurdish issue to the realm of high security. The waters of the Euphrates and Tigris rivers became tools of power once again. In 2014, Turkey allegedly limited downstream flows on the Euphrates again, in order to influence the battle for Aleppo in northern Syria (Shamout, 2014; Vidal, 2014), gradually reducing the water flow to Syria over six days in May before completely cutting off water for eight days in August (Dohrmann and Hatem, 2014: 581). According to Syrian water experts, the cumulative flow during 2014 had been irregular throughout the year: Flows decreased to 80 m^3/s during the month of August, which exhibited the highest temperatures, while aggregate flows increased in the wintertime to meet the threshold.[28]

Summary

Water has been a defining feature in both Syria's historical development and its contemporary interactions with neighboring countries. This chapter presented an overview of these domestic and international relationships, starting with the way that Syria's water legislation

---

[27] Based on author's interview with Syrian water expert on condition of anonymity, London, May 11, 2015.
[28] Based on author's interview with Syrian water expert on condition of anonymity, London, May 11, 2015.

developed over millennia. The sharing of water resources has determined the rise and fall of the great civilizations in the Middle East as well as the development of rules and norms that frame local practices around water-sharing. Local norms were often based on Islamic legal principles and were codified until the introduction, in the late nineteenth and early twentieth centuries, of modern legislations, though these legislations themselves were often inspired by local norms. This chapter traced the local Islamic principles still relevant for modern water management in Syria. The newly independent Syria in the 1940s drew on water legislation from Shari'a law, the Ottoman Majalla Code, and the French Water Code, and featured water-security promotion (quantity, drinkable water, water for irrigation) and environmental security (pollution, quality of groundwater resources), values that date back to the beginnings of Islam. This historical overview also explains how the norms surrounding water set up during early Islam would be treated as best practices now: Social justice, or ensuring that water was accessible to all, and sustainability, or water usage without environmental degradation, were key norms. Although these norms were picked up by later laws when Syria became independent, a shift started in the 1960s when they were no longer adhered to.

The second half of this chapter analyzed Syrian–Turkish relations in order to frame Syria's issues of water security in the context of upstream/downstream interactions over the Euphrates and Tigris. The chapter traces how Syria effectively securitized their shared water issues by supporting the PKK in the 1980s and 1990s, in order to bring about a more equitable and reliable management strategy. The chapter then explored how a shift in perceived threats encouraged Syrian–Turkish cooperation over water rights and other issues. By 2011, the Syrian–Turkish riparian relationship had markedly improved from its Cold War stance, but this was once again to change with the 2011 uprising and the Syrian Civil War.

Having set the historical and regional context for this book, I now return to the HECS framework to explore the key political variable of ideology on water and food security in Syria under Ba'athism as well as under liberalism.

Human–Environmental–Climate Security (HECS)

4 | *Rules of Ideology and Policy*
From Ba'athism to the Liberal Age

I defy anyone to claim that the displaced populations triggered unrest. We Syrians have always lived in arid areas, and climate variability has been historically high. The problem was not about climate change but about the developmental mistakes made by the government. There was no transparency in food-security policies, ideological paralysis, heightened corruption, and the relevant ministries did not recognize their mistakes. No one dared to say anything out of fear. The main triggers of the Revolution were corruption, lack of justice, and the mistakes made in the government's development plans.

(Syrian water expert interviewed by author on condition of anonymity,
Beirut, December 4, 2015)

Syrians have become dependent on "Vitamin W" [for *wasta*, bribe]. It is required for everything.

(Yassin Haj-Saleh, in discussion with author, Istanbul, July 18, 2016)

Of People, Land, Water, and Food

This chapter and the next (Chapter 5) explore the political dimensions of the HECS framework: the ideological and policy drivers of human insecurity that impacted Syria's water and food security. These sections provide an in-depth analysis of key variables such as ideology (Ba'athism, neoliberalism), unsustainable water practices, and unsustainable agricultural practices. I assess water and agricultural policies dating back to the 1970s, which contributed to water scarcity and insecurity under Hafez al-Assad and Bashar al-Assad rule. It evaluates the failure of state farms, government plans to implement intensive "modernized" irrigation schemes for rural constituencies, and the social and economic obstacles to dam construction, including flooding, displacement and failed resettlement of "flooded" populations (*al-maghmureen*) especially within the context of forced Arabization in the Kurdish-inhabited areas of the Jazira

(Hassake governorate). The analysis shows how achieving self-sufficiency in food, a priority under Ba'athism, came at the cost of poor governance from a growing bureaucracy, lack of water sustainability, and decreased soil quality (as measured by the levels of salinity and gypsum). Finally, the chapter explores how liberalizing reforms, culminating in the 2005 shift to a social market economy, increased the vulnerability of rural communities. To better illustrate the relevance and timeliness of policy, Figure 4.1 identifies critical policy decisions on agriculture, land and water resources since the start of the agrarian reform in 1958.

This chapter draws on primary sources collected from within a number of Syrian ministries before 2011, contributions by leading international analysts on the politics and economics of Syria, and debates held in Arabic within the Syrian Association of Economic Sciences (SAES) between Syrian economists, agriculture, and water experts and intended for domestic audiences. By outlining the myths and realities of food security and the problems incurred by large-scale irrigation projects, these sections outline the (mis)management of water resources and provide an overview of the ideological and political drivers behind water scarcity in Syria under Ba'athist ideology. The last sections of this chapter will investigate the motivations behind the historical shift in water and agricultural policy in the 2000s and the difficulties encountered throughout the process. This chapter will analyze the process of liberalization that gradually took place since the 1970s. This will allow us to assess, in Chapter 5, how ideology and policy concretely affected water and food security, and better evaluate the multilayered levels of vulnerability.

The chapter unfolds in a six-part analysis. In the first two sections, ideology is explored as a tool which the regime has historically instrumentalized to consolidate its power, and the specific symbols used by the Ba'ath Party will be introduced. Ideology and Hafez al-Assad's personality cult and peasant origins critically frame how ideology is negotiated by citizens and the regime. The next sections will trace the history of the Ba'athist rural contract and the myth of food security, as well as the "ruralization" of the Ba'ath Party in three distinct phases in the 1950s, 1960s, and 1970s. Food security will then be defined as a primary objective of the Ba'ath Party, and dam construction. Intensive irrigation is identified as the means of pursuing this end. However, these strategies produced a plethora of environmental and social dilemmas, including

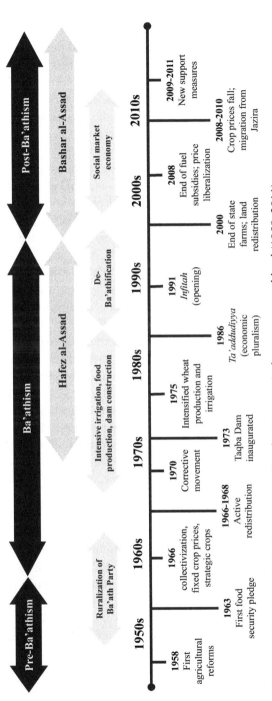

Figure 4.1 Timeline of critical domestic policy decisions: agriculture, water, and land (1958–2011).

the construction of illegal wells, the degradation of water and soil resources, displacement and rural poverty, and the implementation of water, food, and fuel subsidies that distorted market prices. Land-reform policies that furthered Arabization, such as the "Arab Belt" policy, will be shown to have excluded Syrian Kurds from agricultural gains in the second half of the twentieth century. Finally, the rationale and results of the long process of liberalization in Syria will be investigated, with a special focus on the impact on rural communities.

At this point, a simple overview of the historical progression of the Ba'ath and Ba'athist ideology in Syria is helpful before delving into its relevance for agrarian policies and symbols. Delvin describes how the first Ba'athist party, the Arab Socialist (Resurrection) Party, began as a movement that stood for "Arab nationalism, freedom from foreign rule, and the establishment of a single Arab state" (Delvin, 1991: 1396). Its founders, Michel Aflaq and Salah al-Din Bitar, envisaged a movement based on ideals of freedom, unity, and socialism. The development of Ba'athism has not been unidirectional. Batatu, the great historian of Syria and Iraq, contends that Ba'athism is "a mantle for a variety of elements," and observes that "there have been not one but three Ba'ath parties which, though interlinked . . . have been quite distinct in their social base, frame of mind, instinctive responses . . . and the interests they served" (Batatu, 1999: 133). As Batatu notes, from its rise in the 1950s through its ideological decline after 1980, the Ba'ath Party has seen three distinct phases: (1) the old radical leftist Ba'ath of the 1950s, (2) the transitional neo-Ba'ath of the 1960s, and (3) the post-1970s Ba'ath under Hafez al-Assad that saw the consolidation of the regime (1970–1975). Each of the three Ba'athist phases had its own ideological adjustments: For example, the neo-Ba'ath depicted themselves as supporters of the "practical side of Ba'ath ideology," whereas after Hafez al-Assad's rise to power in 1970, the focus shifted to the community networks of the Alawite family instead of ideology (Olson, 1982: 108, 121). The party's direction under Hafez al-Assad deprioritized the early ideology but also reestablished the primacy of the Sunni bourgeoisie. This came to be known as Assad's "Corrective Movement," which "connotes the initiation of reforms rather than any revolutionary break with the past" (Wedeen, 2015: 8).

To continue with this analysis, the concept of ideology must be briefly defined in the Syrian context.

Ideology in Syria: Definitions and Implementation

Ideology is critical in defining the state's social and economic priorities, which in turn impact the way human–environmental–climate security manifests in the country. In the Syrian context, ideologies such as Ba'athism, the personality cult of Hafez al-Assad, and economic liberalization under Bashar al-Assad interacted with state power to initiate agrarian reforms that valued food security over environmental conservation. To understand the role that ideology plays as a core variable in the HECS model, we must first explore the various conceptions of the term. Certain definitions of ideology are more relevant to the case of Syria, and, as such, we will center on three themes: (1) where and how ideology is wielded in a given political climate, (2) ideology's interaction with evolving development plans, and (3) symbols and state mythology used to sway opinion and garner popular support for a given regime.

Ideology as Complicity and Compliance or a Tool of Mobilization

One way to conceptualize ideology is to view it as a form of complicity and compliance; Lisa Wedeen applies this conception of ideology to the cast of Syria.[1] According to Wedeen, although citizens are not required to act according to a belief in national ideology or symbols, they need to "act *as if* " they did (Wedeen, 2015: 67). As citizens are acting as if they believe in a national ideology, they are complicit in its spread and implementation; in fact, all citizens therefore "confirm the system, fulfill the system, make the system, *are* the system" (Wedeen, 2015: 76).

Belief in an ideology of no compromise forces citizens to surrender not only their bodies and minds to the state but their "imaginations" as well; the regime removes from its people the power to create or imagine a vision of what their life would look like outside of the system it has built for them. This leads to a kind of collective depoliticization, in which individual people lose the power of political cognition or agency and become apolitical, without the energy or will to resist, or to exhibit

---

[1] This specific interpretation of ideology provides an interesting parallel with Gramsci's conceptions of hegemony which outline the centrality of consent by the party under hegemony (see Gramsci, 1973).

"dignity" as agents (Wedeen, 2015: 81). If this occurs, adherence to the ideology does not need to be violently enforced, as depoliticization means that obedience is inevitable.

Raymond Hinnebusch posits an alternative understanding of ideology in Syria. Unlike Wedeen, Hinnebusch utilizes a political-organizational framework to explain how Ba'ath ideology was transmitted for mobilization purposes. The party was able to control the society with relatively little constraint on its upper leadership because of its ability to use ideology in framing its interest and recruiting at high levels (Hinnebusch, 2011). For example, the party identified rural populations as its core constituencies and evoked the peasant origins of Hafez al-Assad as a way of mobilizing rural agrarian communities. This process, as well as other tools used by the Ba'ath Party to mobilize citizens, are explored more deeply later in the chapter.

Ideology as Flexible Political Principles

Ideology does not need to be rigid, especially when ideology is put into practice in the foreign-policy arena. Jasmine Gani's nuanced analysis of the role played by ideology in Syria's foreign policy cautions that misunderstanding the place of ideology – particularly, as constructivist International Relations scholars seek to apply ideology to Middle Eastern foreign-policy analysis – can lead to one of two challenges. First, rationality and ideology are seen as incompatible; as Gani phrases it, "to pursue ideological goals at all costs is ... branded as radical, illogical" (2014: 13). Alternatively, ideologies can be seen solely as a "mask [of] the reality of self-interest and personal gain" (Gani, 2014: 13). The former view can lead to essentialism while the latter provides a realist perspective on political behavior.

Problematically, scholars have applied both views in the case of Syria. For instance, Gani notes that Hafez al-Assad, the symbol of Ba'athist ideology, is sometimes considered "to have been a calculated and pragmatic ruler" who neglected ideology (2014: 14), but pragmatism and ideology are not mutually exclusive. Ideology embodies a set of political principles that frame rather than fix policy choices (Gani, 2014: 15). Moreover, ideology was not only instrumentalized by the Assad regime but was negotiated by Syrian citizens who respond to it. As such, ideology can be flexible, and a leader can mold it to fit their needs while still embracing the ideology.

The Ideology of Symbols and Personality

Symbol and rhetoric are central to politics (Wedeen, 2015: ix). Within the Ba'ath Party, the party strategically integrated symbols and personality politics into their ideology. Assad's regime and symbology allowed his image to be used as an archetype and embodiment of an ideal Syrian symbol, both as a peasant and a worker. The importance of the symbols used by the Assad regime and their interactions with ideology will be explored in turn.

The Cult of Personality and Peasant Origins

The new Ba'athist elites of 1963 came from the rural intelligentsia of Latakia, Deraa, Suwayda, and Deir ez-Zor; some say the members' poor background was reflected in the "bitterness" of the resolutions of the Sixth National Congress held in October 1963 (Olson, 1982: 86). Particularly important was Hafez al-Assad's peasant origin, which became central to his narrative of state-centered rural legitimacy (Barnes, 2009: 521). For example, a poster in the town of Hassake shows Hafez al-Assad surrounded by peasants harvesting crops, and projects such as the 8 March Dam have been named after politically or ideologically significant dates and people (Barnes, 2009: 522). Another example is the previously named al-Khabour Dam in the Hassake province, formally renamed the Martyr Bassel al-Assad Dam in 1998, when Hafez al-Assad's heir died in a car accident. Moreover, Assad's discourse repeatedly involved invocations of the importance and power of peasants (Batatu, 1999: 254). Not only was the president's rural background seen as exemplary, but his whole persona became an embodiment of the archetypical citizen in Syrian political art, which was strategically employed to his political advantage (Wedeen, 2015: 46).

Hafez al-Assad even became a symbol of manliness itself, with the example of the October War of 1973, in which the state led an information campaign portraying the leader as a "father" and "victorious 'combatant,'" and later representations went on to stress his "masculinity" (Wedeen, 2015: 54). Significantly, the switch from portraying Hafez al-Assad as a peasant to a masculine military figure occurred in the wake of the 1967 Six Day War, which prompted many thinkers throughout the Arab world to "offer pointed criticisms of leaders, official language, and social practices" (Wedeen, 2015: 54). The military motifs also carried over into the promotion of development and agrarian goals as righteous and just (Barnes, 2009: 524).

Hafez al-Assad's personality cult was also spread by local organizations. Hinnebusch (1976) argues that, in the 1970s, mass mobilization on the part of the Ba'ath Party required that local organizations became diffusers of regime ideology, thereby utilizing local reform and development initiatives to gain popular support. In this framing, Ba'ath ideology became a "blend of egalitarianism and nationalism" that was well received by peasants and the youth, who were less distrustful of the state and even more likely to buy in to change-oriented government programs (Hinnebusch, 1976: 5). In this way, Ba'athist ideology was instrumentalized for mass political mobilization.

Ideology, Legitimacy, and Power

The relationship between ideology, symbols, and legitimacy is an important one. In a sense, legitimacy can be seen as its own kind of ideology – more of a myth to be built and expanded upon than actually defined. Given the apparent ambiguities of the term "legitimacy," one might, alongside Wedeen, call for the abandonment of "legitimacy" as a "social scientific concept." She characterizes legitimacy as "lack[ing] clarity and often obscur[ing] the very processes of power, obedience, consent, and acquiescence that it is intended to explain" (Wedeen, 2015: xi).

Even as we account for the difficulty of defining legitimacy, the Assad regime's primacy was clearly a function of its ideational power. The party drew on early Ba'athist ideals on pan-Arabism and economic equity, turning the agrarian sector into a key pillar of the government's legitimacy in rural constituencies (Hinnebusch, 2013: 3). Barnes notes that this quest for legitimacy drew on "mobilizing agrarian modernist imagery" (2009: 521) because the party supported modernizing development plans that would empower the agrarian peasantry while also putting forward the image of Hafez al-Assad as symbol of this empowerment, given his peasant origins. The themes of social mobility and prosperity through agrarian revolution were therefore key in Ba'athist messaging under Hafez al-Assad. In Syria, therefore, the Ba'athist ideology of economic equality, military might, and a strong agrarian sector, which was supported by the personality cult of Hafez al-Assad, which portrayed him as a peasant worker and victor, created the legitimacy for his regime.

If ideology was key in creating legitimacy, the next step is to understand the relative strength of Ba'athism in Syria from the 1970s to

2011. David Roberts (1987) points out that Ba'athist ideology was never "deeply rooted" when compared to other ideologies, although he uses European nineteenth-century examples in his comparison. According to Roberts, Ba'athist ideology in Syria was useful in that it stopped an "endless" string of coups and waves of political instability (Roberts, 1987: 3). Roberts therefore evaluates a state's prosperity as a function of regime stability; as Ba'athism did bring stability, he argues that it was also prosperous, and therefore strong.

Ba'athist ideology in the 1960s through to the 1980s was grounded in pan-Arab socialism, but with the worsening domestic economic inequality in the 1990s and 2000s, the regime adjusted its ideological grounding to be focused on prosperity for all regardless of the means of achieving this prosperity. Critically, the regime promoted a vision of prosperity, or the "good life" under economic liberalization in contrast to earlier depictions of prosperity as a function of socialism (Wedeen, 2013: 843–844). The new neoliberal ideology envisaged the "good life" in terms of economic well-being, multiculturalism, security, and consumerism – an "elite" life that should have been available to all but in reality was not, leading to public dissatisfaction.[2] Eventually, as demonstrations broke out in 2011, the idea of a "good life" based on free market ideals collapsed (Wedeen, 2013: 845).

In sum, this section has sought to articulate multiple conceptions of ideology in order to better assess the relevance of ideology for the Ba'athist rule of Syria. It examined both the importance of Assad's cult of personality and the role of ideology and symbols in upholding the legitimacy of the Assad regime. Ultimately, this understanding of ideology will prove helpful in conceiving how structural factors in Syrian society interacted with political, societal, and environmental factors to induce an increasingly polarized society and, ultimately, to uprising and revolt.

---

[2] The networks of patronage that characterized the regimes of both Hafez and Bashar al-Assad were known to all. Hafez al-Assad privileged public displays of control, for example by the *mukhabarat*, or intelligence officers, known to roam around cities in large dark cars with tinted windows. The public display of wealth and elite enrichment, however, differed drastically under the Bashar al-Assad era in the mid 2000s, with luxury foreign brands appearing at the heart of Damascus and glamorous neighborhoods, such as Ya'afour, being built exclusively for business elites and wealthy foreigners in the vicinity of the capital, in contrast with the increasing numbers of beggars in the streets.

Ideology and Policy under Ba'athism: A "Green Uprising"

In his seminal analysis of post-World War II Syrian politics, Patrick Seale interestingly attributes the longevity of Adib al-Shishakli's presidency during the pre-Ba'athist turbulent times of 1949–1954 to the remarkable prosperity of agriculture (Seale, 1965: 130).[3] He, however, credits the significant boom in grain production not to state efforts but to investments made by Syrian merchants to mechanize the sector (Seale, 1965: 131).

Promising food security was one way that new Ba'athist elites of the 1960s established legitimacy in their rural constituencies, and fulfilling their promises required new agricultural and economic policies. The next sections explore these policies, drawing upon historical documents, current academic studies, and a discourse analysis of statements by officials and state institutions.

The Ba'athist Rural Contract

The previous sections briefly addressed the importance of the "peasant" symbol in defining the new Ba'athist ideology, crystallizing and empowering its ruling elites. As such, rural agricultural policies were crucial to the political development of Syrian society in the 1960s and 1970s (Hannoyer, 1985: 26; Hinnebusch, 1982: 110), to the extent that Hinnebusch has characterized the Ba'ath Party's rise to power as a "green uprising" (1989: 19). In fact, in one of its first meetings in June 1963, the Sixth National Congress of June 1963 stated that Syria's modernization would be achieved through an agrarian revolution (Olson, 1982: 56). The new regime paved the way for land reform and state-led management of water and agricultural resources inspired by socialism. This led to the intensification of land reclamations starting in 1958, as well as the establishment of state farms and peasant cooperatives to enhance equity in land management and distribution, though active redistribution to peasants did not effectively start until 1968–1969 (Batatu, 1999: 163). Many of these programs relied on narratives of equity, redistribution, and the empowerment of the peasantry, which were part of the Ba'athist rural

[3] I would like to sincerely thank Dr. Kevin Martin for drawing my attention to this interesting historical fact in Seale's book.

contract: The Ba'ath Party promised economic equity and a rural revival, and, in return, agricultural communities supported the new elites.

As such, ideology was at the core of Syria's food and water policies in the 1960s and 1970s. After independence, the countryside and its natural resources were a pillar of socioeconomic development for Syria, but the political elites were not able to stop the overexploitation of water resources by the urban centers at the expense of rural areas. Some politicians responded to this disparity, implementing the major 1958 reforms, which allowed the state to seize gradual control of the country's water resources and rural economic activities. At the same time, the government in the 1960s prioritized food security, which led to the construction of major hydraulic projects on the Euphrates to support intensive irrigation. Ba'athist ideology was therefore used to justify large-scale projects to ensure agricultural production.

Pledging Access to Land and Food: Collectivization and Cooperatization

The focus on agrarian policies came as a response to resource scarcity and a desire for food self-sufficiency (Olson, 1982: 52), as well as a lack of local and foreign capital in Syria that made it unlikely for industrialization to be the main means of modernization (Springborg, 1981: 192). Agricultural reforms therefore begun 1958 and 1962 and intensified under Ba'athist rule in 1963 and 1966, and they gradually implemented a shift from laissez-faire to collectivization inspired by socialism (Batatu, 1999: 163; Olson, 1982: 57).[4] The socialist ideology of the Ba'ath rural policy was embodied early on in the slogan of the 1963 Sixth National Congress: "the land to those who till it, and to each according to his effort" (Olson, 1982: 55). The goal of the reforms was to put an end to the capitalist development of agriculture, decrease the power of large landowners through expropriation and redistribution to the peasants, and foster integrated development through a class of "modern socialist peasants," while accounting for

---

[4] For example, Agrarian Reform Law No. 161 of 1958, which was further refined by Decree No. 88 of June 23, 1963, led to halving ceilings on private landownership, from 80 ha of irrigated land to 40 ha and from 300 ha of nonirrigated land to 150 ha, and the nationalization of private estates to be redistributed to peasants (Olson, 1982: 57).

regional diversities in terms of soil, geography, and irrigated land (Metral, 1980).

The Ba'ath Party did not always have such a rural focus; its "ruralization" began in the early 1950s a few years after the founding of the party and accelerated over a couple decades. When it formed in 1947, the Ba'ath Party was made up of small groups of students and teachers and did not draw significantly from rural areas (Batatu, 1999: 136). The early leaders of the party, including Michel Aflaq, Sala-ed-Din al-Bitar, and Midhat al-Bitar, were born to grain dealers and raised in a climate influenced by "the world of merchants," so that they were likely to favor "large and expanding markets, unencumbered by tariffs and custom duties or by a multiplicity of economic rules and regulations" (Batatu, 1999: 134). In his writings, Michel Aflaq showed little interest in peasants, and the early cadres of the party were mainly schoolteachers such as himself. Their recruits, however, were students who came predominantly from peasant families.

The process of ruralization began with the Ba'ath Party's merger with Akram Hourani's Arab Socialists in 1952 (Hourani being of peasant origin himself), the formation of the party's military committee in 1959, whose members were mostly of peasant origin, and the post-1963 "peasantification" of the officer corps, the armed forces, and the state bureaucracy (Batatu, 1999: 142, 145, 155, 157). This "transformation" of the officer corps, armed forces, and state bureaucracy into bodies that were ruled, or heavily inundated with rural influence, seeped into the Ba'ath Party itself (Batatu, 1999: 156). Using the party's documents of the time, Batatu was able to identify a deliberate strategy, to consolidate the party's rural peasant support base, in order to garner political favor rather than to actually address peasant needs (Batatu, 1999: 162; Olson, 1982: 51). Olson (1982) identifies the primary focus on Ba'ath policies as issues of Palestine, pan-Arabism, socialist revolution, and modernization rather than rural agriculture.

The ruralization of the military was in part due to the ability of wealthy urban Sunnis to buy their way out of compulsory military service. Alawis and peasants were not able to afford this, which increased their proportion in the military and ultimately allowed more Alawite officers to climb the ranks and fill positions that had previously been held by the urban Sunni military class. The shift in relative numbers cinched Alawite dominance of the military, putting Alawi recruits in positions "of direct relevance to the making and unmaking of military coups," further increasing their standing in later state formation (Batatu, 1999: 157, 159).

The party's legitimacy had been gained through a social contract that increasingly included rural communities and was maintained through peasant organizations and corporations. These organizations identified constituencies that were interested in statist policies such as cooperative agriculture, regulation of the market, and consolidation of the public sector, and implemented policies to ensure their support (Hinnebusch, 2015: 23). When the left wing of the party came to power in 1966, the corporatist popular organizations were decentralized, and local committees were established to distribute land to farming cooperatives (Metral, 1980). These cooperatives gave state-funded loans at preferential rates, distributed seeds and mechanized tools with 5 percent refund rates, and allocated a public subsidy to reduce transportation costs of equipment by 25 percent (Batatu, 1999: 251; Hinnebusch, 2013: 10). In exchange for governmental support, the cooperatives accepted fixed crop prices and planted crops based on the Ministry of Agriculture's preference for "strategic crops" for which that state had a marketing monopoly, such as wheat, barley, cotton, sugar beet, tobacco, lentils, and chickpeas (Batatu, 1999: 47).

More generally, land reform was a "mobilizational technique" through which the regime was able to organize mass support among the peasants while building a new agrarian administrative bureaucracy (Hinnebusch, 1976: 4). Since peasants were already invested and had expertise in local infrastructure, the regime was able to capitalize upon this through corporatist peasant organizations (Hinnebusch, 1976: 5). These organizations were both an instrument of domination and cooption of peasants by the state as they established a "pro-Ba'ath sub-elite" empowered to participate to decision-making (Barnes, 2009: 522; Metral, 1980; Springborg, 1981: 202). Hinnebusch characterizes this model of mobilization as quasi-Leninist because of the way influence was spread both from above and from below (Hinnebusch, 1976: 1).

Hafez al-Assad's coup of the 1970s was a turning point for the Ba'athist regime that established new symbols and norms (Batatu, 1999: 134). The government started framing their economic policies as pragmatic rather than ideological in nature; for example, the land tenure system gradually moved toward decollectivization as the government discarded some of its socialist ideological roots in favor of a more efficient approach (Springborg, 1981: 197–199). This pragmatism was expected to translate to a more open economy that would benefit commerce over agriculture so that, as Batatu notes, "no element of the population greeted [Assad's military coup] with greater enthusiasm than the urban merchants" (1999: 175). At the same time, the regime continued to promote expensive projects that were symbolically important, such as the Euphrates land-reclamation project (Hinnebusch, 2011: 5).

Under Hafez al-Assad, the symbol and rhetoric surrounding Ba'athist ideology gradually crystallized around the objective of food security. This national priority was financed by rents from Syria's domestic oil industry, which had grown significantly by the mid 1980s, and from the Soviet Union and Arab Gulf states in the aftermath of the 1973 October war. Interestingly, the Syrian state constituted a peculiar type of rentier state that allocated most external rents to the expansion of its agricultural sector (Selby, 2018: 9).[5] In 1975, the state further consolidated its control over the agricultural sector with a law that gave the Higher Agricultural Council authority to enforce "a planned compulsory crop rotation" (Barnes, 2009: 553). This allowed the state to massively increase wheat production to the extent that it became Syria's main crop and also to implement intensive irrigation to increase production yields and expand cultivated areas.

The new policies came at a price for water resources and soil quality. According to Allan, water resources across the Middle East began to dry as early as the 1970s as a result of political and economic choices regarding food security (Allan, 2000: 5). This was exceptionally true of Syria, which had historically been food secure and even self-sufficient in the production of staple crops. Syria's food self-sufficiency was predicated on intensive irrigation; however, that came at a cost of overuse of groundwater resources and the deterioration of soils.[6] The country's water resources were therefore subject to poor institutional

---

[5] Oil rents peaked to 60 percent of Syria's revenues in 2001 (Selby, 2018: 9). Despite a steady decline in the following decade, oil revenues still contributed up to 9.5 percent of GDP in 2010 (Daher, 2018: 6).

[6] Based on the author's interview with Nadim Khouri, an independent researcher on food security in the Arab world, actively involved with the Global Agriculture and Food Security Program at the World Bank and the International Food Policy Research Institute (IFPRI), Washington, DC, February 10, 2016.

and economic decisions in terms of water management, such as over-pumping of groundwater resources, inefficient irrigation techniques, and upstream extractions. In the next section, I analyze the Syrian government's narratives around food self-sufficiency, the tools they used to achieve this goal, and the institutional, environmental, and social problems that confronted them in the process.

The Securitization of Food Production: Narratives and Practices

Chapter 3 discussed at length international debates about definitions of water and food security and the discursive and political processes that securitize climate, water, and food policies. Now, we can trace how food and water were securitized in Syria under Ba'athism. In Syria, both food and water took on a symbolic importance under Ba'athism as means to achieve autonomous development (Postel, 1996: 13). Syria's ambitious food production goals in the 1970s should be considered in the context of broader myths and misconceptions regarding food self-sufficiency, which allow political considerations to prevail to the detriment of economic efficiency (Allan, 2000: 39; Biswas et al., 1997: 45).

Syria's political, social, and economic objectives under the Ba'ath Party need to be evaluated in the context of the new elites' quest for socioeconomic development and the necessity of feeding a rapidly growing population. Barnes notes, however, that issues of food, water, and income security have frequently been framed as "crisis narrative[s]" in Syria and in the region more broadly (Barnes, 2009: 510). Chapter 2 showed how debates on modernization and development still grapple with the concept of food security, which has evolved from a narrow focus on food availability to a more multidimensional approach that includes food availability, affordability, basic needs, entitlement programs, and sustainability. All these parameters are crucial to understanding Syria's water and food security goals, which have been a central objective of Ba'athist agrarian policies since the 1970s. In fact, the Ba'athist goal of food security dates back to the Sixth Regional Congress of the Arab Ba'ath Socialist Party in 1975 (Barnes, 2009: 523). Party officials were concerned that grain-producing Western countries could use their control of food supply as a "food weapon" to counter the Arab countries' "oil weapon" in the aftermath of the 1973 oil-price increases so the officials established control over planting decisions aimed at achieving food self-sufficiency (Hinnebusch, 2013: 4).

Food Security vs. Water Sustainability: Views from Within

Food security and self-sufficiency are separate but interrelated concepts. The aim of food security is, broadly, to be able to domestically produce enough food to guarantee that the population's minimal nutritional needs will be met for the foreseeable future. On the other hand, the aim of food self-sufficiency is for a country to domestically produce all of its food, to attain a form of international autonomy or independence, and is equivalent to the "economic situation of a community that supports its [food] needs without resorting to trade" (Fenelon, 1991: 46).

There are inherent security ramifications to this distinction. According to official narratives in the 1980s and 1990s, food security in Syria was matter of national security because it meant that the country would not be cut off from importing necessary resources for strictly political reasons.[7] For example, the Ministry of Irrigation phrased this as "food security and water security are fundamental pillars of national security" that amount to "issues of survival" (Syrian Arab Republic, 1996). The World Bank and other development organizations have also highlighted Syria's need for food security as a key element in ensuring Syria's "internal stability" and "buffering Syria's exposure to market fluctuations or political dynamics beyond its borders" (Barnes, 2009: 523).

Increasing domestic food production therefore became a strategic goal for the Syrian state, in part because it allowed them greater political independence from Western countries but also in part because of fears of being able to feed a projected population of 30 million by 2025. An official publication, intended for an external audience, clearly links the issue of food security to population growth and global trade patterns: The report predicts a significant increase in population followed by more imports of primary foodstuffs and the leveling of import and export volumes of oil (Syrie et Monde Arabe, 1987: 7). Unfortunately, achieving food security was prioritized at the expense

---

[7] Based on the author's interview with Syrian Minister of State for Foreign Affairs (Nasser Kaddour), Damascus, November 27, 1999.

of sustainable water-management practices. The goal of food security led to water-intensive agriculture focused on irrigation so that until the end of the 1990s, more than 90 percent of water resources were allocated to agriculture.

Definitional debates over food and water security can be seen in the SAES's discussions between economists and water experts during the 2006–2010 drought. Most experts focused on definitions of food security that do not actually require self-sufficient domestic production of staple crops. For example, George Soumi puts forth two definitions of food security: first, food security according to need, defined as the ability of individuals to obtain complete nutrition at 2,500 calories a day; and, second, food security according to supply, defined as the state having sufficient purchasing power to ensure the domestic supply of food at reasonable prices. He points to Japan and the Gulf states as examples of countries that have ensured food security without significant amounts of domestic agricultural production (Soumi, 2009: 2).

Other experts highlighted that not all countries are able to produce enough to be self-sufficient, especially when global markets are artificially distorted by OECD countries' agricultural subsidies, making tempered calls for ensuring food security while recognizing Syria's resource limits and the need for a competitive and liberalized economy (Bakour, 2009: 4; Qatna, 2009: 8). Bakour criticizes an "international" definition of food security that focuses on sufficient production to feed a global population, guaranteeing distribution of sufficient food at the global level and maintaining stores in case of low production in some years. He argues, in line with Ba'athist concerns of early 1970s, that profit-seeking capitalism and imperialist states' dominance of global trade mean that the food will not be distributed equitably and certain countries will therefore be able to use their food supply to pressure other countries (Bakour, 2009: 5). Bakour therefore calls for an "Arab" definition of food security that would guarantee food security at the regional level through cooperation between Arab states. Atieh Al-Hindi called for the Syrian government to partner with the Food and Agriculture Organization of the United Nations (FAO) to create new projects to ensure food production (Al-Hindi, 2011: 30) matched by appeals to strengthen government responses to basic food supplies for emergency food assistance to families in the eastern provinces (Al-Muheissin, 2010: 5). Finally, some advocated in favor of renewed attention to policies that both increased productivity and maintained sustainable use of resources, as most of the policies to increase food production had also led to the overexploitation of water resources (Al-Hindi, 2011: 30; Nasr, 2010: 9; Soumi and Ma'an, 2010: 14–17). Caught between myths of food and water self-sufficiency and the reality of resource overuse and mismanagement, the Syrian goals of food security seemed somewhat utopian.

Tools and Dilemmas of Food Security: "Strategic" Crops, Intensive Irrigation, Dams with Institutional, Environmental, and Social Problems

In Syria, the rate of food self-sufficiency fell from 78 percent in 1970 to 48 percent in the early 1990s, and the resulting food deficit was the gap between the population's food needs and national production (Khouri, 1990: 11). Many have argued that these deficits resulted from policies that prioritized high yields of "strategic crops" for export to the detriment of crops for domestic consumption; for example, new strains of high-yield American and Egyptian cotton were prioritized even though they took space away from other crops and consumed large quantities of water (Barnes, 2009; Batatu, 1999: 88).

Chapter 5 details the water deficits and resulting decline in food production as the country faced recurring droughts in 1998–2001 and 2006–2010. While these droughts can be explained by changing climatic conditions, other explanations exist that show mismanaged national plans for the expansion of irrigated surface areas, worsening the effects of the droughts. For example, wheat is Syria's main crop, and although it does not require irrigation, intensive irrigation had been deployed to the point of saturation to increase yields to unsustainable levels. This intensive irrigation helped consolidate gains and profits for certain members of society while oversaturation of the market resulted in price hikes as Syria became a net exporter of wheat (Batatu, 1999: 88).

The framing of specific crops as "strategic" was a pillar of Ba'athist food-security policies. Syrian experts define "strategic crops" as those that are critical for civilian food supply and overall food security, many of which were produced in the eastern region, which was more dependent on rain for water (Bakour, 2009: 6). The FAO more specifically defines these strategic crops in Syria as those for which the government set producer prices: wheat, barley, lentils, chickpeas, cotton, and sugar (FAO, 2003). These producer prices were artificially inflated; for example, the government bought wheat from farmers at 60 percent higher than the world prices (Barnes, 2009: 524).

Intensive Irrigation: Plans and Problems

Until the mid 1980s, 90 percent of cultivated land in Syria relied on rainwater, and its irregularity influenced agricultural production (Hannoyer, 1985: 24). There was a marked decline in cultivation during the 1980s as a result of unmitigated groundwater use, low rainfall, and the spread of salinity from mismanagement of irrigation or poor drainage, especially in the Euphrates basin and the al-Ghab region (Batatu, 1999: 77). As a result, the government made securing water resources for agriculture a priority in 1985, prioritizing the country's most important river, the Euphrates, because its basin contains more than 65 percent of the country's overall hydraulic resources.[8] The government favored two tools for this purpose: (1) the construction of dams and networks of irrigation and (2) the introduction of optimization technologies in order to increase productivity per irrigated hectare (Ghadban, 1995: 40, 47). Figure 4.2 provides an overview of the country's water projects by the early 2000s.

The transformation of rain-fed to irrigated agriculture happened in three stages, with the goal of yielding high profits from irrigation and agricultural exports (Barnes, 2009: 521). From 1966 to 1984, the state focused on expanding irrigation systems mainly for wheat and cotton. From 1985 to 2000, new mechanisms were put into place to expand irrigated surfaces, primarily in the northeastern part of the country, like the manipulation of prices of crops to ensure yearly targets and the allocation of subsidies for seeds, fertilizers, farm equipment, and fuel. The projects were successful: Between 1985 and 2000, Syria's irrigated areas doubled to 1,347,000 hectares (Daoudy, 2005: 85; Aw-Hassan et al., 2014: 206; Selby, 2018: 7). The net increase in irrigated surface area can be attributed to groundwater irrigation, which increased from 49 percent of total irrigated surface area to 57 percent during this period (Mualla and Salman, 2002: 3).

---

[8] Based on interview by the author with Aziz Ghadban, Director of Irrigation, Ministry of Irrigation, Damascus, November 15, 1995.

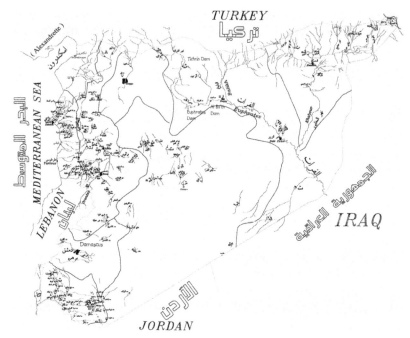

Figure 4.2 Water projects in Syria.
Source: Syrian Arab Republic, 2001

Finally, from 2001 to 2010, large-scale public investment was directed to irrigation, with 20–25 percent of total public investment going to agriculture and 70 percent to irrigation (Aw-Hassan et al., 2014: 207; Barnes, 2009: 524).

By 2010, therefore, the country was experiencing a severe depletion of groundwater resources encouraged by government fuel subsidies that allowed farmers to pump groundwater at low cost from unlicensed wells. Broadly speaking, the country's water deficit was a result of ideological preferences that allowed for overpumping because of fuel and food subsidies, though it was also aggravated by the mismanagement of water resources by inefficient bureaucracies and public perceptions of water as a free good. The impact of this irrigation expansion is best illustrated by the case of the Khabour River, whose flows drastically decreased from 60 m³/s to 0 m³/s in 2001 (Ababsa, 2015: 205; Daoudy, 2005: 124) after irrigation consumed 300 percent of the basin's "safe yield" (Selby, 2018: 7).

Excessive Pumping of Groundwater: The Problem of Unlicensed Wells

Syrian experts note that government policies encouraging the spread of agricultural land also encouraged the overexploitation of groundwater resources due to large increases in the number of wells (Qatna, 2009: 8; Seifan, 2009a: 12; Soumi, 2009: 5). Since the 1960s, many laws were devised to stop the proliferation of wells illegally dug by farmers.[9] Despite these bans, the FAO estimates that in 1997 there were 122,276 wells in the country, of which 53,453 were unauthorized (FAO, 1997). In 2002, official sources estimated that out of a total of 172,687 wells, 95,910 were illegal (Mualla and Salman, 2002: 4). According to a renowned Syrian economist, Samir Seifan, by 2009 there were 102,000 government-sanctioned wells and an additional 108,000 unsanctioned wells (Seifan, 2009a: 12). The authorities realized the magnitude of the phenomenon and issued more licenses for illegal wells. The condition for obtaining a license was that well-owners would resort to modern irrigation techniques so as to ensure that annual irrigation would not exceed 7,000 m^3/hectare (Syrian Arab Republic, 2001: 5).[10] Likewise, the digging of new wells was made illegal with the exception of areas in the coastal basin. Figures 4.3 and 4.4 show escalating trends in the number of unlicensed and licensed wells and surfaces irrigated by wells.[11]

The use of groundwater from licensed and unlicensed wells has considerably increased since 1990 for several reasons. First, irrigation from these sources is relatively cheap, requiring only the costs of construction and a pump. Second, 75 percent of farmers run small operations of less than 10 ha that are easily irrigated using wells (FAO, 1997). Third, the central government has a low monitoring capacity because of bureaucratic proliferation and core–periphery divides. Fourth, farmers perceive water to be a free public good. These last two incentives for overpumping are the focus of the next section.

---

[9] For example, Decree No. 721 of 1969, Decree No. 2,808/61 of 1978 which forbids illegal wells and Decree No. 2,537 of 1991 relating to the Barada and Awaj (Damascus).

[10] This was codified in Decision No. 2,165 taken by the Ministry of Irrigation, on August 16, 2000.

[11] The question of unlicensed wells in the northeastern and eastern governates will be discussed in Chapter 5.

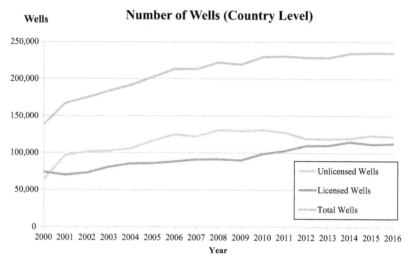

Figure 4.3 Number of wells (country level).

Source: Elaborated by author on the basis of Syrian Arab Republic, 2017a

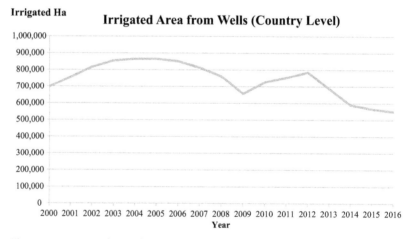

Figure 4.4 Irrigated area from wells (country level) (in hectares: ha).

Source: Elaborated by author on basis of Syrian Arab Republic, 2017a

Institutional Dilemmas: Bureaucratic Proliferation and Core–Periphery Divide

A divide between central authorities and the remote countryside makes implementation of water policies and oversight unreliable. Although Law No. 16 of July 11, 1982, unified all decrees relating to water management covering development, conservation, and investment, there still remained a large number of administrative bodies in charge of water management. Roles were redundant and overlapping, and most employees had low levels of expertise. This is largely due to a government decree to prevent brain drain mandating engineers to work for five years in a public ministry after graduation (Japan International Cooperation Agency and Syrian Ministry of Irrigation, 1996: 27). While this policy was rescinded in 1996, most of the country's 50,000 engineers still work in the public sector and are often compelled to leave urban centers for the countryside, working on large-scale hydraulic projects for low pay. The urban–rural divide causes internal fragmentation in the state apparatus (Hannoyer, 1985: 39) and creates conflict between the central water administration's top-down approach with rural areas' traditional and autonomous methods. According to a Syrian water expert speaking on condition of anonymity, the government sends unskilled engineers to monitor agricultural projects. The farmers, expecting to "receive water, not speak to an agricultural *murshid* [adviser]," obstruct governmental plans; overall, this means that the government fails to educate peasants while expanding infrastructure.[12]

Ideological Dilemmas: The Effects of Subsidies (Food, Fuel, Water) on Overpumping

In a previous section, I outlined how fuel subsidies increase the proliferation of wells by making pumping cheaper, but food and water subsidies also create incentives for farmers to overexploit water resources. Since the proclamation of decrees 144/S (Lebanon) and 299/S (entire Levant) of 1925 during the French Mandate, water has been considered a part of the "public domain," a resource without costs associated with its use (Hirsch, 1956: 185). In 1972, Law No. 46 finally set an annual cost for irrigation at 70 Syrian pounds per hectare per year (SYP/ha/y) , as well as 5 SYP/ha/y for operational, maintenance, and irrigation system energy costs.[13] However, these consumption costs represented only a small fraction of the real costs of water provision. In 1989, Law No. 19 raised these rates to 1,075 SYP/ha/y and 200 SYP/ha/y for maintenance costs, and Decree No. 128 of

---

[12] Based on author's interview with a Syrian water expert, on condition of anonymity, Beirut, December 4, 2015.

[13] The official rate of the Syrian pound was approximately equivalent, at the end of the 1990s, to 1 USD for 40–50 SYP.

1982 mandated fees of 1,075 SYP/ha/y for users of small and medium-sized dams (Bakour, 1991: 60).

Nevertheless, the task of evaluating the cost of water made available by large-scale irrigation projects has proven insurmountable. In agriculture, costs exist not only in terms of the direct costs of extraction and distribution but also in terms of opportunity costs, which are the water's value to other sectors of the economy compared to its value to the farmer (Allan, 2001: 275). The concept of opportunity cost of water relates to a broader debate around issues of economic efficiency and the need to ascribe a cost to water consumption that reflects its real value. This has been difficult in Syria, however, because of the understanding that water is a public good with mere symbolic pricing. This conception is common in agricultural societies, which prefer for the state to assume direct control whereas more developed societies tend to see water as a private good. A third option has also been put forth between total state control and privatization (Meinzen-Dick and Bruns, 2000: 34).

Syria falls firmly in the first category. As elsewhere in the Arab world, water has traditionally been perceived as public property that must remain accessible to the majority of the population. Thus, no cost has been associated with the use of groundwater nor any limit imposed to regulate the quantities extracted or the depth of the pumping, with the exception of issuing mandatory licenses. This makes excessive pumping possible. Moreover, fees applied to the use of surface water have remained nominal and unrelated to an evaluation of real costs. Water is thus distributed at very low prices subsidized by the government, which also shoulders the entirety of the costs of constructing dams and irrigation systems. Indeed, the true cost of distribution is around 0.03–0.05 US dollars (USD) per cubic meter, bringing the cost of irrigating a hectare of wheat to about 360–600 USD, with a yield of 4 tons of grain.

The Syrian government therefore supported wheat producers through water subsidies but also through direct subsidies per ton of wheat, which gave farmers prices that were two to three times higher than international prices. In the late 1990s, this meant that Syrian farmers received somewhere between 360 and 661 USD per ton of wheat, whereas the price on international markets was closer to 200 USD per ton (Biswas et al., 1997: 26). Prices were maintained at this level to ensure that low-income groups from the agricultural sector retained access to the water market.

The government also planned for large investments and expend-itures for the construction of dams for irrigation, though this time with the aim to generate returns on investment so as to partially compensate spending. Under Law No. 45 of 1972, the beneficiaries of cost-retrieval mechanisms must pay certain fees (Japan International Cooperation Agency and Syrian Ministry of Irrigation, 1996: 24). However, these mechanisms were usually unsuccessful, as irrigation taxes were set in relation to the irrigable surface area rather than the quantity of water used, so the fees only covered a small share of the real value of the water supply (Bakour, 1992: 153). In the end, landowners only paid 20 percent of the real cost of irrigation (Bakour, 1991: 62). The fees are set by the Supreme Council for Agriculture and can be paid in install-ments, without interest, over a period of thirty years. In 1996, the annual fee was set to 2,500 SYP/ha/y irrigated, and all unlicensed extraction was subject to a fine. This rate was incredibly low, as water fees were no more than a symbolic contribution to the public distribu-tion network, according to Decision 3072 of 1990. The rates for domestic consumption were equally low, at 1.25 SYP for a consump-tion of 1–20 m^3/month to 6 SYP for a consumption of 60 m^3/month on top of a fixed rate of 36 SYP/month.

The Construction of Dams: The Tabqa Dam as the Emblem of Agrarian Revolution[14]

Large-scale irrigation intensified through the construction of dams and the reclamation of land with the help of Soviet investments. In the early 1960s, there were no dams in Syria, but their construction quickly increased as the Ba'athist regime prioritized the agricultural sector. By the late 2000s, Syria had 166 dams, the most important of which were located on the Euphrates and served a dual purpose of irrigation and electricity production (FAO, 2008; see Table 4.1).

The launch of the Tabqa Dam project in 1968 was a symbol of the agrarian transformation and performance of the new Ba'athist regime. Following the country's independence in 1946, the Syrian government commissioned a British company to study the costs of constructing a

---

[14] The Taqba Dam is officially called al-Thawra ("Revolution" in Arabic) but is usually referred to as the Tabqa or Euphrates Dam because it is located in the city of Taqba.

Table 4.1 *Main dams on the Euphrates river (millions of cubic meters: mcm; megawatts: MW; hectares: ha).*[15] *Source: Elaborated by author on basis of official sources (Syrian Arab Republic, 1996) and official news for the Bassel al-Assad and Sajur Dams (Al-Thawra, 2005; Syria Report, 2002).*

Dams	Province	Storage Capacity (mcm)	Electricity (MW)	Planned Irrigation (ha)
Taqba (1973)	Raqqa	14,100	800–1,100	644,000
Al Baath (1990)	Raqqa	90	75	NO
Tishrin (1999)	Aleppo	1,900	630	NO
Martyr Bassel al-Assad Dam (2002)	Hassake	605	NO	8,200
Sajur (2005)	Aleppo	9.8	NO	N/A

dam near the village of Youssef Basha on the Syrian–Turkish border. These plans remained idle until their revival in 1968, when the Syrian government decided to construct the large Taqba Dam on the Euphrates, located 40 kilometers upstream from the city of Raqqa, where the bed of the Euphrates shrinks considerably. The dam was completed with the technical and financial assistance of the Soviet Union and inaugurated in July 1973 (Bourgey, 1974: 346). In official discourse, the Tabqa Dam represents a "cornerstone in the construction of a solid economic base" (Syrie et Monde Arabe, 1978: 1), as its purposes are numerous: the elimination of flood risks, the irrigation of enhanced lands, and the production of electrical power (Syrie et Monde Arabe, 1978: 1).

Although each of the dams on the Euphrates river were built for different purposes, many had irrigation components. Originally, operational plans for the Taqba Dam focused primarily on irrigation in the Euphrates basin. Of the 640,000 hectares surrounding the Taqba Dam, 110,000 hectares were irrigated by gravity from the al-Assad reservoir, with a storage capacity of 11.6 billion m³ (Ghadban, 1995: 42). Moreover, an additional 400,000 hectares of irrigated land is

---

[15] During the Syrian conflict, the Tishrin and Tabqa dams were captured by rebel groups and the Islamic State of Iraq and the Levant in 2012 and 2013 respectively, before being reconquered in 2015 and 2017 by the Syrian Democratic Forces with the help of the US-led international coalition.

planned in the Khabour basin, which would result in more than a million hectares of irrigated land in the Euphrates valley. The al-Baath Dam, downstream on the Euphrates, and the Tishreen Dam, on the Syrian–Turkish border, were built to maintain a constant flow for the larger dam, even though they do not directly irrigate land. On the Tigris river, dams also exist primarily for irrigation. The Bassel al-Assad Dam, launched in 1980 and revived many times, has the ultimate goal of irrigating 150,000 ha in Hassake (Syria Report, 2010f).

Delays in Implementing Irrigation Projects: Water and Soil Quality

The implementation of irrigation projects in the Euphrates basin faced numerous setbacks aggravated by traditional irrigation techniques: gradual salinization of soil and water from excessive agricultural usage, evaporation along surface networks, and continued tension between the government bureaucracy and farmers.

The Middle East, and Syria in particular, is a region in which the soil is subject to salinization and gypsum accumulation. The overexploitation of groundwater has led to problems of decreased quantity and quality of these waters, and even deterioration in soil quality. Canals have even collapsed following the discovery of gypsum-powder accumulation, which itself is largely the result of the use of these same lands over millennia (Furon, 1963: 61; Ghadban, 1995). Quantity losses from irrigation are estimated at around 5 m^3/s (or 157 million m^3/y), and the efficiency of distribution networks was only 60 percent in the 1990s (Bakour, 1992: 154; Medzini, 2001: 81). In the 1980s, these effects of overuse came to the forefront – with land reclamation, the growth of alkali flats east of the Euphrates, and gypsum accumulation – causing decelerating land and irrigation development (Batatu, 1999: 81).

Official Syrian reports dating back to the 1990s already mentioned problems related to traditional irrigation, which covered 80 percent of the irrigated surface area (Bakour, 1991: 67). These methods allow farmers to irrigate at a low cost with simple technology, but they lose 50 percent of water inputs to evaporation, which causes the remaining water and soil to become more saline (Japan International Cooperation Agency and Syrian Ministry of Irrigation, 1996: 37–38). Some farmers further decreased the quality of the soil by recycling drainage water on their fields. Finally, traditional irrigation contributes to

Table 4.2 *Irrigation networks and surfaces in Euphrates Basin (2000) (hectares: ha). Source: Calculated by author on basis of various sources from the Syrian Arab Republic, 1999.*

Project	Province	Planned (ha)	Irrigated (ha)
Pilot Project	Raqqa	21,200	1969–1986 19,600
Section (1) of Bir Al Hachim	Raqqa	10,031	1976–1984 10,031
Middle Euphrates Valley	Raqqa	23,872	1976–1984 23,872
Irrigation and drainage in Balikh basin	Deir ez-Zor	4,000	1997–1999 4,000
Farm of April 7th	Deir ez-Zor	10,000	1986–1987 750
West Meskeneh, Step 1	Alep	23,285	1988–1990 16,142
Remaining Section (1) in Balikh basin	Raqqa	10,667	1984–1993 10,667
Al-Assad Project on Meskeneh	Raqqa	21,325	1971–1993 20,951
Section (7), Step 1	Deir ez-Zor	7,142	1992–1996 7,142
Total		**131,522**	**113,155**

microbiological and chemical contamination, which can bring about water-related diseases. Water-purification stations have been built in larger cities, but more stations are needed. Traditional irrigation projects have faced a number of obstacles, including the worsened soil and water quality that they helped bring about. It is estimated that half the irrigated land in the Euphrates valley is affected by salinization, though exact numbers are unknown, as they question the long-term feasibility of the Ba'athist rural contract (Syrian Arab Republic, 1988). Additionally, the quantity of water available for irrigation from the Euphrates depends on Syria's negotiations with Turkey, as described in Chapter 3.

Tables 4.2 and 4.3 outline the projected irrigated areas and their finalization in the late 1990s based on calculations drawn from official sources. The surface area being irrigated in the Euphrates basin reached 449,237 ha in the late 1990s, of which 117,528 ha was from

Table 4.3 *Delays in irrigation plans on the Euphrates (hectares: ha).*
Source: Calculated by author on basis of various sources from the Syrian
Arab Republic, 1999.

Project	Province	Irrigation (ha)	Achievement Rates (%)
Step (2) of West Meskeneh	Alep	17,692	86
East Meskeneh	Alep	17,800	73
Portion of Section (2) of Balikh basin	Raqqa	10,000	40
Portion of Section (2) of Balikh basin	Raqqa	10,000	80
Section (5)	Deir ez-Zor	5,000	94
Section (3) of Upper Euphrates	Deir ez-Zor + Raqqa	5,000	78
Total		**Planned: 67,800**	**Finalized: 48,884 ha**

government-operated systems, 187,830 was from wells, and 89,879 was from rivers and springs (Syrian Arab Republic, 2001). According to other sources, only 170,000–250,000 ha were actually irrigated (Syrian Arab Republic, 1999). In 2010, the General Establishment for the Investment and Development of the Euphrates Basin officially confirmed that, since 1981, it had reclaimed only 216,000 hectares of land in the Euphrates basin (Syria Report, 2010b).

The Ba'ath Party saw irrigation plans along the Euphrates as major revolutionary projects and state farms as a model for agricultural production and livestock improvement. However, as shown in Tables 4.2 and 4.3, the Euphrates projects did not meet their goals in terms of expanding irrigation (Foy and Tabeaud, 2012: 45). This was blamed on the lack of efficient irrigation networks, therefore prioritizing the modernization of irrigation above the management of water resources and the agricultural sector.

The Modernization of Irrigation: Objectives and Obstacles

The modernization of irrigation is part of a new international approach to political economy that attempts to manage water demand rather than water supply and to reallocate resources toward more productive sectors (Allan, 2000: 156, 310–311; Falkenmark, 1986: 88). Management of water demand depends, in general, on curbing demographic growth, restructuring the economy, and developing water-conservation techniques. While the Syrian government nominally embraced the modernization of irrigation as a necessary step, they did not seem prepared to take concrete action toward water-management reform. This action could have included introducing an operational cost for farmers and ensuring a fair price for the export of agricultural products; if exports increased, surplus agricultural income would allow investment in cutting-edge irrigation methods. These measures required a complete restructuring of the state-dominated agricultural sector, which the government was not prepared to sponsor.

In the late 1990s, the Syrian government decided to encourage farmers to use modern irrigation techniques, with the intended goal of replacing drainage irrigation networks with drip irrigation systems (Bakour, 1991: 59; Bakour and Kolars, 1994: 142). Drip irrigation was expensive, however, and only a few farmers had the means to invest, even with loans from the Agricultural Bank.[16] The government also supported the replacement of open irrigation systems to pressurized conduit systems, which can reduce the quantity of water lost in the distribution. In 2001, the Ministry of Irrigation launched a four-year 600-million-dollar renovation plan. According to official Syrian sources, 30 percent of the national irrigation network already used this technique by 1999, but this figure has been disputed by experts within the Ministry of Irrigation speaking under conditions of anonymity.[17] These experts raise two primary obstacles to this widespread diffusion: high investment costs as well as the time needed to train farmers in new techniques. In 1992, an estimated 1 percent of irrigated land benefited from efficient methods, and it seems much more likely that by the late 1990s only 13 percent of overall irrigated surface area benefited from these optimized techniques (Bakour, 1991: 64).

Solutions do exist to combat salinization of the soil; drainage structures, for instance, allow excess salt to be drawn off from the soil. Drainage structures only work with traditional irrigation systems

---

[16] Based on author's interview with Aziz Ghadban, Director of the Irrigation Department, Ministry of Irrigation, Damascus, November 15, 1995.
[17] Based on author's interview with Abdel Aziz Masri, Director of International Waters, Ministry of Irrigation, Damascus, November 28, 1999.

when there is enough water, however, and there was not enough water for these structures to be implemented in most of the country. Fortunately, drip-irrigation techniques do not face the same problem of needing a certain amount of water to use this cleaning technique, and now 90 percent of drip-irrigation systems are equipped with drainage structures. Drainage infrastructure therefore has helped with the salinization of the soil in certain areas, but they come with other environmental problems: The highly salty byproduct can run off into rivers and be a pollutant if not closely monitored.

Official sources have alluded to the opportunity to implement a more efficient national water strategy now that the sustainability of water resources must be maintained as agricultural productivity increases. However, state officials have appeared unmotivated to apply a demand-management approach in light of the yet unexhausted resources of the Euphrates and Tigris, preferring instead to advocate for more efficient irrigation techniques. The goal of expanding irrigation in the Euphrates basin has also been instrumental in Syria's negotiations with Turkey. Syria was able to back its claims for minimal water allocations across the border on the basis of existing irrigation needs (Daoudy, 2005). In the 2000s, the state had not yet completed the modernization of irrigation networks and continued to launch state-funded projects. The expansion of irrigated land was still a priority in conjunction with the implementation of more efficient techniques such as drip irrigation (Syria Report, 2002). Discussions within the SAES offer insight into dilemmas that confronted the agricultural sector. Several experts note that the government made claims about modernizing irrigation infrastructure but failed to follow through, arguing that it was a clear example of the failure to implement policy into reality (Nasr, 2009: 10; Qatna, 2009: 5–6). In 2006, the government announced a 72 billion SYP plan to modernize irrigation infrastructure over a five-year timeline (Qatna, 2009: 6). In 2010, it issued Decree No. 21, which stated that any cotton-related activity would require a license, thereby indicating an effort at curtailing the expansion of water-intensive crops (Syria Report, 2010e). But by 2009 only 1 billion SYP out of a planned 50 billion SYP budget had been spent (Seifan, 2009a: 11–12).

The previous sections highlighted the ideological, institutional, and economic dilemmas facing the agricultural and water sectors in Syria, and the failure of the government to address these problems. Beyond the economic costs to the government's water-management approach were social costs; in particular, intensive dam construction forced local populations to relocate.

Social Implications of Dam-Building: Displacements and Rural Poverty

The construction of the Taqba Dam led to the evacuation, sometimes forced, of 60,000 inhabitants from forty-three villages submerged by the reservoir. The government had acknowledged that those relocated should receive a hectare of irrigated land for each hectare lost, but some of these *maghmurin* ("flooded" in Arabic) never received their compensation and were left without prospect of future stable rural employment (Metral, 1987: 11–145; Meyer, 1995: 303). The government attempted to create jobs for the newly displaced with experimental state-owned farms that attempted to improve the yield of existing crops and introduce new ones. However, poor soil quality in the newly irrigated land meant that these pilot project farms were not that successful and unable to employ many of those who had relocated. After twenty years, nearly two-thirds of the relocated population still had not been reintegrated into the economy (Meyer, 1995).

The social ramifications of the experimental state farms were considerable, most significantly for the affected communities that suffered when they were not successful. An analysis of the al-Assad state farm, from the perspective of local actors, demonstrates its detrimental social implications. While locals welcomed the development of irrigation, they criticized the management of the farm, its bureaucratic hierarchical organization, lack of productivity, and land expropriation (Foy and Tabeaud, 2012: 47–52). Furthermore, the economic insecurity allowed existing tribal quarrels to be revived. While the state farm enabled access to water resources from al-Assad Lake through irrigation, the top-down development of the farm did not encourage locals to take initiative and was seen as an exogenous project imposed by the state that resulted in land expropriation and population displacement (Foy and Tabeaud, 2012: 46, 54). Ultimately, lack of effective management due to water loss, exorbitant water consumption, and a lack of a long-term vision led to the failure of the pilot farm and its closure in 2000 (Foy and Tabeaud, 2012: 51–52). In the end, state farms failed in their objectives of economic opportunity for the relocated and the spread of the Ba'athist ideology (Ababsa, 2013: 94).

The negative social consequences of the state's agricultural policies were not just limited to those displaced by the construction of the Taqba Dam, however: Syrian Kurds were excluded from agricultural gains, which led to their economic disenfranchisement.

An Arab Encirclement: The Agrarian Revolution and Syrian Kurds under Ba'athism

The "Kurdish Question" has occupied much of the Middle East, including Syria, as a historical, geographic, and demographic issue for most of the twentieth century, and reemerged in the public eye when parts of the population rebelled in Jazira in 2004 and later joined the opposition forces after the 2011 uprising (Ababsa, 2015: 217; Gauthier, 2009: 119; Tejel, 2014). Under the French Mandate, Syrian society first had to grapple with the place of the Kurds in their country. Many Kurds moved to the Jazira province (later named Hassake governorate) in Syria from 1938 to 1962, first because of forced migration under the French Mandate and later because of land-redistribution incentives under the United Arab Republic's agricultural reform (Arab Center for Research and Policy Studies, 2013: 27–28).[18]

The French Mandate did not respect the autonomy of the Kurds, enacting oppressive policies that lead to widespread migration. In fact, according to archival research, the French Mandate required Kurds to carry a card identifying their ethnicity between 1938 and 1939 (Tejel, 2009: 4). At the same time, France had transferred the Iskandaroun (Alexandretta) province from Syria to Turkey, an unpopular move that Syrians still consider as illegal.[19] Among the thousands of Kurdish refugees moving from Turkey to Syria in the late 1930s, many were the initiators of a Kurdish movement in Turkey (Tejel, 2009: 4). Figure 4.5 shows the areas inhabited by Syrian Kurds in the northeastern provinces.

Starting in the 1960s, the Syrian government tried to change the demographics of the Jazira province. In 1962, the Syrian Ministry of

---

[18] This book (in Arabic) provides a unique collection of studies and perspectives by Syrian and Arab experts on the contentious question of Syrian Kurds. Refer to the map shown in Figure 1.1 (Chapter 1) to situate the location of the Hassake governorate in Syria.

[19] See Chapter 3.

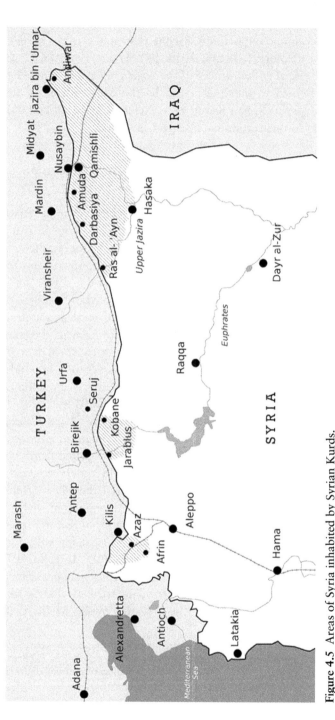

Figure 4.5 Areas of Syria inhabited by Syrian Kurds.
Source: Tejel, 2009: xiv

Interior conducted a census in the province and removed citizenship and civil rights for most Kurds (Arab Center for Research and Policy Studies, 2013: 28, 30–35). The classifications of the census stipulated that Kurds who were registered before 1945 were considered Syrians, yet those after 1945 were "foreigners," which problematically led to 120,000 Kurds losing their citizenship and becoming "stateless" (Arab Center for Research and Policy Studies, 2013: 36, 155). Kurds were also discriminated against in terms of redistribution of public land, which was limited to sons of Arab clans and farmers actively cultivating the land. Some farmers even stole land from Kurds by claiming they were Turks, even though they possessed identity cards showing otherwise (Arab Center for Research and Policy Studies, 2013: 30–32).

It is crucial to note that Ba'athist discourses were central to the policies that excluded Kurds from agricultural gains. The Ba'ath Party justified these policies with Arab nationalism (Arab Center for Research and Policy Studies, 2013: 35) and sought to increase Arab influence in northern regions under the pretext of land reform. Land distribution therefore served the ideological purpose of Arabization. The "Arab Belt" policy of the 1960s and 1970s codified the Arabization of Kurdish areas. Geographically, the Arab Encirclement/Belt refers to about 3 million acres of land from Malakiya to the border between the governorates of Hassake and Raqqa. Most of the residents were Kurds who had migrated from Turkey, but the Syrian government wanted to "Arabize" the region. As such, it built Arab villages on public land and expropriated Kurdish lands. The goal of the project was to solve the "Kurdish question" through Arabization, even though it entailed the displacement of thousands of Kurds. The policy aimed to move 20,000 Arab families from the al-Assad Lake flood zones to public housing in Arab Belt villages, though, in the end, only 4,000 families relocated (Arab Center for Research and Policy Studies, 2013: 41). The Arab Belt policy was more rhetorical than effective in changing demographics, but it provides insight into the ways in which Syrian Kurds were denied access to land as early as the 1970s. As will be seen in the next chapter, the land-tenure restrictions entailed in Decree No. 49 of 2008 further marginalized Syrian Kurds.

While the agrarian reforms initiated in the early 1960s under the new Ba'athist regime did positively impact large parts of the country by reducing poverty, some populations – like the Kurds – suffered more than others. As such, the results have been mixed, which eventually led the state toward decollectivization and liberalization of the economy.

The Move to Decollectivization and Liberalization

The Mixed Results of Ba'athist Collectivization

Ba'athist collectivization saw the dismantlement of large land ownership and the establishment of peasant unions, which empowered rural communities (Hinnebusch, 2013: 13; Metral, 1980). This "revolution from above" created greater equality in rural villages, and the more vulnerable areas of the country gained access to basic human infrastructure, like safe water networks, as a result of state investment. By 1980, 54 percent of the rural population and 97 percent of the urban population had access to piped water (Batatu, 1999: 66). The state also reaped benefits: Each new set of agrarian reforms allowed the party's elites to break up the power of the previous oligarchy and build a base among the country's "middle peasantry" (Hinnebusch, 2013: 10). Syria was also able to trade agricultural products with its historic trading partners in central and eastern Europe, as well as to the European Union and neighboring partners such as Jordan and Lebanon (Barnes, 2009: 525).

The reforms were not entirely successful, however. First, they failed to adjust income disparities, which actually increased in the 1970s and 1980s as the party shifted away from radical socialism and the economy opened up (Batatu, 1999: 43). Second, they left many small farmers without land to cultivate (Batatu, 1999: 170; Hinnebusch, 2013: 10). Third, they did not combat the gendered aspect of rural economic insecurity. Across various labor sectors, regions, and communities, women were paid less than half of the wages of their male counterparts, or, in many cases, simply compensated in the "old traditional manner" – a bucket or basket of the day's proceeds (Batatu, 1999: 44). Fourth, the reforms tried to slow the rural exodus to burgeoning cities, which were so successful that after 1989 there was actually "reverse migration" from the cities and towns back to villages (Batatu, 1999: 188).[20]

Ending the Social Contract: De-Ba'athification and Decollectivization

In the early decades of Hafez al-Assad's rule, Ba'athist elites gradually moved away from radical Ba'athism to decollectivize the economy and the agricultural sector. Since the mid-1970s – earlier than widely assumed – Syria experienced repeated expansions of the private sector

---

[20] Chapter 5 looks more extensively into migration patterns back to the cities during the 2006–2010 drought.

(Haddad 2012: 73–76). In the face of a series of economic crises, liberalization "proved ... inescapable," leading to a "neo-patrimonial" model of society (Hinnebusch, 1995: 305). Over forty years, the process brought together the ruling elites and merchant classes in four stages: (1) after 1970 with Hafez al-Assad's Corrective Movement, which signified the move away from Salah Jadid's leftist and progressive Ba'athist ideology of the 1960s; (2) after 1986 with the era of *ta'addudiyya* (economic pluralism); (3) after 1990 with the *infitah* (opening); and finally, (4) after 2005 with Bashar al-Assad's rise to power, in the most visible stage of de-Ba'athification (Dahi and Munif, 2011: 323–326). In 2005, the "new" Bashar al-Assad regime abruptly shifted from a centrally planned economy, by cutting fuel and water subsidies, to the detriment of social constituencies in the rural peripheries.

The Multiple Infitahat *(Openings) since the 1970s*

Hafez al-Assad's coup of 1970 initiated a turning point for the Ba'athist regime, which had previously been led by the leftist Salah Jadid (Batatu, 1999: 134). Although Hafez al-Assad continued to cultivate a persona of championing the peasants, the majority of state revenues were still not coming from the agrarian sector. As a result, the state turned to the private sector for support, implementing policies that were much more popular with urban merchants (Dahi and Munif, 2011: 324). The alliance between former General Hafez al-Assad and major commercial actors lead to the creation of a new "military-mercantile complex" (Seale, 1988: 456).

Many of Hafez al-Assad's early policies were still relatively socialist, while the economy was stronger. For example, the 1975 law that created compulsory planting guidelines of strategic crops was passed during a time of unusually high profit margins (Batatu, 1999: 47). Strong economic performance allowed the government to further large social projects, such as the Euphrates Dam to provide electricity to rural constituencies. However, when the Syrian economy began to struggle, the gradual move toward de-Ba'athification and liberalization intensified. In 1986, for example, a foreign-exchange crisis led to reduced subsidies and more freedom for the private sector (Dahi and Munif, 2011: 325). The economy grew with increasing oil revenues. In 1991, the process accelerated when the state issued Investment Law No. 10 of 1991, exempting new investments from taxes for several years. The Damascene middle merchant class reemerged and established new social and economic alliances with the regime, thereby accomplishing Hafez al-Assad's goal of "bridging many of the rural-urban cleavages" (Perthes,

1995). Nevertheless, until 2000, the economy remained "essentially socialist" according to Olson (1989: 145).

In June 2000, Hafez al-Assad died, creating an opportunity for even more economic liberalization. As Bashar al-Assad took over from the Ba'ath Party in the mid 2000s, Syria shifted to a post-Ba'athist regime (Hinnebusch, 2011). Without the ideological and symbolic connection to the old rural base, the regime suffered as income inequality continued to increase (Hinnebusch, 2015: 21). The following years saw intense in-fighting and sabotage between income groups as well as policies designed to further enrich the wealthy at the expense of poorer groups in society. Public–private partnerships allowed the regime to maintain its standing while promoting its interests (Seifan, 2011: 24). The state grew increasingly dependent on the private sector as a "new bourgeoisie" grew out of the ranks of the "military junta" (Dahi and Munif, 2011: 328). Wedeen refers to the regime during this period as a "neoliberal autocracy," as the makeup of the society fundamentally changed. In communities, Ba'ath Party cadres were replaced with a "social army" of government-organized nongovernmental organizations, creating a strong "third sector" beyond the public and private sectors (Wedeen, 2015: xi).

The liberalization policies that aimed to increase the role of the private sector, including in the provision of welfare services, involved introducing market mechanisms; limiting the role of state intervention; offering a place in decision-making to business elites rather than trade unions and other corporations; and increasing privatization while keeping public ownership (Abboud, 2015: 53).

The Social Contract Ends: Syria's "Social Market Economy" (2005)

In June 2005, just five years after Hafez al-Assad's death, the Ba'ath Party dramatically broke with tradition by labeling Syria a "social market economy" during the Tenth Regional Command Conference. In the words of a member of the ruling elite, a "revolution of minds" had been set in motion.[21] In Chapter 5, the consequences of this move on the Syrian population's human security will be examined, but first the concept of the social market economy will be explored. The Ba'ath

---

[21] Based on author's interview with former brigadier general Manaf Tlass of the Syrian Republican Guards and member of Bashar al-Assad's entourage, Damascus, June 20, 2005. During the discussion, Tlass, who defected in 2012, depicted the new president as a Syrian nationalist rather than Ba'athist.

Party aimed to model their new economic transition on Germany's economic model after World War II.

The German Social Market
The Ba'ath Party saw the German social market as a potential model because of its success in achieving economic development and low inequality in post-World War II Germany. The concept of reconciling "competitive market forces and social cohesion" was not new to Germany, and had first been proposed by Gustav von Schmoller in the late nineteenth century (Ebner, 2006: 207). Shattered and divided after World War II, West Germany attempted to put these ideas of a socially conscious yet still competitive economy into practice.

Following Germany's remarkable economic recovery, analysts extolled the "German Model" as a "unique and highly successful, synthesis of capitalism and social democracy" (Albert, quoted in Betz, 1996: 303). The German social market model had been the result of a compromise between two factions in the German Christian Democratic Party: the neoliberal wing, which favored a minimal state role, and the socially oriented wing, which desired a corporatist restructuring of social security where "welfare state responsibilities would be transferred to occupational bodies" (Betz, 1996: 304). A combination of these two visions led to a "third way" that blended laissez-faire capitalism with state socialism, where the state was neither interventionist nor minimalist. Hans-Georg Betz praised the model, in particular for the way it enabled collective bargaining and saw comparatively low inequality (Betz, 1996: 305, 307).

Still, analysts temper the optimism around the German social market by exposing its serious structural weaknesses, evident in Germany's large manufacturing sector (which exists to the detriment of its service sector), mediocre economic growth and productivity, and the exclusion of subsections of the labor force (Betz 1996: 309–311). More specifically, Betz contends that the German social market was "severely biased" against women, foreigners, and older workers in the 1970s when there was high unemployment (1996: 312). Despite these weaknesses, the Syrian regime was inspired by the German social market.

The Leap toward the Social Market Economy: Official Narratives and Rationale
In a speech to the nation in July 2007, Bashar al-Assad advocated for a transition to the social market economy to "achieve social justice, combat poverty and unemployment and enhance social security

networks," placing particular importance on the agricultural sector (Syria Report, 2007c). These official narratives did not always correspond with the reality of the transition. The shift toward a social market economy was a product of a series of complex negotiations between many public, private, and international actors with different interests. While many of the players claimed to advocate for marginalized populations, the policies often aggravated the plight of such groups. This section will trace the proximate cause of the shift – an oil shortage – as well as the larger context of pressure from international organizations and a shift in the ideological grounding of the party.

The decision to adopt the social market economy followed a severe diesel shortage in preceding years, which was blamed on the smuggling of cheap diesel to neighboring countries where it could be sold at higher prices (Syria Report, 2005c). This in turn, led to calls within the government for an increase in oil prices by eliminating state support, to dissuade smuggling, while increasing state salaries and safety schemes to avoid the negative social impacts of increased fuel prices (Syria Report, 2005d). On September 2007, the government announced its decision to reduce subsidies for oil by-products the following year, within a period of five years (Syria Report, 2007d). These measures were allegedly to combat smuggling that made fuel inaccessible to the poorest parts of the population, and domestic sources indicate the government was concerned about "fear of protests from the population" because of declines in standards of living for two decades (Syria Report, 2007d).

The results of this policy, as well as other contemporaneous policies, hit rural agrarian populations hard. This policy resulted in increased production costs and agricultural commodity prices. A separate government program cut by 20 percent the prices of "strategic crops" (cotton, tobacco, and sugar beet) that used to be bought exclusively by the Syrian government. This lowered profit margins for farmers, threatening their survival at a time when the Price Stabilization Fund, the equivalent of the food stamp scheme, was also terminated. Although the fuel subsidy-reform was supposed to take place gradually from 2007 to 2013, all fuel subsidies ceased abruptly in May 2008. Agrarian communities purportedly supported the measure, but its impact on farmers who needed fuel to operate their machinery was devastating. Only seventeen months after the subsidy cuts, the government launched a new plan with cash payments for heating gas (*mazout*) for about 1 million families in need (Syria Report, 2009e).

However, the decision was still too late in support of an already decimated community in the northeastern regions.

External actors, especially the International Monetary Fund (IMF) and the World Bank, pushed strongly for Syria's liberalization, arguing that the existing subsidies benefited the rich more than the poor. In its 2005 annual assessment of the Syrian economy, the IMF recommended a host of measures such as increasing taxes, freezing wages and reducing subsidies on oil and other consumer products (Syria Report, 2006). In 2007, the IMF reiterated its recommendation to lift subsidies on oil products, which were 15 percent of Syria's GDP (Syria Report, 2007b). In the same year, the World Bank encouraged the Syrian government to pursue subsidy reforms before they could join the World Trade Organization, because the subsidies mainly benefited wealthy farmers and encouraged unsustainable water use and noncompetitive crops such as cotton (World Bank, 2008: 20, 49, 50). According to World Bank calculations, diesel price subsidies to agriculture represented 2.6 percent of GDP, cotton price subsidies represented 0.9 percent of GDP, and wheat price subsidies were entirely absorbed by the increase in the world price of the same crop in 2007 (World Bank, 2008: 43–45). While the World Bank argued for drastic cuts to these subsidies, it also advocated for improved access to credit for farmers, which the government only implemented several years later in 2010 and 2011.[22]

While the state did follow the IMF and World Bank's recommendations of subsidy reform, it did not adopt their prescriptions to undertake a gradual approach, for instance by starting with institutional reforms in order to prepare the market for liberalization and by focusing on "growth from within" (Barout, 2012: 50, 58). Syrian analyst Muhamad-Jamal Barout notes two conflicting factions of powerful actors: "traditional reformers/Syrian bureaucrats" who found the liberalizing reforms incompatible with the Syrian way of doing things and an emergent class of "new businessmen" who wanted change as soon as possible (Barout, 2012: 60–61). Each faction had its own interpretation of reforms, as the traditionalists saw the change as an opportunity to exploit public resources for personal economic benefits, and the new businessmen wanted a fast transition at the expense of vulnerable

---

[22] The Agricultural Cooperative Bank took the decision to double the ceiling on loans in 2010, followed by Presidential Decree No. 22/2011 of December 12, 2011, which eased lending restrictions to farmers (Syria Report, 2010d, 2011b).

communities. Although the traditionalists managed to include policies to support the poor and marginalized in the shift toward a social market economy in the Tenth Five-Year Plan of 2006–2010, in reality, the new businessmen won the battle for reform, resulting in an abrupt opening of the market without social safety nets.

The decision to lift subsidies had support not only from international organizations but also from ideological powerhouses within Syria. Abdullah Dardari was a major liberal player in the Syrian government in the 2000s and the key figure behind the reformist Tenth Five-Year Plan.[23] Dardari was a major opponent of the subsidies, qualifying them as "unfair" because "almost 40% go to the 15% richest segments of the population" (Syria Report, 2005a). The reforms that eliminated these subsidies fell under the Tenth Five-Year Plan, and Dardari argued that the reforms were not undertaken because of foreign pressure but because of their social ramifications in Syria. He outlined three objectives for the reforms: (1) to pursue the support of the most vulnerable parts of the population; (2) to reduce the costs of subsidies; and (3) to make the economy more efficient, including raising agricultural productivity (Syria Report, 2005a). In 2009, Dardari argued that the reforms were successful because economic growth from 2005–2007 generally exceeded the growth projections, and the poverty rate decreased from about 14 percent in 1998 to 11 percent in 2007 (Dardari, 2009: 41).

By 2015, it was clear that the reforms had not been as successful. In an interview with the author, Dardari blamed the relative failure of the social market economy model on the 2006–2010 drought as well as government mismanagement and corruption.[24] According to his calculations, without the drought, the social market economy would have decreased poverty rates from 11 percent in 2005 to 7 percent in 2010, whereas in reality the poverty rate increased to 12 percent. Dardari claims that he wanted to postpone the reduction of agricultural subsidies until after the drought, but he did not have the authority do so. On top of the obstacles posed by the drought, some of the reforms

---

[23] Dardari served as head of the State Planning Commission from 2003 to 2005, deputy prime minister of economic affairs from 2005 to 2006, and minister of planning from 2006 to 2008. His appointment fits within the regime's strategies of "co-option" of Syrians outside of the country through selective recruitment and engineering of Western-educated technocrats (Zintl, 2015: 115).

[24] Based on the author's interview with Abdullah Dardari. Beirut, December 10, 2015.

encountered ideological and economic resistance from existing rural powerholders. The direct sale of products by farmers posed a direct challenge to the monopoly of farmers' unions in the countryside while the fuel subsidy reform attempted to eliminate smuggling. Local push-back over the reforms compounded the government's refusal to act on the drought, in his view, partly leading to the "explosion" of 2011.

Evaluating the Social Market Economy: Domestic Perspectives

While the government eventually recognized that the shift to the social market economy had not been successful, Syrian experts – particularly the renowned economists, water engineers, agricultural experts, and others involved in the SAES – had been debating its success for years. In a series of papers presented from 2005 to 2010, the members of the SAES evaluated the effectiveness of the social market economy in terms of agricultural production, social welfare, employment, competition, crisis management, corruption, migration, and poverty, particularly during droughts. Their opinions and critiques were freely voiced, in stark contrast with the brutal government repression of dissent in later years, and provide valuable insights on the state of the water and agricultural sectors, and, more generally, the political and economic situation of Syria in the years that preceded the uprising of 2011.

While the assessments of the social market economy started rela-tively positive, they grew increasingly critical over the years. In 2005, many saw benefits to the new system. Suleiman, for example, charac-terized the social market economy as a technical concept that sought to use markets as a tool to stimulate demand and production to achieve economic growth. To him, it was a good mix of the best of both capitalism and socialism because its three goals were to promote competition, create equality of opportunity, and ensure state interven-tion in the case of market failures (Suleiman, 2005: 1–3). Additionally, official reports showed unemployment dropping from 12.3 percent in 2004, to 9 percent in 2008, which at face value seemed to indicate a positive impact of the reforms (Suleiman, 2005: 17).

The dissent, which grew steadily between 2005 and 2010, started by disputing the official employment statistics, claiming that the social market economy had actually negatively impacted employment, espe-cially in key demographic areas. By 2009, the papers and discussions grew increasingly pessimistic as the world faced a global economic crisis and Syria faced an extreme drought and increasing rural poverty. Sharf drew on broader criticisms of free markets and unbridled capitalism in fomenting the global economic crisis to point out the ways in which a more liberalized economy could hurt Syrian people (Sharf, 2009: 3), and Al-Shaib pursued a similar line of thought, arguing that the global economic crises indicated a larger failure of neoliberalism and the rule of the market (Al-Shaib, 2010: 6). Other criticisms centered around the failure of the social market economy to deliver its goals. A common critique was that the government did not account for the risks of reform, and decisions were made for political rather than pragmatic reasons (Seifan, 2009a: 2, 2011: 12). In particular, many emphasized the fact that the social market economy had not done enough to help the poor because the Syrian government did not accompany economy reforms with institutional reform (Nasr, 2009: 2, 13). As Abboud writes, the "social" in the social market economy turned out, in the end, to be "quite peripheral," as the private sector saw massive gains, often at the expense of the public sector (2015: 50, 64). By 2009, virtually every Syrian expert was agreed on the detrimental impacts of the end of subsidies to the poor and the working classes and called for their reintroduction (Nasr, 2009: 12; Qatna, 2009: 10; Seifan, 2009b: 12).

A final key theme in the evaluation of the shift to the social market economy was the need to eradicate corruption, which had become more prevalent as business elites grew more powerful, yet which represented a major obstacle to meaningful change in support of the poorest citizens. Official and unofficial corruption illustrate the role of elite business networks in creating and maintaining human insecurity, and the next section will explore this in the Syrian context from the 1970s to the 2000s.

Corruption: From Ba'athism to Liberalism

This section will explore the distinction between corruption and patronage networks, both of which are important in the Syrian context, before reviewing the causes and consequences of corruption under Ba'athism and the social market economy. Generally, corruption can be understood as a broad range of activities in politics and business that involve "misuse of public office for private gain" (Rose-Ackerman, 1999). Larmour defines seven varieties of corruption, emphasizing the need to disaggregate between the *types* and *toolsets* by which political actors commit corruption and misappropriate public resources for private gain (Larmour, 2012: 100). By not lumping different types of corruption together but rather by treating them as separate phenomena, we get a clearer view of how and why these types of corruption take place, especially in developing economies, as well as which are the most detrimental. Larmour's six definitions include: (1) kickbacks (i.e., extra payments on routine transactions designed to facilitate a beneficial relationship), (2) "greasing the palms" (outright unprompted bribes), (3) nepotism/cronyism (favoritism in recruitment or hiring), (4) rank pulling (using high political status to bend public rules), (5) unethical decisions in procurement (using policy for political interference), and (6) misuse of public funds (stealing or mismanaging funds in a way that leads to personal gain) (Larmour, 2012: 101, 102). All of these forms were deployed under Hafez and Bashar al-Assad, generally by means of *wasta* (bribes).

Political patronage and clientelism, on the other hand, is a system in which seemingly legitimate or legitimately elected persons in power distribute material and political benefits to groups or individuals in exchange for political or electoral support, to ensure their continued power. Singer argues that patronage is more likely to occur in countries with "high levels of poverty, weak democratic institutions, short democratic histories, and a large state economic presence" (2009: 2). Haddad (2012), speaking to the Syrian case, traces an increase in patronage as the country evolved from a state-centered economy to state–business alliances from the late 1980s to early 2000s. His definition tracks closely to most accepted versions of political patronage, in which "networks of bureaucrats and capitalists consolidated around public sector patronage" (Haddad, 2012: 10). Perthes (1995) attributes this to Hafez al-Assad's ability to monitor corruption – that is, the ability of state employees to co-opt material resources for private gain – but not patronage, which is often legal and much more common. This allowed members of the existing protected elite business–political class to maintain a monopoly on power during and following the *infitah* period; as this business class grew wealthier and more powerful, the lower strata of state employees suffered (Perthes, 1995: 145). The networks of political patronage extended throughout all branches of government and were exceptionally strong in the water and agricultural sectors. As Sadowski argues, "farmers who demonstrated their loyalty to the regime or who had good times ties to the party had an easier time getting land than those who did not" (1987: 448).

The origins of corruption in Syria has been the object of many studies, which will be explored in Chapter 5 in the context of human insecurity. The theory that Hafez al-Assad tolerated corruption among key aids to make them weaker and more reliant on him has been widely promulgated, but Batatu questions this, pointing out that, in the end, corruption "eroded" some of the leader's legacy and added to "cynicism" of Syrians about the regime (Batatu, 1999: 243). Under Ba'athism, therefore, corruption was not a grand top-down scheme but rather an aggregation of bureaucratic mishaps and poor planning inspired by poor salaries, brain drain, and emphasis on bonuses/allowances; it was therefore not as much of a major threat to the country and to vulnerable populations (Hinnebusch, 2011: 6). Under Bashar al-Assad's liberalized economy, however, corruption became much more a money-making game among elites, that served to concentrate power in the hands of supporters of the regime. The actors in corruption changed too: It was no longer low-level bureaucrats seeking to making a little extra cash but rather a wealthy Sunny bourgeoisie concentrated in chambers of commerce and other public–private organizations (Ababsa, 2015: 315). This new political and economic nexus created a form of "authoritarian upgrading" (Heydemann, 2007). The regime had no reason to check rampant corruption, as it could threaten its strength, so corruption increased (Ababsa, 2015: 308).

In Syria, the new form of corruption under liberalization mainly served to exacerbate existing inequalities. Haddad identifies power networks that developed between "offspring" of the regime officials and private sector actor, which ensured policies were drafted and implemented to benefit those who were already well connected (Haddad, 2012: 177). Syria's legacy of state–business mistrust produced a particular form of state–business cooperation – that is, "selective and informal economic ties (networks) between state officials and private actors" that generated further mistrust and informality in network trading (Haddad, 2012: 3). The networks solidified the divide between urban elites and rural vulnerable parts of the population, which will be a primary focus of Chapter 5.

Summary

This chapter has presented an in-depth analysis of Ba'athist and neo-liberal ideological and political drivers of human insecurity in Syria from the 1960s to the late 2000s. The discussion showed that ideology impacted political decision-making by defining priorities, even as it was strategically employed by the regime to achieve legitimacy. In tracing the history of the Ba'athist rural contract and the myth of food security, this chapter also revealed the strategic importance to the Syrian state of food security, dam construction, and intensive irrigation. Ultimately, however, investments in irrigation led to overuse of groundwater and soil, resulting in salinization, and land reforms that often ended up confiscating land, mostly at the expense of the rural poor or Syrian Kurds. Finally, the chapter followed the gradual liberalization under Hafez al-Assad and Bashar al-Assad, culminating in the abrupt shift to a social market economy in 2005. This process exacerbated the divide between rural Syrians and business elites, privileging the latter at the expense of the former while increasing patronage networks and corruption. Most significantly, the new reforms of the mid 2000s compounded the effects of the 2006–2010 drought to make it nearly impossible to grow and sell crops at reasonable prices. From the 1960s onwards, Ba'athist ideological discourse served to justify policies pursued by the Syrian regime that adversely affected rural communities and increased their vulnerability to climatic changes such as the 2006–2010 drought. The next chapter will trace more explicitly how the interplay of water, food, economic, and social vulnerability combined with deficient resilience mechanisms, at the core of our HECS framework, paved the way for human insecurity in the decades that preceded the 2011 uprising.

5 | Vulnerability and Resilience
Human–Environmental–Climate Security in Syria

We suffered from drought and lack of water in Deir ez-Zor. The Turks cut the waters of the Euphrates and Khabour and the government did nothing to help us. They forbade us from digging wells unless people paid a bribe (wasta) of 500 USD. If we built illegal wells, they would put us in prison. Deir ez-Zor is empty, three-quarters of its populations is gone.[1]

(Farmer from Deir ez-Zor, Refugee Camp Shaher, Bekaa Valley, Lebanon, interviewed by author, December 12, 2015)

When I am asked: What motivated you to join the Syrian Revolution as your living conditions have been acceptable? My answer is no, we have not been living a normal situation. We've been living like slaves on a plantation from 1963–2011. There was no karama (dignity), no freedom, and many obstacles to our development. We want to be able to live like others.

(Civil-society activist Raed Fares of the United Revolutionary Bureau, Kafr Nabl, province of Idlib, interviewed by author, Washington, DC, November 15, 2015)[2]

Chapter 4 examined the effect of political ideology on resilience in Syria up until the 2011 uprising. Chapter 5 now brings together this understanding of resilience and vulnerability and applies the HECS framework to my case study. Chapter 4 traced how the ideologies of Ba'athism and the social market economy translated into specific

---

[1] Based on author's interviews from December 2015 in the Bekaa Valley with Syrian refugees from Deir ez-Zor, as well as civil-society activists exiled to Beirut, the migrants from the northeastern provinces did not contribute to the initial mobilizations in Deraa that later spread to the rest of the country. One activist mentioned specifically that the uprising did not start in the northeastern provinces but in front of the Tunisian and Egyptian embassies in Damascus on March 15, 2015, and the populations from Deraa who took the streets on March 18, 2011, were part of well-known established families of Deraa. Beirut, December 7–15, 2015.
[2] Raed Fares was assassinated on November 23, 2018.

150

policies with different types of insecurities, such as intensive irrigation and dam construction, and identified the consequences of Ba'athist and liberal preferences in terms of water waste, soil erosion, land-tenure disputes, and, ultimately, human insecurity in the form of population displacement and exclusion from the benefits of agricultural reform.[3] In Chapter 5, I discuss how these consequences tie directly into the themes of vulnerability and resilience at the core of the HECS framework.

Chapters 1 and 2 set up the theoretical background for this analysis, by defining climate security in human-security terms, as a series of threats and vulnerabilities posed by variation in climate conditions as well as elite decisions to human and ecological life. Climate vulnerability was defined according to the IPCC and the United Nations Development Program (UNDP) as "sensitivity or susceptibility to harm and lack of capacity to cope and adapt" (IPCC, 2014: 5), with the three core components of (1) exposure to hazards and perturbation; (2) sensitivity of the affected environment to these perturbations, which is context-specific; and (3) adaptive capacity of a society depending on various social factors such as class, gender, age, etc. (UNDP, 2010: 20). Applying these definitions to the Syrian case, I measure vulnerability to environmental instability and change in the daily impact of non-elites, whose sources of income, food, and services are primarily agricultural, taking into account community-level resilience – i.e. how communities respond to and cope with these disruptions on a daily basis.

To offer a clearer picture of the environmental context that preceded the Syrian uprising, this chapter starts by engaging with the extensive scholarly debates that took place outside Syria regarding the applicability of a climate-conflict nexus to Syria following the 2006–2010 drought. It also contrasts the claims made by international experts with domestic sources and expert discussions. A careful assessment of the environmental, water, food, and socioeconomic impact of this 2006–2010 drought will be carried out, before comparing these with another breakpoint drought in Syria's history which lasted from 1998 to 2001.[4] The scale of these comparisons will first be national,

---

[3] See Figure 4.1 for a detailed timeline on critical policy decisions regarding agriculture, water, and land from 1958 to 2011.

[4] Based on official documents originating from various Syrian ministries and the papers presented within the SAES from 2005 to 2010 (all sources in Arabic). In addition, additional insights will be drawn from international sources, such as

then regional (northeastern and eastern provinces), and finally sub-regional (Deir ez-Zor, Jazira/Hassake, and Raqqa). Special attention will be paid to human-insecurity factors such as the renewability of water sources, variations in precipitation and temperature, agricultural output and economic growth, unemployment, corruption, and mass migration – indicators of high vulnerability and low resilience.

The International Debate

Due to the domestic and international implications of the Syrian conflict, as well as the hotly contested global debate on climate change, the international community engaged in a lively discussion concerning the origins of the conflict, with some experts identifying the roots as climate-related. As a result of its attention from Western academics, scientists, and politicians, Syria became the reference of analysis in a series of journal articles that triggered this climate-conflict discourse. A plethora of articles explored the central issue of whether climate change "contributed to," "led" or "caused" unrest and conflict in Syria (Ababsa, 2015; Burke et al., 2014; De Châtel, 2014; Eklund and Thompson, 2017; Femia and Werrell, 2012; Fröhlich, 2016; Gleick, 2014, 2017; Hendrix, 2017; Hoerling et al., 2012; Kelley et al., 2015, 2017; Selby, 2018; Selby et al., 2017a, 2017b). These discussions focus on several points of contention: the 2006–2010 drought and the role played by climate change in precipitating the extreme weather event; the mismanagement of water resources by the Syrian government; the vulnerability of Syria's breadbasket Jazira region (Hassake governorate) to drought; the impacts of the drought on unusual patterns of internal migration; and the decimation of the rural economy that drove agricultural labor to the cities, possibly exacerbating social tensions.

Environmental Factors: Droughts, Patterns of Rainfall, and Temperatures

The most recent drought in Syria is broadly understood to have occurred between the winters of 2006–2007 and 2009–2010, despite

databases relating to Syrian politics (Syria Report) and international organizations (the World Bank, the International Labor Organization [ILO], the FAO).

varying opinions on the length of the drought due to the use of different metrics (Fröhlich, 2016; Kelley et al., 2015: 3241). Most scholars use precipitation levels to determine if there was a drought, but this does not mean that the effects of the drought are confined to rain-fed systems, as precipitation levels also impact runoff, ground-water levels, and soil moisture (Eklund and Thompson, 2017; Gleick, 2017: 249; Kelley et al., 2015: 3243; Selby, 2018: 2). Another helpful measure of drought is temperature, as temperature increases lead to increased water demand and evaporation, and subsequent reductions in soil moisture, surface, and ground water (Gleick, 2017: 249; Kelley et al., 2015: 3243). Soil moisture has a direct effect on agricultural productivity and is therefore an important variable for examining drought (Kelley et al., 2017: 246). Indices that combine several indirect factors can also quantify droughts. For example, Eklund and Thompson (2017) analyzed precipitation levels, land productivity trends, and vegetation anomalies to find that 20 percent of randomized points in Syria's agricultural areas had a negative trend whereas points in Iraq and Turkey had positive trends of 1 percent and 5 percent, respectively. These negative vegetation trends indicate land degradation in croplands due to land overexploitation, which can be a sign of decreasing groundwater aquifer tables and land degradation (Eklund and Thompson, 2017).

While there is widespread consensus that a drought occurred some time during the second half of the 2000s, the exact dates of the drought and whether it was "multi-year" is still contested. Kelley et al. (2015) define a "multi-year drought" as having "three or more consecutive years of rainfall below the century-long normal," but since the 2009–2010 winter witnessed above-average rainfall, they did not classify this as a multi-year drought (Kelley et al., 2015: 3243–3244). Eklund and Thompson (2017) take this argument further by claiming that 2008 was the only real drought year. Selby et al. (2017a) contend that despite the decline in precipitation from 2006 to 2009 in eastern Syria, these were not abnormally dry years in the context of the past sixty years.[5] The authors point to data of above-average rainfall in

---

[5] Selby et al. (2017a) find an overall decrease of 20 percent of precipitation in eastern Syria, with 2007–2008 as the driest year on record. In that year, the eastern city of Qamishli received just 25 percent of its 1961–1990 average rainfall, while Deir ez-Zor received only 12 percent of its twentieth-century rainfall (Selby et al., 2017a: 237). Francesca De Châtel had previously assessed

Aleppo, Damascus, and Homs from 2006 to 2009 (De Châtel, 2014: 524–525; Selby, 2018: 2; Selby et al., 2017a: 234).

The question of whether there is a long-term drying trend in Syria and the Fertile Crescent is also debated. Kelley et al. use the Palmer Drought Severity Index to advocate for this drying trend and use tree-ring climate proxy data to suggest that 1998–2012 was the driest fifteen-year period in the previous 900 years (Kelley et al., 2015: 3243–3244; 2017: 246).[6] However, Selby et al. argue that a long-term drying trend is not present in the precipitation data, which shows that rainfall in the region is "highly variable," with the decade between 1999 and 2009 being an abnormality (Selby et al., 2017a: 235). This topic is of high importance because it could signal long-term climate-change effects on the region. For example, Kelley et al. point to the long-term drying trend – in combination with data showing Syria has experienced warming at a faster rate than the global average and a long-term reduction in winter rainfall in the region – to suggest that climate change is already affecting Syria (Kelley et al., 2015: 3243–3244; 2017: 246).

Overall, while there is consensus on the existence of a drought, the role of climate change is less widely accepted. Kelley et al. (2015) argue that while climate change did not cause the drought, it increased its severity. However, according to Francesca De Châtel, the majority of evidence suggesting climate change caused the 2006–2010 drought is based on climate models, and that these models are inadequate predictors of drought (De Châtel, 2014: 523). Selby and his coauthors echo this critique by pointing to conceptual problems in attributing the drought to climate change. Despite significant evidence that climate change has increased the probability of drought in Syria, the evidence does not support the claim that climate change caused the most recent drought of 2006 (Selby et al., 2017a: 235; 2017b: 254). Selby et al. also question the models used to determine causality between climate change and the 2006 drought and further argue that linear modeling by Kelley et al. (2015) may be a problematic way of measuring precipitation, citing the misleading conclusions about rainfall in the Sahel

---

the 2007–2008 winter with Hassake's rainfall decreasing 66 percent, Deir ez-Zor's rainfall decreasing 60 percent, and Raqqa's rainfall decreasing 45 percent (2014: 524).

[6] The Palmer Drought Severity Index combines precipitation and temperature to produce an estimate of soil moisture.

that had been produced through linear modeling (Selby et al., 2017a: 235). As a result, the long-term drying trend caused by climate change identified by Kelley et al. (2015) may be a "statistical artifact" (Selby et al., 2017b: 254).

Mismanagement: Government Resource Policy

While the specifics of the drought remain contested, consensus emerges among these authors that mismanagement played a role in exacerbating the severity of the drought. Water tables across Syria have been in decline since the 1980s, and by 2001 the majority of the country's water basins were experiencing withdrawal deficits (Selby, 2018: 7). The basins were victims of a massive irrigation expansion between 1985 and 2010, with irrigated land doubling from 651,000 ha to 1.35 million ha (De Châtel, 2014: 529–530). Approximately 80 percent of this irrigation employed flood irrigation methods (Selby, 2018: 7). The impact of this irrigation expansion is best illustrated by the case of the Khabour River, where flows drastically decreased from 60 m^3/s in the mid twentieth century to 0 m^3/s in 2001, after irrigation consumed 300 percent of the basin's "safe yield" (Ababsa, 2015: 205; Selby, 2018: 7).

Water policies also increased well construction within the northeastern and eastern provinces (comprised of Hassake, Deir ez-Zor, and Raqqa), which saw a significant rise from 135,000 in 1999 to 213,000 wells in 2007 (Ababsa, 2015: 204). This increase in well construction made the region heavily dependent on river and groundwater extraction, with 94 percent of Hassake's water, 75 percent of Deir ez-Zor's water, and 50 percent of Raqqa's water coming from these sources (Ababsa, 2015: 204). In 2005, the government attempted to regulate the construction of new wells, but enforcement efforts were plagued by corruption and failed to stymie the building of new wells (Ababsa, 2015: 205; De Châtel, 2014: 532; Kelley et al., 2015: 3241). This resulted in water extraction exceeding sustainable available resources by over 3.5 billion cubic meters (bcm) (Ababsa, 2015: 205; De Châtel, 2014: 539).

Although most experts accept the negative repercussions of mismanagement on the region's water situation, several of these authors disagree on the extent to which this mismanagement has impacted agricultural production during drought years. Generally, regions that rely on irrigation – and therefore groundwater – are expected to be less affected by drought than regions that are dependent on rainfall. Kelley et al. believe that two-thirds of Syria's agriculture is dependent on rainfall, with only one-third reliant on irrigation, making it more susceptible to drought (2015: 3241). As previously noted, however, Ababsa has contended that the vast majority of the Jazira region's water comes from groundwater sources (2015: 204), and that the drying up of the Khabour river forced farmers to move their production into areas where there was comparatively less rainfall, making them more reliant on groundwater resources (Selby, 2018: 7). For Selby and his coauthors, Hassake and the broader governorate's reliance on groundwater resources indicates that mismanagement, not climate change, was the primary cause of the region's agricultural hardships. Wheat production relied on irrigation, which insulated the crop from the precipitation changes experienced in the 2006–2010 drought, and a decline in production therefore is a signal of mismanagement and not drought (Selby et al., 2017a: 239). The linkage between water source and susceptibility to drought is not as clear-cut as these authors suggest, however, as declining precipitation and rising temperatures increase groundwater extraction. Satellite imagery shows that there were reductions in groundwater during the drought (Kelley et al., 2015: 3241), which consequently impacts agricultural regions that are not rain-fed (Gleick, 2017: 249). In addition, higher temperatures also negatively impact soil moisture, which is crucial for wheat production (Kelley et al., 2015: 3243). These relationships imply that drought can still impact areas that are not dependent on rainfall.

Mismanagement: The Elimination of Farmers' Subsidies

Northeastern Syria was already vulnerable to drought, and government policies clearly compounded the vulnerability of its rural populations and communities. Even proponents of the climate-conflict thesis note that the government policies heightened the vulnerability of Syrian communities (Kelley et al., 2015: 3241), yet the Syrian government readily deployed narratives of environmental problems to explain the country's water scarcity (De Châtel, 2014: 528–529). The government claimed that the 2006–2010 agricultural crisis was the result of the global financial crisis and climate change, and not government mismanagement for political purposes (De Châtel, 2014: 527–528).

The Syrian state manipulated the climate-conflict thesis to absolve itself of any responsibility for the crisis, and later sections of this chapter will delve into this political aspect of the climate-conflict thesis (De Châtel, 2014: 532).

In examining the vulnerability of marginalized populations to weather events, it is important to note that according to the most recent records from 2004, the majority of the country's poor – about 58 percent – lived in rural agrarian northeastern Syria (Selby, 2018: 7). Although the intervening seven years had seen a reduction in poverty across the country, northeastern Syria had actually experienced an increase in poverty (De Châtel, 2014: 525). For example, the aforementioned Jazira (Hassake) region experienced an unemployment rate of 25 percent, significantly higher than the nationwide standard of 11 percent (Ababsa, 2015: 201). Government policies adversely affected the region's agricultural sector, which was the primary livelihood for most people.

In Jazira, a large part of the poverty increase had been due to the removal of subsidies under the shift to the social market economy (Ababsa, 2015: 206–207; Kelley et al., 2015: 3242). When the fuel subsidies were removed in 2008, diesel fuel prices rose approximately 350 percent from 7 SYP to 25 SYP. This price spike coincided with farmers' increased need to pump water because of declining soil moisture and precipitation from drought, and farmers needed the diesel to run their pumps. These subsidy cuts also were implemented immediately prior to the harvest, negatively impacting the ability of farmers to irrigate their crops and transport their harvest to the market (Ababsa, 2015: 206–207; De Châtel, 2014: 525–526). The removal of fuel subsidies also caused livestock loss: International and national assessments revealed that the sheep population fell 33 percent, from 18 million to 12 million (Selby, 2018: 3). The Hassake area was particularly affected, with its sheep population falling 44 percent (Selby, 2018: 3). Overgrazing had already contributed to significant desertification of the Jazira steppe (De Châtel, 2014: 523) so the removal of fuel subsidies further hindered the ability of shepherds to transport their herds to water or to bring them water (Ababsa, 2015: 206). In addition, animal feed prices increased 75 percent by 2010, further contributing to significant herd loss (Kelley et al., 2015: 3242). In 2008, the government also ended its subsidies of chemical fertilizers, resulting in price increases of 200–450 percent (Selby, 2018: 9). Given the low wages for farmers, this meant fertilizers were consuming up to 20 percent of the average farmer's monthly salary (De Châtel, 2014: 526). Compounding these price increases was the need for more fertilizers as years of irrigation mismanagement had taken its toll on soil fertility (Fröhlich, 2016: 40).

Three other government policies also increased the vulnerability of agriculturally-dependent communities. In December 2000, Decision No. 83 dismantled state farms that had played a central role in Syrian agriculture for decades. Land was distributed in 3-hectare parcels of irrigated land and 8-hectare parcels of nonirrigated land to former owners, farm workers, and state employees. Multiple distribution methods remained on the books, so there was significant confusion regarding the rights to these newly privatized lands (Ababsa, 2015: 213). The Jazira region bore the brunt of this confusion as the majority of state farms had been in the region (Selby, 2018: 8).

The government also relaxed tenancy protections under Law No. 56 in 2004, which allowed landowners to end tenancy contracts and shift to temporary contracts (Ababsa, 2015: 200–211). Workers under these contracts only received compensation for termination if the contract contained both signatures and fingerprints. Most contracts, particularly those for workers from Jazira who were employed in the coastal Tartous and Lattakia regions, were oral contracts, and the initial drafting of the law provided no compensation for the termination of oral contracts. Significant protests to the law eventually resulted in the government amending the law to allow testimonies in support of oral contracts, offering farmers marginally enhanced legal protections. Ababsa notes that most of the workers who in the Jazira region were not, though Jazira migrants working in other were disenfranchised by the lack of legal protections. Such disenfranchisement would have likely impacted remittance flows back to families in the Jazira region; however, this linkage remains unexplored in the literature. The implementation of these laws also caused significant land speculation, driving some land prices over 1,000 times the original costs. The price increases and sales allowed landowners to expel farmers from the land that they had developed and cultivated for years, indicating another point of marginalization and dispossession of Syria's poorer communities (Ababsa, 2015: 211; Selby, 2018: 8).

Finally, Decree No. 49, passed in 2008, restricted communities' ability to buy and sell land along the border (Ababsa, 2015: 216).

Government approval was required for all land sale transactions, and while the policy technically only applied to border areas, in practice, the entire Hassake governorate was subject to these restrictions (Ababsa, 2015: 216). The decree was part of Syria's larger Arab Belt policy, which promoted the Arabization of Kurdish-inhabited areas and frequently discriminated against Kurdish inhabitants (discussed in more detail in Chapter 4).

Although championed under the broad banner of economic liberalization, these reforms hurt the agricultural sector upon which the Syrian economy heavily depended. Official estimates indicated that in 2005–2006 the sector employed nearly 20 percent of the country's labor market, while unofficial estimates placed that number as high as 50 percent (De Châtel, 2014: 526). There is consensus among analysts that the agricultural workforce decreased substantially during the drought, though the exact numbers vary: De Châtel cites a decrease of 460,000 jobs between 2001 and 2007 (2014: 526), whereas Ababsa cites a decrease of 600,000 jobs between 2002 and 2008 (2015: 200). De Châtel notes that the largest declines in agricultural employment occurred during the non-drought years of 2003 and 2004, although declines in the sector's employment still happened during the 2006–2010 drought (2014: 526). In addition to job losses in 2003 and 2004, Selby notes significant job losses in 2008 (2018: 8) and that the Central Bureau of Statistics may have had political motivations for failing to provide the data from 2008.

Mismanagement: Migration

Mass internal migration in Syria prior to 2011 has led some analysts to reflect on whether drought-induced migration was a significant factor in the outbreak of violence. While contributors to this debate account for many factors, such as unemployment, corruption, and inequality, that resulted in protests, the unique role played by climate change in exacerbating a broad set of contentious issues remains relatively unexplored in the literature (Kelley et al., 2015: 3242).

While other trends undoubtedly precipitated violence, the role of migration remains hotly contested, largely because there are no comprehensive studies on the matter (De Châtel, 2014: 527). Some authors have cited figures of 1.5 million migrants as a result of the drought (Kelley et al., 2015: 3242). This number is called into question by other analysts as likely being based on the total number of people impacted by the drought rather than the number of people displaced (Selby et al., 2017a: 237). While drought-induced migration may have not totaled 1 million people – certain studies estimate 300,000 people or 65,000 families – there is consensus that it was substantial (Ababsa, 2015: 209; De Châtel, 2014: 527). More importantly, this migration of whole families was a "relatively new phenomenon" in the region as it only began a few years before the onset of the most recent drought (De Châtel, 2014: 526–527). The highest estimate of migrants is 600,000 people, reported by the United Nations Special Rapporteur (Selby et al., 2017a: 238). This migration reportedly left 160–220 villages in the Jazira region empty (Ababsa, 2015: 199), while other estimates have indicated that the migration emptied 60–70 percent of the villages in Hassake and Deir ez-Zor (De Châtel, 2014: 527).

Such migration, however, must be seen in the context of broader internal and international migration in and out of Syria throughout the decade preceding the drought. Seasonal migration from Hassake, Deir ez-Zor, and Raqqa to southern Syria was common, and workers would frequently travel for the summer before returning home in the fall (De Châtel, 2014: 526–527; Fröhlich, 2016: 43). The temporary nature of seasonal migration, however, means that it was likely not enough to cause social tension emanating in conflict, as suggested by some (Kelley et al., 2015: 3242; 2017: 246). In fact, there is relatively little evidence for the theory that demographic change sparked conflict (Selby et al., 2017a: 239).

In addition to disputes over the rate of migration, there are conflicting accounts as to where internal migrants traveled. Estimates from the United Nations Office for the Coordination of Humanitarian Affairs (UNOCHA) stated that 300,000 people migrated to urban centers, including Damascus, Aleppo, Hama, Raqqa, and Deir ez-Zor (Ababsa, 2015: 199, 209). Surveys by the United Nations Children's Fund, however, reported that internally displaced persons were working in Tartous, Lattakia, and Deraa (Ababsa, 2015: 209–210). Fröhlich's research also indicates that a substantial amount of the internal migration in Syria was from rural areas to other rural areas, and she notes that this complicates the migration-conflict narrative as such narratives rest on clashes between rural and urban communities (Fröhlich, 2016: 44).

Critics of the migration-conflict linkage also note that the amount of internal migration pales in comparison with broader demographic trends that took place prior to the conflict. In the years before the uprising, Syria received 1.5 million refugees from Iraq and experienced a population growth of 3 million people (Selby et al., 2017a: 239). The country also experienced a youth bulge, resulting in 800,000 people entering the labor market between 1998 and 2002 (Fröhlich, 2016: 43), while rural–urban migration from 2000 to 2005 was already significant at approximately 135,000 people (Selby, 2018: 4). Some skeptics also contest the link between internal migration and conflict by arguing that the migrants did not participate in protests. In Deraa, migrants from Hassake were perceived as "too poor to get politicized" (Ababsa, 2015: 210) and avoided the local protests (Ababsa, 2015: 210; Selby et al., 2017a: 240). Fröhlich's migrant interviews further reiterated the apolitical nature of this migrant population, with one interviewee reporting that the migrants "had nothing to do with politics" (Fröhlich, 2016: 46). Migrant participation in the protest would be unusual, as they were not integrated into Deraa communities, and they did not share their "common identity" (Fröhlich, 2016: 46).

This is consistent with the fact that the demands made by the initial protesters in Deraa were unrelated to the drought. Fröhlich does note that individuals displaced by environmental change will likely attribute the displacement to economic rather than environmental factors, but in Deraa the protests were not even just about the economy (Fröhlich, 2016: 41). Demands were predominantly related to the security services and the government's repression, though there were some demands related to land sale and fuel-subsidy policies (Selby et al., 2017a: 241). The variety of demands makes it difficult to draw a causal link between climate change and the people's decision to engage in protests and violence (Hendrix, 2017: 251). In their response to Selby, however, Kelley et al. note that the lack of explicit drought-related grievances is not proof that the drought was not an underlying cause of the protests (Kelley et al., 2017: 246).

International Perspectives, Diverse Conclusions

International scholars are clearly divided on the exact nature of the drought, the role of climate change and government policies in precipitating drought, and the impact of drought on internal migration and conflict. The following sections will carefully examine these questions using data from domestic and international sources over two key periods of drought: 1998–2001 ("Drought 1") and 2006–2010 ("Drought 2"). This comparison will allow us to better understand the nature of Syria's climate vulnerability prior to the 2011 uprising. The application of the HECS framework here helps to show how different factors contributed to environmental, economic, and social vulnerabilities.

Environmental Vulnerability: Drought, Temperature, Precipitation, and Surface and Groundwater Quality and Quantity

By 2010, the ongoing drought had revealed water-related problems and government management of water resources to be major issues. Key challenges included annual water deficits for agriculture (Soumi and Ma'an, 2010: 2), the drought and its impact on river flows and rainfall (Al-Muheissin, 2010: 4), the failure to modernize irrigation infrastructure and illicit digging of wells (Al-Hindi, 2010: 27), and general overextraction of groundwater due to a lack of government oversight and planning (Al-Shaib, 2010: 4). These stem from a variety of causes, including national water demand; increases due to demographic growth hovering around 2.55 percent per year; unequal precipitation over time, which prevented a constant replenishment of ground and river water; deficient irrigation systems that brought about substantial water losses; low quality soils that required higher volumes of water for drainage; and agricultural policies based on intensive irrigation. Although many of these trends began before the 2006–2010 drought, they accelerated during that period, and, in response, most Syrian experts called for the reinstallment of agricultural subsidies.

Precipitation is needed both directly for agriculture and for replenishing groundwater resources. Thus, lack of precipitation heavily impacts agricultural areas with poor resource management. It therefore represents a key indicator of the region's vulnerability to the effects of climate change since changes in precipitation and drought are fundamental aspects of climate change. Indeed, the IPCC AR4 report considers climate change to be comprised of rising temperatures, which can lead to, among other things, changing precipitation patterns and increased severe weather phenomena (IPCC, 2007: 4–7). Droughts, in turn, are related to precipitation and temperature variability and have significant implications for variation in water resources, specifically the quantity and quality of water available to citizens in different regions of the country. Under these conditions, the country can face severe deficits when there is a gap between available water resources and population needs.

Variation in Temperature

Although records suggest that temperatures have always been variable, we have seen accelerating increases in average yearly temperatures since 1950. Some experts have identified this phase of unprecedented rising temperatures as the "Great Acceleration" of the Anthropocene, creating a fundamental and unique shift in global conditions that changes the environments in which we live (Steffen et al., 2007: 614).

Variations in average temperatures constituted a serious form of vulnerability during Drought 1 in Syria, by interacting with precipitation levels to affect crop output and water security (see Fig. 5.1). From 1991 to 1997, the yearly average temperature in Syria was 17.94°C, while from 1999 to 2001, the yearly average temperature was 18.85°C, revealing an overall 5.07 percent increase from the pre-Drought 1 period. During July months from 1991 to 1997, the average temperature was 28.9°C, while July months from 1999 to 2001 showed an average temperature of 30.7°C, a 6.23 percent increase from the pre-drought

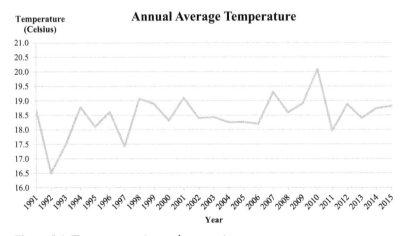

Figure 5.1 Temperatures (annual average).
Source: Elaborated by author from World Bank, 2018a

period. Finally, during August months from 1991 to 1997, the average temperature was 28.9°C, while August months from 1999 to 2001 had an average temperature of 30.1°C, a 4.15 percent increase from the pre-drought period. These rising temperatures significantly impacted soil moisture and other factors pertaining to successful agriculture.

During Drought 2, the mean variation in temperatures in Syria continued to rise at a steady rate. From 2004 to 2005, the yearly average temperature was 18.3°C, whereas from 2006 to 2010, the yearly average temperature was 19.02°C, a 3.93 percent increase from the pre-drought period. In the post-Drought 2 period from 2011 to 2012, however, the yearly average temperature was 18.45°C, a 3.00 percent decrease from the drought period. This seems to suggest that the fluctuation in drought temperatures was slightly higher during Drought 2 than Drought 1 (19.02°C compared to 18.85°C, a 0.90 percent increase), but that there was a sharper percentage increase in temperature from the pre-drought period of 1991–1997 to the drought period of 1999–2001 than from the pre-drought period of 2004–2005 to the drought period of 2006–2010 (5.07 percent compared to 3.93 percent). There was also a smaller percentage decrease in temperature from the drought period of 1998–2001 to the post-drought period of 2002–2003 than from the drought period of 2006–2010 to the post-drought period of 2011–2012 (2.39 percent compared to 3.00 percent). This higher percentage increase in the post-drought period would explain heightened consequences of the more recent drought.

These two comparisons suggest that the effects of the earlier drought were felt more strongly than the effects of the latter drought. For Syrian experts, however, Drought 2 was identified as having disproportionately impacted the eastern and northeastern provinces, including Deir ez-Zor, Raqqa, and Hassake, and covered roughly 60 percent of Syria's land area (Seifan, 2009a: 12). Western Syria still averaged 600 millimeters (mm) per year of rain during the drought years of 2007–2008, demonstrating the differentiated impact of the drought by region (Bakour, 2009: 5).

Drought 2's major impact was to reduce arable land, harm pastoral livelihood, cause health problems due to dust storms, lower the water table, increase irrigation costs, precipitate a drop in reservoirs, increase air and water pollution, raise imports of basic food items, and cause outward migration (Qatna, 2010: 1–6). Because the drought meant not just increased temperatures but also decreased precipitation, it was threatening to rain-fed agricultural areas, such as the wheat-producing regions of the Northeast (Bakour, 2009: 6).

Evaluating Historic Rates of Precipitation

Syria is divided into five climatic zones based on annual precipitation levels. As a country with low annual precipitation rates, rainfall represents a highly variable source of water for Syria, with the rainy season spanning from October through May (Abou Zakhem and Hafez, 2010: 2643). Average rainfall approximates 46 billion cubic meters per year (bcm/y), though it fluctuates between 30 and 55 bcm/y of rainfall (Khaddam, 2011: 64). While precipitation levels have experienced significant variability, there has been a general decline over the previous half century. Precipitation data from stations in Damascus indicates that annual precipitation peaked in 1945 and 1953 at 360 mm and was lowest in 1999 at 60 mm (Droubi, 2009: 4). Additionally, the mean annual rainfall from 1919–1979 was 212 mm, whereas it was only 180 mm from 1980–2008 (Abou Zakhem and Hafez, 2010: 2643). This decline in precipitation heightens the effect of detrimental agricultural and water policies such as the removal of subsidies, land-sale inequalities, and rising prices.

Rainfall: Country Levels
Figure 5.2 helps us begin the comparison of Droughts 1 and 2 by measuring annual rainfall, revealing the variable rates of precipitation in the region over time. A comparison of precipitation levels in Syria prior to Drought 1 in 1997 shows levels of 371.96 mm, followed by a drop during Drought 1 with a minimum of 135.6 mm in 1999; this represented a tremendous decrease of 63.5 percent to this lowest year, as visually represented in the table above. The post-Drought 1 year of 2002 saw an increase back up to 301.54 mm, or a percentage increase of 55 percent, and average precipitation stabilized somewhat in the years leading up to Drought 2, with the pre-drought year of 2005 showing rainfall of 248.9 mm. However, the period from 2006 to 2010 saw another sharp drop, reaching 172.2 mm in 2008, before again stabilizing somewhat in 2012. The data for Drought 2 shows an overall decrease of 24.5 percent over the drought period, and a decrease of 36 percent from the beginning of Drought 2 to the lowest year of precipitation during the period. According to this data,

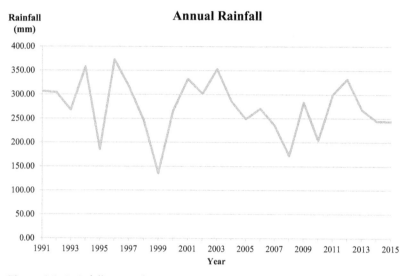

Figure 5.2 Rainfall (annual).
Source: Elaborated by author from World Bank, 2018a

therefore, both the variability of and mean of precipitation were less extreme during Drought than Drought 1.

The National Rainfall Index (NRI) is also informative in determining long-term trends. During the pre-Drought 1 period of 1988 to 1992, for example, the average NRI was 454.7 millimeters per year (mm/y), decreasing to 434.5 mm/y during the immediate pre-Drought 1 years of 1993 to 1997, with an overall decrease of 4.4 percent. Drought 1 saw NRI numbers of 375.8 mm/y, for a further decrease of 13.5 percent. Although the NRI is not available for Drought 2, inferring from other measurements of precipitation during this period seems to confirm that a similarly drastic drop would have occurred during Drought 2 and that such trends were part of overall long-term trends (FAO, 2016b). These figures suggest that precipitation levels in Syria are generally variable but that there were intense periods of low precipitation and high temperature during Drought 1 and Drought 2. These trends imply a systematic link between below-average precipitation and severe drops in agricultural activity, which in turn has adverse effects on sustainability and food security.

Regional Variance: Northeastern and Eastern Provinces

The majority of eastern Syria receives very low annual precipitation, especially in contrast with its major cities to the West. In order to properly evaluate regional variation, Edwards and McKee (1997) developed a widely used Standardized Precipitation Index (SPI), which measures the variation of precipitation levels in a given region from an average. Table 5.1 provides a more specific examination of how the SPI indicator is calculated.

As seen in Droubi's visualized data in Figure 5.3, distribution of rainfall varies across the country's five rainfall zones. Evaporation of water resources is a significant problem in the eastern and southern region of the country, resulting in yearly water deficits of 2,000 mm. The water deficit in the eastern part of the country fluctuates throughout the year, peaking at 1,600 mm during the dry season and falling to 600 mm during the rainy season (Khaddam, 2011: 64). In terms of general historical trends, arid land (less than 200 mm/y of rain) increased by 6 percent from 1970 to 2008 in the eastern part of the country, and semi-arid land area (200–250 mm/y of rain) increased by 50.7 percent during the same period (Soumi and Ma'an, 2010: 22). Although there is a lack of sufficient data to makes conclusions with certainty, it appears that the SPI in Syria had no clear trend starting in Drought 1, probably because the SPI indicator is more influenced by individual drought episodes than overall trends in precipitation (Droubi et al., 2011). The SPI also includes projections, with a high

Table 5.1 *SPI calculator. This index is calculated from the relation: SPI = Xi − X̄. Where: Xi is seasonal precipitation and X̄ is the average precipitation for each station. Source: Droubi et al., 2011: 4–5.*

SPI Values	Category
2.0 and above	Extremely wet
1.5 to 1.99	Severely wet
1.0 to 1.49	Moderately wet
−0.99 to 0.99	Near normal
−1.0 to −1.49	Moderately dry
−1.5 to −1.99	Severely dry
−2.0 and less	Extremely dry

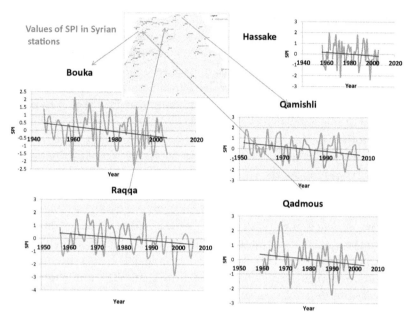

Figure 5.3 Regional variations: variation of SPI in selected Syrian stations.
Source: Droubi et al., 2011: 6

likelihood of lower precipitation in the Northeast region and heightened precipitation in coastal areas by 2025.

In terms of the critically vulnerable Jazira region, rainfall during the drought periods was more highly variable, ranging from less than 150 mm/y to over 600 mm/y. This is particularly critical since 63–68 percent of agricultural land in Hassake is rain-fed, so drought means more arid land (Soumi and Ma'an, 2010: 22). Provinces therefore known for their historical grain production experienced large decreases in precipitation, reducing the success of rain-fed agriculture. Reduced agricultural output not only reduced Syria's food self-sufficiency in terms of strategic crops but also hurt individual people.

Water Availability and Stress: Water per Capita, Irrigation, and Extractions

Given large annual fluctuations in rainfall, relying on precipitation remains hazardous. Rivers and groundwater resources, therefore, are critical resources for the country and serve as the primary source of

Syria's available water (Bazza and Najib, 2003: 6). Syria has relied on four principal sources for its hydraulic supply: the Euphrates, the Yarmouk (before the occupation of the Syrian Golan Heights by Israel in 1967), the Orontes, and groundwater (Syrian Arab Republic, 1999). Calculations of available water resources varies in domestic sources, possibly due to differences in data sources and different methods in calculation. For example, some calculations assume that Syria consistently receives its full share of Euphrates water from upstream Turkey or they include Iraq's share of the Euphrates, which likely overestimates the available water resources in a given year. Nevertheless, all assessments show significant increases in groundwater extraction in 2003 as compared to 2002 and an increase in the usage of agricultural and industrial wastewater between 2000 and 2003.

Official sources show that, while Syria receives 62 bcm/y of water, only about 14–16 bcm is available for use. At the end of the 1990s, the country's total water volume, combining surface water and groundwater, was evaluated at 22.9 bcm on average, except for during Drought 1. During this time, the total water volume fell to 16.134 bcm, nearly a 45 percent decrease from 1995 (Daoudi, 2001; Mualla and Salman, 2002: 1; Syrian Arab Republic, 2001). The resources of the Damascus basin, for example, were affected to the extent that the Barada, the capital's primary source, completely dried up. As a result, local authorities resorted to groundwater, pumping as deep as 100 meters in order to provide the capital and its 4 million inhabitants with 95,000 m^3 per day. The rest was ensured by the Fijeh source, the principal tributary of the Barada. This water crisis generated daily water shortages in the Syrian capital, for which the water deficit was estimated to be nearly 60 percent.[7] The crisis continued from about 1999 to 2002, when abundant rainfall in the winter of 2002–2003 restored water tables and the Barada came back to life.

[7] Following the drying-up of the Fijeh spring, outages that had previously reached sixteen hours a day increased to twenty hours a day as early as summer 2001. This was in order to compensate for the capital's daily deficit of 433,000 m^3 compared to the total need of 750,000 m^3. According to a Syrian government official cited in *Tishreen*, an official Syrian newspaper, the overarching reason was the drop in precipitation since 1997 and the increase in pumping from the Fijeh spring by the seventy-five wells present in the Damascus region (article referred to in *al-Mustaqbal*, July 25, 2001).

Between 1995 and 1998, Syria used 42 percent of its total volume of water of about 29 bcm annually. This situation was compounded during the drought of 1999–2000, when overall consumption reached a peak of 19.6 bcm (Daoudi, 2001; Syrian Arab Republic, 2001: 7). According to criteria set by the Falkenmark Index (see Chapter 2), which ranks countries on the basis of renewable water volume per capita, Syria qualifies as a country experiencing elevated water stress (Commission on Sustainable Development, 1997). The difference between renewable and nonrenewable water resources, though small, is also significant: It reveals the degree to which water resources were impacted by changes in irrigation and water-collection patterns, especially in relation to dam capacity. More contextual policy analysis is needed to determine how to interpret data regarding renewable vs. nonrenewable resources, yet Syria's vulnerability is evident.

The available water volume is estimated, on average, at 159 liters per person per day (Japan International Cooperation Agency and Syrian Ministry for Irrigation, 1996: 6). This quantity is situated halfway between the scales of certain Western countries, evaluated at 400 liters/person/day (Beaumont, 1994: 13) and the urban standards of 100 liters/person/day set by the World Health Organization as criteria for "acceptable quality of life" (Falkenmark, 1997: 30).

Tables 5.2 and 5.3 show the sectoral breakdown of water usage leading up to and during Drought 1. As a result of the prioritization of irrigation, by the end of the 1990s, more than 90 percent of water resources were allocated to agriculture (see Table 5.2). Starting in 2000, this portion declined to 80 percent, but the country incurred a considerable water deficit with withdrawals reaching 121 percent (Table 5.3).

Table 5.2 *Sectoral water allocations (1995–1998) (million cubic meters per year: mcm/y). Source: Calculated by author on basis of official sources (Syrian Arab Republic, 2001).*

Domestic/Drinking	844.4	7.5%
Agriculture (irrigation)	11,136.5	91%
Industry	194.7	1.5%
Total water use	29,014	100%
Total volume/annual availability	12,175.6	Withdrawal: 42%

Table 5.3 *Sectoral water allocations (2000) (mcm/year) (million cubic meters per year: mcm/y). Source: Calculated by author on basis of official sources (Syrian Arab Republic, 2001).*

Domestic/Drinking	1,277	6.5%
Agriculture (irrigation)	15,867	80.8%
Industry	480	2.4%
Evaporation	1,990	12.3%
Total water use	19,614	Withdrawal: 121%
Total volume/annual availability	16,134	Deficit: −3,481

Based on water withdrawal rates and deficits, it becomes evident that Syria went from a situation of medium water stress in 1995 (with 42 percent of water withdrawal) to a situation of elevated water stress in 1999 (with 121 percent withdrawal), leading to serious deficit in the 2000s. These deficits also demonstrate the increased dependency on groundwater as extraction surpassed their rate of renewal. Prior to the conflict, the country's consumption of water resources exceeded the available amount by 3 bcm annually (Al-Hindi, 2011: 16–19). The country thus found itself in a situation of dire water deficit with a consumption level of over 120 percent of available water resources (see Table 5.3).

Meanwhile, the total nonrenewable water resources per capita in the country in the pre-Drought 1 period (1993–1997) was at 1,109 m³/y, and dropped to an average of 988.4 m³/y during Drought 1 years (1998–2001), for a 10.87 percent decrease. From the pre-Drought 2 years (2002–2005) to Drought 2 years (2006–2010), total resources per capita went from 988.4 m³/y to 864.8 m³/y for a decrease of 12.51 percent. This led to a larger drop in total resources in Drought 2 than in Drought 1, a difference of 1.64 percent. The total internal renewable water resources per capita, measured in cubic meters per person per year (m³/p/y) was at an average of 470.7 m³/p/y for the pre-Drought 1 period and 419.6 m³/p/y during Drought 1, with a drop of 10.8 percent. Meanwhile, during the Drought 2 years, the total internal renewable water resources dropped to 367.1 m³/p/y, a decrease of 12.51 percent. The percentage of internally available water resources dropped to lower levels during the Drought 2 years, and dropped by a larger amount – a difference of 1.71 percent. This suggests that the

Table 5.4 *Water resources in Syria (1995–1999) (billion cubic meters: bcm; million cubic meters: mcm). Source: Calculated by author on basis of official sources (Syrian Arab Republic, 1999).*

Precipitation/year	49,705 bcm
Groundwater	8,227 bcm
Surface Water	22,149 bcm[a]
Total volume	30,376 bcm
Availability/person/year	1,791 mcm

Note: (a) Mentions that volume includes Iraq's share of the Euphrates.

water loss from the first drought compounded the effect on the second drought, increasing its severity.

Data on total water resources available per sector in Syria shows that the average of total available water resources from 1993 to 2003 varied by sector, with the highest water types coming from Syria's share of the Euphrates river, ground resources, and surface resources (Daoudy, 2005: 65, 67). Later, during the post-Drought 1 year of 2001, groundwater and surface resources had dropped to 4,613 million cubic meters (mcm) and 2,359 mcm, respectively, while the share of water available from the Euphrates remained constant. The total volume of these groundwater resources was estimated at around 8.227 bcm in the late 1990s and 5.8 bcm in 2005 (see Tables 5.4 and 5.5). The groundwater resource rates can be compared to annual consumption, which fluctuates between 4.5 and 7.5 bcm (Khaddam, 2011: 64). The pre-Drought 2 period from 2001 to 2005 also showed significant increases in groundwater extraction, and a drop in the usage of agricultural and industrial wastewater from 2000 to 2003.

Groundwater: Overpumping around the Country and in the Eastern Provinces

Experts within the SAES saw overextraction of groundwater resources as the primary failure of government water policy (Al-Hindi, 2010: 27; Al-Muheissin, 2010: 4; Al-Shaib, 2010: 4; Soumi and Ma'an, 2010: 2). The total water deficit in all of Syria was 3.5 mcm, and the eastern provinces made up 2.5 mcm of that, over two-thirds of the total deficit (Al-Hindi, 2010: 27). The unregulated building of unofficial wells and the government's failure to restrain it interacted with other climate and economic factors to drastically reduce water access and human security

Table 5.5 *Available water sources (2000–2005) (billion cubic meters: bcm). Source: Al-Hindi, 2011: 20, citing Syrian Arab Republic, Ministry of Agriculture and Agrarian Reform, Status Quo of the Agriculture Sector 1992–2003.*

Water Type	2000	2001	2002	2003	2004	2005
Groundwater	3	3.75	4.37	6.11	5.9	5.8
Surface Water	6.42	6.67	7.13	7.48	7.3	7.1
Surface and Groundwater	9.42	10.42	11.5	13.59	13.2	12.9
Other sources (e.g., waste water)	3.1	3.24	3.41	4.51	3.4	3.3
Total	12.52	13.66	14.91	17.1	16.6	16.2

during Drought 2. Soumi and Ma'an assert that warnings on the overextraction of groundwater began as early as 1985 (Soumi and Ma'an, 2010: 18), and Chapter 4 showed how this overextraction could be attributed to an increase in groundwater irrigation through (mostly unlicensed) wells (Mualla and Salman, 2002: 3). These wells drew unsustainably on groundwater resources: Approximately 7.5 to 8.5 bcm of the total 15–16 bcm used for agriculture came from groundwater sources, whereas only 2.3–2.5 bcm of groundwater extraction a year is sustainable according to recharge rates (Soumi, 2009: 5). This meant that overextraction of groundwater was approximately 150–230 percent of recharge rates in an average year in terms of precipitation whereas overextraction reached 250–300 percent in drought years, which has been the norm since 1995 (Soumi, 2009: 5).

Drought 2 had more dramatic adverse effects on human security than Drought 1, not because the climate stress was significantly greater but because specific policy measures created additional vulnerabilities. From this comparison, we can therefore see the vast importance of effective resource management in climate-vulnerable regions, such as Syria.

In some cases, groundwater also served as the only reserve in the event of a deficit in surface waters. The compound effect of this rolled over from Drought 1 to Drought 2 where continued and new patterns of unsustainable water-pumping and water use accelerated the impact of this loss on economic vulnerability. This trend augmented in the Jazira region in the 2000s, where in Hassake the number of new

Table 5.6 *Extension of wells in Khabour Basin. Source: Soumi and Ma'an, 2010: 16.*

Year	1984	1991	2006
Number of wells	232	1,652	2,391
Land irrigated from these wells (ha)	2,400	34,265	44,550

unlicensed wells increased from 682 in 2000 to over 11,000 and 10,000 in 2007 and 2008 (see Tables 5.6 and 5.7).

The trend also accelerated during the 1999–2000 drought when aquifers in the Khabour–Tigris basin were tapped extensively (Daoudi, 2001). These developments were exacerbated in recent years due to the drought, as the average rainfall in the eastern provinces only amounted to 131 mm of rain in 2007–2008, the lowest since the drought of 1959–1960 (Al-Shaib, 2010: 4). Furthermore, the Dajla and Khabur basins received only 70.4 mm of precipitation the same year (Soumi and Ma'an, 2010: 23) The extension of irrigated land, outlined above, contributed to the digging of new wells starting in 1984. This led to the total decline of water output from the Ras al-Ain spring in the region from 45.83 cubic meters a second (m³/s) in 1970 to 5.93 m³/s in 2000 and forced the beginning of pumping in 2001 (Soumi and Ma'an, 2010: 15–17).

Economic Vulnerability: Agricultural Production, Food Prices, Poverty, Unemployment, and Urban–Rural Divides

The environmental vulnerabilities defined in the second part of this chapter fed into existing economic vulnerabilities created by Syria's high dependence on the agricultural sector. A key economic vulnerability facing Syria was, therefore, food security, which, in Chapter 2, was defined from a human-security lens using Amartya Sen's (1981) entitlement approach that focuses on socioeconomic dimensions of accessibility instead of scarcity. This section will discuss economic vulnerabilities related to agriculture in Syria, particularly in the northeastern provinces, during two drought periods, as well as poverty and employment – specifically in the agricultural sector – and unequal access to water. These vulnerabilities can be understood as a measure

Table 5.7 Licensed and unlicensed wells in Syria's Northeast. Source: Elaborated by author from Syrian Arab Republic, 2017a.

Year	Deir ez-Zor			Hassake		
	Unlicensed Wells	Licensed Wells	Total Wells	Unlicensed Wells	Licensed Wells	Total Wells
2000	2,806	1,530	4,336	682	18,694	19,376
2001	3,155	2,245	5,400	10,351	18,747	29,098
2002	4,286	1,036	5,322	9,390	23,162	32,552
2003	4,286	1,036	5,322	8,028	21,974	30,002
2004						
2005	3,345	1,977	5,322	8,018	21,974	29,992
2006	5,498	1,465	6,963	11,246	20,738	31,984
2007	4,620	1,465	6,085	11,246	20,738	31,984
2008	3,420	1,355	4,775	10,789	20,738	31,527
2009	4,102	1,355	5,457	9,743	18,095	27,838
2010	4,100	1,357	5,457	13,346	25,769	39,115
2011	4,100	1,357	5,457	9,140	29,975	39,115
2012	4,100	1,357	5,457	2,483	36,632	39,115
2013	4,100	1,288	5,388	2,483	36,632	39,115
2014	4,100	1,288	5,388	2,483	36,632	39,115
2015	4,100	1,288	5,388	6,481	34,797	41,278
2016	4,100	1,288	5,388	6,481	34,797	41,278

of (in)security for rural populations in the context of the HECS framework, and exacerbating the urban–rural divide.

Food Production: Overall Trends

Food production is a key measure of insecurity in the HECS framework as it amplifies other environmental and economic insecurities. Variability in food production per capita is directly related to the stability of environmental factors, such as precipitation and temperature variability, as well as policy choices and the stability of employment in the agricultural sector. Using food production per capita, we can quantify the impact of droughts on different regions. In general, rain-fed areas were perceived to be hit harder by the drought than irrigated areas, though both were identified as having lower production during times of drought (Al-Shaib, 2010: 1–2; Qatna, 2010: 2–4; Soumi and Ma'an, 2010: 5, 7–8).

Previous chapters explained how agricultural output is strongly linked to water availability, which in turn is affected by government policies. Chapter 4 outlined domestic perceptions relating to food security, which can be defined in terms of self-sufficiency of production in key crops (Bakour, 2009: 5), or in terms of the ability of a country to sustain itself without significant imports (Soumi, 2009: 2). The next sections will analyze food production and price trends to gain insight into food (in)security in Syria prior to 2011.

From 2006 to 2008, the overall agricultural area decreased, with irrigated areas shrinking 2.5 percent from 1,229,000 ha to 1,168,000 ha, and nonirrigated areas shrinking 2.3 percent from 2,596,000 ha to 2,476,000 ha. This mostly impacted the production of basic crops such as wheat and corn (Qatna, 2009: 10). However, since 85 percent of irrigation uses traditional inefficient methods that lose about 50 percent of water through evaporation (Seifan, 2009a: 12), the loss of agricultural output probably results in an increased use of inefficient water methods for crop production. The reduction in irrigated areas was not uniform, with some areas actually seeing an expansion that increased pressure on groundwater resources (Soumi and Ma'an, 2010: 9). Since roughly 75 percent of production on irrigated land is dependent on unsustainable extraction of groundwater, the increase in irrigation in certain areas heightened the stress on water use that was already at a peak during Drought 2 (Soumi and Ma'an, 2010: 8).

Production of cereals, which includes many of the strategic crops defined as critical to Syrian food security (including wheat, barley, and corn) is another helpful indicator of food production trends during these two periods. From 1991 (pre-Drought 1) to 2001 (Drought 1), cereal production in Syria increased 19.4 percent from 4,322,487 tons to 5,161,232 tons. Then, from 2001 (Drought 1) to 2007 (Drought 2), overall cereals production dropped 47.9 percent to 2,684,688 tons (FAO, 2017a). By 2010, cereal production had increased again and stabilized at 3,900,866 tons, but the post-Drought 2 period saw another severe drop to 2,696,855 tons. While Drought 1 saw a marginal decrease in cereal production (2.1 percent), Drought 2 saw a dramatic 38.1 percent decrease. This suggests that although food capacity was built and remained strong in certain sectors, key climate factors interacted with policy and production to disproportionately endanger the food security of average citizens in Syria during Drought 2 (FAO, 2017b).

Production of Strategic Crops

The droughts had a disproportionate effect on the production of strategic crops. Increases in irrigation-fed agriculture during Drought 1 alongside fluctuations in temperature and precipitation had a strong impact on output and production patterns for Syria's strategic crops. Syrian economists and agricultural policy-makers have defined these crops as those that are the main source for the civilian food supply, that are usually grown in the grain-producing eastern region, and that tend to be dependent on rainfall (Bakour, 2009: 6). The FAO has further defined these strategic crops in Syria as those for which the government sets producer prices: wheat, barley, lentils, chickpeas, cotton, and sugar (FAO, 2003). Wheat and cotton are the most critical of the strategic crops in terms of job creation, use of irrigation, and overall agricultural revenue (FAO, 2003). Strategic crops use 70 percent of irrigated land and are considered a "pillar of the food security policy" (FAO, 2003).

The overall loss of precipitation during the drought periods threatened the self-sufficient production of Syria's strategic crops, especially wheat, forcing the country to import 1 million tons of wheat in 2007 and 2008 (FAO, 2003: 5). By 2008, 50 percent of imports into the Arab world were going to Syria (Bakour, 2009: 9). Decreases in crop production during Drought 2 were a result of different combinations of agricultural and policy changes. For example, in 2005, approximately 70 percent of nationally cultivated land was rain-fed and 30 percent was irrigated (Al-Hindi, 2011: 16) although wheat production relies extensively on irrigation, with over 75 percent of wheat production in Jazira using irrigation (Ababsa, 2015: 204). In Hassake, 45 percent of the region's agricultural land produced strategic crops using rain-fed land, with 11 percent growing barley (Soumi and Ma'an, 2010: 4–5). While both rain-fed and irrigated agriculture are impacted by droughts, rain-fed agriculture is on the whole more susceptible to periods of low precipitation.

Wheat: The Most Strategic of Crops

Figures 5.4 and 5.5 provide an overview of the production of wheat from 2000 and its breakdown between irrigated and rain-fed areas. Wheat is considered the most important strategic crop in Syrian agriculture, occupying up to 34 percent of the cropping area, with 55 percent of this production coming from irrigated farming (Droubi et al., 2011: 11).

Both Drought 1 and Drought 2 had significant impacts on national wheat production in Syria. Figure 5.4 illustrates this trend, and, while data is not available prior to 2000 (or prior to 2007 at the governorate level), the impacts of Drought 1 are still evident as the yield per hectare in 2000 is particularly low at 1,850 kilograms per hectare (kg/ha). This inefficiency is only surpassed by 2008's yield per hectare (1,440 kg/ha). These two numbers are in comparison to an average yield per hectare

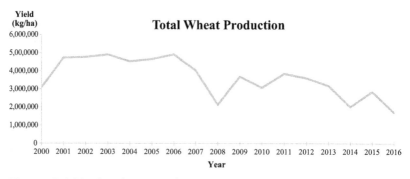

Figure 5.4 Total wheat production (country level) (kilograms: kg; hectares: ha).

Source: Elaborated by author from Syrian Arab Republic, 2017b

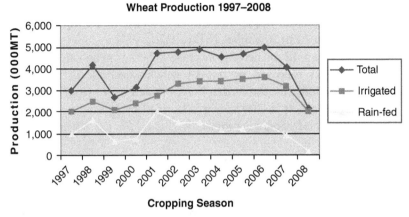

Figure 5.5 Rain-fed and irrigated wheat production in Syria (1997–2008).
Source: UNOCHA, 2008: 5

from 2000–2010 of 2,391 kg/ha and reflect a significant deviation from the mean. Absolute production in 2000 and 2008 is also substantially lower than the ten-year average with yields of 3,105,489 megatons and 2,139,313 megatons respectively in comparison to the ten-year average of 4,058,323 megatons (Syrian Arab Republic, 2017b: 1).

The most drastic declines in wheat production occurred in rain-fed land, which is consistent with the claim that abnormally low precipitation levels (or drought) caused declines in agriculture. The 10-year average for rain-fed land production is 1,085,522 megatons; rain-fed production in 2000 was well below this average at 708,916 megatons, and rain-fed production from 2006 to 2010 was also below average. Rain-fed production reached its lowest point in 2008 at 165,407 megatons, which was well below even the average from Drought 2. According to 2009 estimates, Syria's wheat imports that year reached a record high level of 1.5 million tons (Syria Report, 2009a). Significant declines in rain-fed production began when 2007 harvest yields dropped to 911,090 megatons from 1,363,854 megatons in the previous year, representing a 33 percent decrease (Syrian Arab Republic, 2017b: 1).

Production from irrigated land also exhibits declines during Drought 2; however, these declines are not as drastic, and reported yields from irrigated land in 2007 and 2009 are above the ten-year average (2,972,800 megatons) at 3,130,010 megatons and 3,037,582 megatons respectively. Yields from 2008 are the lowest of the decade at 1,973,906 megatons, approximately 33 percent below the ten-year average (Syrian Arab Republic, 2017b: 1).

In summary, a 12.56 percent increase in wheat production during Drought 1 was followed by a 6.14 percent decrease in the post-Drought 2 period, suggesting that compounded losses from the crash in the wheat harvest in 2007 were intensified by specific non-climate issues during the Drought 2 years.

Other Strategic Crops: Barley and Cotton

The trends seen in wheat production during the two droughts were replicated in production of other strategic crops, such as barley and cotton. From 2002 to 2005, total yearly yield of barley averaged 648 kg/ha, a 22.02 percent decrease from the last two years of Drought 1. During Drought 2, the yearly total yield average was 555.6 kg/ha, a 14.26 percent decrease from the pre-drought period. From 2011 to 2016, the yearly total yield average was 763.33 kg/ha, a 37.38 percent increase from the Drought 1 period. Barley is grown predominantly on irrigated land but significantly more susceptible to annual changes in precipitation levels than wheat, which likely explains the crop's annual variability (Syrian Arab Republic, 2017c: 2). Data on barley production from 1999–2011 show declines, with the two lowest reported yields during this time frame occurring at the height of both droughts in 2000 and 2008 at 211,905 megatons and 261,136 megatons, respectively. These yields were 74.8 percent and 68.9 percent below the ten-year average. However, while drought conditions clearly impacted barley production in 2000 and 2008, the drought effects in other years do not appear to be as significant (Syrian Arab Republic, 2017c: 2). Drought 2's barley yields in 2008 were higher than 2000, due to the expansion of irrigation that occurred from 2000 to 2005: Irrigated yields in 2008 were 89,271 megatons in comparison with 2000 when yields were 14,223 megatons (Syrian Arab Republic, 2017c: 2). While the low yields from 2000 and 2008 are consistent with claims of drought, 2004 and 2005 also experienced below-average barley production at 527,193 megatons and 767,416 megatons, respectively. These figures are also below production from the drought years of 2007 and 2009, which experienced yields of 784,479 megatons and 845,669 megatons, respectively, though the 2004 and 2005 figures are still well above the 2000 and 2008 levels. These below-average yields highlight the difficulty in attributing declines in barley production only to drought conditions.

Cotton production also reflects similar trends. Nationally, cotton production peaked in 2004 and 2005 at just over 1 megaton before declining considerably in 2006 and 2007 when national production was approximately 700,000 tons. The average amount of cotton produced in 2003–2007 was approximately 850,000 tons but from the limited sample size it is difficult to determine if 2004 and 2005 or 2006 and 2007 are statistical outliers (Al-Hindi, 2010: 9). National cotton production continued at approximately 2006 and 2007 levels in 2008, indicating that cotton production was more resilient to the environmental changes that occurred during this time period than were other crops (Al-Hindi, 2010: 9).

Regional Vulnerability: Agricultural Impact in the Northeast and East (Irrigated Areas, Wheat, and Barley)

The northeastern and eastern provinces (Deir ez-Zor, Hassake, and Raqqa) were the most dependent on agriculture, particularly strategic crops, and were therefore the most heavily impacted by the droughts. In particular, the Hassake governate – the most northeastern province, which shares a border with Turkey and is primarily inhabited by Kurds – has been framed as the most important agricultural region in Syria, containing 42 percent of arable land in Syria and 54–56 percent of total irrigated area (Al-Hindi, 2010: 5; Al-Shaib, 2010: 1; Soumi and Ma'an, 2010: 8). Hassake's intensive irrigation has also been critical in Syria's claims to a greater portion of the Euphrates river in negotiations with upstream Turkey.[8]

The 2006–2009 drought severely impacted agricultural production in the region, and 2007–2008 was said to be the worst drought year in forty years, particularly for winter crops such as wheat and barley (Al-Shaib, 2010: 1; Qatna, 2010: 1, 3). The drought, the failure to modernize irrigation infrastructure, and ineffective agricultural policy were said to be the main cause of this phenomenon (Nasr, 2010: 9). Urban spread also represented a threat to agricultural land (Khudour, 2010: 5–6). In terms of agricultural production, the eastern provinces had

---

[8] See sections of Chapter 3 on transboundary water interactions over the Euphrates waters between Syria and Turkey.

produced roughly 56–58 percent of total national wheat production since 2003 (Al-Hindi, 2010: 8), yet wheat production steadily fell from 4.9 million tons in 2006, to 4 million tons in 2007, to 2.1 million tons in 2008 (Al-Shaib, 2010: 1–2; see Table 5.8). Barley experienced similar losses, from 1.2 million tons in 2006, to 785,000 tons in 2007, to 261,000 tons in 2008 (Al-Shaib, 2010: 1–2). However, it is important to note that while wheat production in the eastern provinces fell proportionately to national wheat production, production did not appear to be more severely impacted in the East than in the rest of Syria (Al-Hindi, 2010: 8). Furthermore, corn production actually increased by nearly 40 percent in 2008 in comparison to the average production from 2003–2007 (Al-Hindi, 2010: 10). Cotton production remained steady from 2006 to 2008, although it was roughly one-third less than the height of production in 2004–2005 (Al-Hindi, 2010: 9).

Animal-agricultural resources are also impacted by fluctuations in temperature and food production, and the country's growing reliance on animal agriculture created distinct food and climate vulnerabilities.

Food Production: Impact on Animal-Agricultural Vulnerability to Drought

Livestock production is particularly affected by the failure of feed crops (Qatna, 2010: 2). By one account, 70 percent of livestock were lost in the East during Drought 2 due to the prohibitively high costs of feed and lack of grazing land (Al-Shaib, 2010: 2). However, other statistics show little change in production of livestock from 2003 to 2008 (Al-Hindi, 2010: 13–15). Goat production actually increased slightly in 2008, in line with a steady increase of production from 2003 to 2007. Sheep, who are highly dependent on the steppe, increased in numbers significantly during Drought 1, rising 73 percent between 2000 and 2006 (Khaddam, 2011: 74). In other words, while both droughts saw a direct impact on animal-agricultural, Drought 2 likely had a larger impact. This is possibly due to different policy decisions in the intervening years that accelerated the desertification of certain land resources and increased likelihood of migration by those who with agricultural livelihoods. Differential declines in livestock production might have changed the diets of people, especially those living in the eastern regions, possibly altering overall food accessibility. More broadly, however, food accessibility mostly pertains to

Table 5.8 *Wheat production in Deir ez-Zor and Hassake compared to country levels (2007–2011). Source: Elaborated by author from Syrian Arab Republic, 2017b.*

Year	Total			Nonirrigated			Irrigated		
	Yield (kg/ha)	Production (mt)	Area (ha)	Yield (kg/ha)	Production (mt)	Area (ha)	Yield (kg/ha)	Production (mt)	Area (ha)
Country Level									
2007	2,580	1,816,397	703,984	1,171	410,818	350,970	3,982	1,405,579	353,014
2009	1,573	947,848	602,713	382	115,708	302,581	2,773	832,140	300,132
2009	2,923	1,581,834	541,202	1,339	367,295	274,241	4,549	1,214,539	266,961
2010	2,372	1,307,144	550,958	1,327	371,276	279,758	3,451	935,868	271,200
2011	2,846	2,043,813	718,113	1,045	334,960	320,668	4,300	1,708,853	397,445
For Deir Ez-Zor									
2007	3,632	96,192	26,484	–	–	700	3,731	96,192	25,784
2008	2,937	123,531	42,059	–	–	–	2,937	123,531	42,059
2009	4,385	96,641	22,040	–	–	–	4,385	96,641	22,040
2010	3,625	105,268	29,038	–	–	–	3,625	105,268	29,038
2011	4,218	167,606	39,738	–	–	–	4,218	167,606	39,738
For Hassake									
2007	2,328	510,420	219,234	1,107	120,984	109,308	3,543	389,436	109,926
2008	1,046	158,148	151,186	–	–	81,755	2,278	158,148	69,431
2009	1,749	219,954	125,783	208	16,562	79,666	4,410	203,392	46,117
2010	2,207	277,668	125,808	–	–	–	3,625	105,268	29,038
2011	2,109	527,278	249,995	351	43,897	125,168	3,872	483,381	124,827

cereals and is a strong indicator of the health of a community's economy and agricultural sector, and can be measured as a function of per-capita food-price variability.

Food Prices: Durum and Soft Wheat

Although Syria experienced rising production costs, official prices outpaced these increases during Drought 2. The largest price increase for durum wheat occurred from 2007 to 2008, when the official price rose 30.6 percent from 1,180 SYP to 1,700 SYP, and prices continued to increase to 2,000 SYP in 2009 and 2,050 SYP in 2010.

In order to determine overall changes in food prices in Syria, however, soft wheat will be used as a representative of overall prices since it is so critical to consumers, particularly in more vulnerable regions. At the beginning of Drought 1, the official price of soft wheat was at 1,080 SYP, and the Ministry of Agriculture and Agrarian Reform reports this number to have stayed constant during the Drought 1 period, as shown in Figure 5.6.

This trend changed during Drought 2, which saw a dramatic 85.2 percent increase from 1,080 SYP in 2007 to 2,000 SYP in 2010. Where costs reached 2,167 SYP in 2010, exceeding the official price (Syrian Arab Republic, 2017d: 3, 4). For soft wheat, at least, there was a clear effort from the Syrian government from 2006 onwards to ensure that

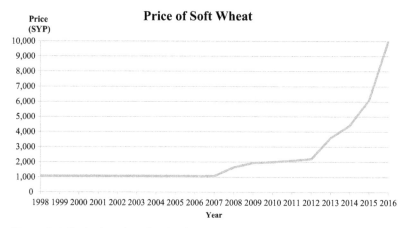

Figure 5.6 Peaks in price of soft wheat.

Source: Elaborated by author from Syrian Arab Republic, 2017d

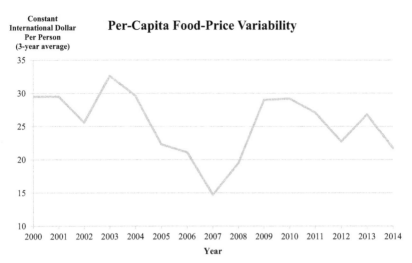

Figure 5.7 Per-capita food-price variability.
Source: Elaborated by author from FAO, 2014

the official price covered production costs, which more than doubled from 2007 to 2010 (Syrian Arab Republic, 2017e: 5). In fact, in 2010, production costs reached 2,167 SYP, exceeding official prices. These figures suggest that although food prices remained relatively stable during Drought 1, the losses compounded as a result of production trends during and after Drought 1, leading to a disproportionately more severe impact on wheat prices during Drought 2.

Per-Capita Food-Price Variability
Per-capita food-price variability adds another dimension to the analysis, allowing food prices to be compared across time.[9] Figure 5.7 illustrates food-price per-capita variability from 2000 to 2014, which reached a peak of 32.6 USD per person in 2003 and a low of $14.7 per person in 2007. Although there was a strong recovery from the major 2004–2008 dip, the figures were still lower in 2014 than in 2000. The end of Drought 1 saw a decrease of 13.22 percent while Drought 2 saw an increase of 38.4 percent. To summarize, food-production variability

---

[9] Per-capita food-price variability corresponds to the variability of the "food net per capita production value in constant 2004–2006 international $" as disseminated in FAOSTAT. The per-capita food-price variability compares the variations of the per-capita food production across countries and time.

during the Drought 2 period showed a steady deceleration, indicating overall instability in food security during this period.

Syria's population is highly vulnerable to variation in climate conditions and policy choices, as agriculture is its main economic sector in the country and is very dependent on water resources.

Value Added of Agriculture (Share to Gross Domestic Product)

The value of economic sectors to national productivity is usually measured by their contribution to the GDP. In developed economies, the industrial sector provides the biggest share. In Syria, however, agriculture has traditionally contributed significantly to GDP. Examining how agriculture's value added to the economy – represented by share of GDP – changes during periods of drought, we can understand the indirect impact of environmental factors on the economy as a whole and gain insight into how rural employment will be affected. The share of agriculture in the country's GDP is also a measure of the relationship between food insecurity and the state's structural vulnerability, outlined in Chapter 2 (Jones et al., 2017: 340). A state's structural vulnerability is its capacity and susceptibility – share of agriculture in GDP – which suggests that Syria had a relatively high structural vulnerability.

Official sources from the Syrian Central Bureau of Statistics show an increase of agriculture's contribution to GDP from 29 percent in 1988 to 32 percent in 2002, employing nearly 31 percent of the labor force (Syrian Arab Republic, 1999: 533; Mualla and Salman, 2002: 2). However, this data must be analyzed cautiously given that the GDP contribution includes overall agricultural activity, also beyond irrigated crops. Other non-official domestic sources evaluate the share at an average 22 percent of GDP from the 1990s to 2004 (Suleiman, 2005: 8). Table 5.9 synthesizes the share of agriculture in GDP from the rise of Ba'athism in 1963 to the early stages of Drought 2 in 2007.

Table 5.9 *Share of agriculture to GDP by percentage. Source: Seifan, 2009a: 7.*

1963	1970	1980	1990	2000	2007
33%	24%	22%	22%	22%	17%

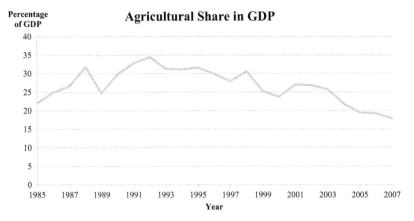

Figure 5.8 Value added from agriculture.
Source: Elaborated by author from World Bank, 2018b

The share of agriculture in GDP declined consistently from the period of the early Ba'ath days to the late 2000s, beginning in 1963 at 33 percent of GDP, dropping to 22 percent by 1980, while remaining consistent at 22 percent from 1990 until 2004, and finally reaching a low of 17 percent in 2007. These calculations are based on debates within the SAES, and do differ from the figures reported by external sources, such as the World Bank, which draw on governmental data. Most results, however, suggest an overall decline in the percentage contribution of agriculture to GDP during Drought 1.

Figure 5.8 shows agriculture as a percentage of GDP from 1985 to 2007; in the pre-drought period, it peaks in 1993 at 31.21 percent while sharply declining during Drought 1 from 29.9 percent to 27.1 percent. Meanwhile, the value added from agriculture continued to decline throughout the years prior to Drought 2 and during Drought 2 itself. The share of agriculture in GDP represented anemic growth in the sector, which was only 1.3 percent from 2005 to 2009 (Ibrahim, 2010: 9).[10] Although data for the years leading to 2010 is not available, trends suggest that agriculture continued to decline as an overall share of GDP, altering livelihoods and shifting key industries,

---

[10] Growth was not always slow during this period; in fact, in 2006, the agricultural sector grew 10.63 percent, but in 2007 there was a negative growth rate of 11.25 percent, matched by another 11 percent decrease in 2008 (Nasr, 2009: 5), leading to overall small growth.

particularly in rural areas of the country during the discussed periods of drought.

The declining trend of Figure 5.8 has been attributed to a wide range of factors, including not only the decline in agricultural output but also increases in industrial activity (Nasr, 2009: 5). Some economists connect the decline in agricultural output to the drought while others are more partial to explanations located at the intersection of drought and government policy, including marketization, food security, and land fragmentation after Syria left the United Arab Republic in 1961. This last factor is key because it reallocated land to medium-sized farms, bringing their share of arable land from 15 percent in 1963 to 52 percent in 1968 (Al-Qadi, 2009: 64; Seifan, 2009a: 11). Syrian economists note that global preferences for larger, capitalized farms meant that the smaller, traditional farms lost out, decreasing the overall role of agriculture nationwide. Understanding the role of agriculture at the local level is also critical, particularly in the case of the vulnerable Jazira region. Major transformations occurred from 2000 to 2009 in the agricultural sector, which gained productivity but lost large numbers of jobs, to the tune of approximately 20 percent of the total labor force (Aita, 2009: 3).

In conclusion, both national trends and regional data demonstrate that the role of agriculture in the Syrian economy as a share of GDP declined during both periods of drought, with Drought 2 undergoing a more significant decline. The implications of this for employment and individual economic security, symbolized by displacement and perceptions of corruption, will be discussed more in detail in the next sections of this chapter, both as an indicator of vulnerability and as a measure of (lacking) resilience.

Poverty as a Measure of Human Security

Poverty is an essential measure of human security and is intimately linked with employment and migration trends. Rural populations in Syria are most likely to seek employment in agriculture to achieve economic security as it is the largest sector of the economy, so employment in agriculture can be a proxy for the ability to maintain a livelihood. Poverty has been categorized by Syrian economists into three types: (1) human poverty, which is based on lack of health, education, or opportunities; (2) absolute poverty, which is based on the national poverty line; and (3) material poverty, which is based on both income and quality of life (Nasr, 2009: 3).

The face of poverty in Syria has changed over the past twenty years but was still a major national issue in the buildup to the 2011 uprising. In fact, for the prominent Syrian writer and dissident Yassin Haj Saleh, extreme poverty and unemployment were the main triggers of the uprising. While poverty had appeared to be decreasing throughout the second half of the twentieth century after the liberalization market reforms in the mid 2000s, poverty spiked, encompassing 37 percent of the population with an income under 2 USD/day and 11 percent under 1 USD/day.[11] The trend identified by Haj Saleh can be traced through an analysis of poverty levels during Drought 1 and Drought 2 at the national, regional, and local levels. Consistent and rigorous regional data regarding average incomes and relative poverty is generally not available before 2005, but existing data does suggest that poverty decreased in the late 1990s and early 2000s before increasing again. The national poverty ratio was reported at 20.1 percent in 2004 and 35.2 percent in 2007, suggesting drastic rises in poverty levels during the Drought 2 years (World Bank, 2019). Regional-level data shows that the increase was universal: The urban poverty ratio increased from 28.5 percent to 30.8 percent over 2004–2007, while the rural poverty ration increased from 31.8 percent to 36.9 percent in the same years. The increase in poverty has been attributed to widespread unemployment, which was a key part of debates around the failure of the liberalizing reforms.

Unemployment

The Debate around Unemployment Numbers

Under a more market-oriented system, the pecuniary effects of increased employment is meant to replace the need for social support through government transfers to vulnerable populations. Employment levels were therefore hotly debated as a marker of the success of reform initiatives; predictably, official data showed falling unemployment after 2005 while many impartial experts found a rise in unemployment during the same period. For these Syrian economists, the shift to small

---

[11] These metrics are widely used as international baselines for absolute poverty. Based on author's interview with Yassin Haj Saleh, Istanbul, July 18, 2016.

and medium-sized enterprises compounded the effect of the drought to produce overwhelming job loss in the agricultural sector, which was not offset by adequate official retraining programs (Seifan, 2009a: 17, 28). The result, therefore, was increasing total unemployment as well as a shift in the demographics of the unemployed. In 2004, the official unemployment rate was 12.3 percent, and in 2006 it had officially dropped to 8.2 percent (Suleiman, 2005: 17). In 2009, it was supposedly 11.5 percent, with 16 percent of employed individuals actually only working two days a week or less, though nongovernmental experts have suggested it was closer to 23 percent (Aita, 2009: 17; Ibrahim, 2010: 11). However, by 2009, 24 percent of the unemployed were between twenty and twenty-four years old, a high proportion, since it suggests these people are unable to enter stable long-term careers (Seifan 2009a: 17; Soumi and Ma'an, 2010: 33–34). Additionally, the increases in unemployment had predominantly been in the agricultural sector, which disproportionately affected rural areas.

Unemployment in Agriculture: Overall Trends

Figure 5.9 illustrates the stark decline in agricultural employment from 2000 to 2010 using data from the International Labour Organization (ILO). Although this decline has been attributed to the two major droughts, much of the decline occurred during the non-drought years

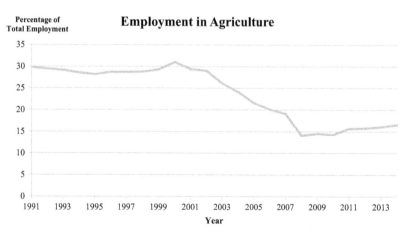

Figure 5.9 Employment in agriculture as a percentage of total employment (country level).
Source: Elaborated by author from ILO, 2019

from 2002 to 2006. The downward trend in the 2000s was part of a larger trend of declining agricultural dependence in Syria; in the 1960s, almost 60 percent of the jobs were related to agriculture, but this number declined as the country industrialized. However, through the 1990s, agriculture provided 30 percent of all jobs in Syria, which shows that it was still an important sector and that job losses in agriculture could endanger the livelihoods of much of the population (Daoudy, 2005: 106).

Looking at actual employment figures, we can see the extent to which the population was affected. In 2006, 951,000 people were employed in agriculture, but by the second quarter of 2009 there were only 761,000 agricultural jobs (Qatna, 2009: 12). Drought 2 clearly had an impact, as it had the single largest decline in agricultural employment, down from 19.1 percent to 14.1 percent between 2007 and 2008 (ILO, 2019). Literature from 1995 suggests that agricultural employment was 28.2 percent, actually increasing slightly throughout the Drought 1 years to 29.4 percent. After the end of Drought 1, however, agricultural employment dropped quickly, with the decline continuing through Drought 2. During this second drought, agricultural employment declined 5.8 percent from 20.1 percent to 14.3 percent. This suggests that Drought 2 constituted a much harsher set of conditions for agricultural employment than Drought 1.

The stark change in agricultural employment from 2000 to 2009 mirrored other major transformations occurring in the sector. While productivity increased by 60 percent, about 20 percent of jobs were lost; notably, these losses had a differentiated impact across gender. Unsurprisingly, women were more likely to work in the agricultural and informal sectors so about 50 percent of women lost their jobs during this period (Aita, 2009: 3–4). Meanwhile, in the years 2001–2007 the net average creation only amounted to 36,000 jobs yearly: Men gained 65,000 jobs per year while women lost 29,000 jobs. Outside the agricultural sector, about 105,000 jobs were created every year. Data shows that 98,000 jobs were lost in 2008 in the combined agricultural and public sectors with men losing 141,000 jobs while women gained 43,000 jobs. In particular, over six years during the post-Drought 1 and Drought 2 periods, women lost 57 percent of their jobs in agriculture, which constituted 65 percent of overall female employment (Aita, 2009: 3–5).

Decreasing employment in agriculture can be understood as a vulnerability factor for the most rural sectors of Syrian society. This suggests that while food production was declining so too were employment opportunities in agrarian communities that were dependent on food production. This left rural populations with two choices: Move and try to find work elsewhere, or stay and be unemployed. The difficult choice was even more common for populations in the most vulnerable rural areas of Syria, as in the eastern and northeastern provinces.

Regional Vulnerability and Impacts: Northeast and East

Unemployment

The poorest people in rural Syria have historically suffered most under drought conditions, particularly as 20 percent of the rural population works in animal production (Hidou, 2010: 1; Qatna, 2010: 2). Animal production is often even harder hit than agriculture during droughts; for example, 70 percent of animals died or were slaughtered during Drought 2 and then sold at low prices, due to lack of feed, which meant that 59,000 of the smallest producers lost all of their animals (Al-Shaib, 2010: 2). By 2010, the drought had caused high unemployment and lack of sufficient work opportunities in the eastern and northeastern provinces, a circumstance actually recognized by the government (Al-Hindi, 2010: 28; Al-Muheissin, 2010: 4; Dardari: 2009: 46; Hidou, 2010: 1; Qatna, 2010: 4; Soumi and Ma'an, 2010: 6). According to Syrian economist Samir Seifan, the massive impact of drought on the Jazira region as well as the overall governorate of Hassake in which it is located signifies the region's low resilience as a result of agricultural erosion, frequent droughts, and land fragmentation, which led to government neglect and inequality (Seifan, 2009a: 10).

Figures 5.10 and 5.11 illustrate official agricultural employment data by governorate from multiple different datasets provided by the Central Bureau of Statistics. One dataset covered 1994 and 2000–2006, while others covered individual years from 2006 to 2010. While the two types of datasets were not perfectly calibrated – the numbers for 2006 in some governorates varied slightly – when aggregated they provide reasonable insight into official employment figures and can be usefully compared to estimates from Syrian economists.

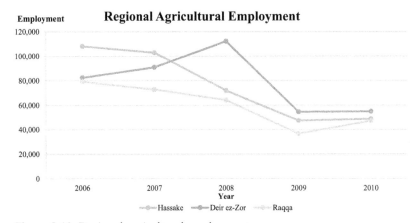

Figure 5.10 Regional agricultural employment.
Source: Elaborated by author from the Central Bureau of Statistics, 2018a, 2018b

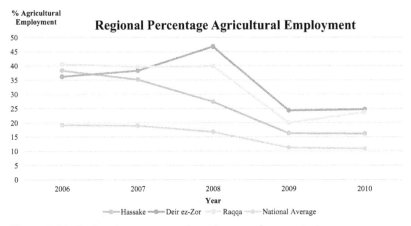

Figure 5.11 Regional percentage of employment from agriculture.
Source: Elaborated by author from the Central Bureau of Statistics, 2018a, 2018b

These figures show decline in agricultural jobs in all three eastern cities, with the biggest declines in Hassake. Earlier datasets over agricultural employment in Hassake show a significant decline in jobs from 2003 to 2004 when the percentage of workers decreased from 44.5 percent to 36.3 percent, a decline that continued through the peak of the Drought 2 between 2007 and 2009 when the percentage fell again from 35.2 percent to 16.3 percent, representing a loss of nearly 60,000 jobs in four years (Central Bureau of Statistics, 2018a, 2018b).

However, numbers from Deir ez-Zor are markedly different from those in Hassake. They show an increase in the percentage of agricultural workers from 2000 to 2002 when employment peaked at 66.7 percent, suggesting that agricultural employment in Deir ez-Zor was more resilient to pressures from Drought 1 (Central Bureau of Statistics, 2018b). Similar to the evolution of agricultural employment in Hassake, employment declines significantly between 2003 and 2004, falling from 61.7 percent to 43.5 percent, and then rebounds in the first half of Drought 2, with an increase from 36.2 percent in 2006 to 46.8 percent in 2008 (Central Bureau of Statistics, 2018a). After 2008, however, agricultural employment fell significantly from 46.8 percent to 24.3 percent. In total, less than 30,000 jobs were lost in Deir ez-Zor from 2006 to 2010, but the region underwent its biggest annual loss of almost 60,000 jobs between 2008 and 2009.

Poverty

Poverty in Syria is concentrated in the northeastern regions of Idlib, Aleppo, Raqqa, Deir ez-Zor, and Hassake with the highest rates of poverty seen in the northeastern rural areas at 17.9 percent, followed by the northeastern urban areas where they remain significant at 11.2 percent (Marzouk, 2013: 59). Similarly, 62 percent of the urban poor and 52 percent of the rural poor live in the three northeastern regions. The region is also less affluent in general with household expenditure in Hassake amounting to a mere 75.4 percent of the national average in 2013 as compared to Damascus where it was 148.6 percent (Marzouk, 2013: 61). This drastic variation in poverty across regions underscores the inequality between the poorer, more vulnerable eastern cities and the wealthier urban capital and its immediate periphery. Hassake has the highest rate of poverty and unemployment in all of Syria (Khudour, 2010: 8).

Drought 2 destroyed the livelihood of over 50 percent of farmers nationwide of whom 486,312 lived in Hassake, 155,000 in Raqqa, and 41,000 in Deir ez-Sor (FAO, 2016a: 12; Qatna, 2010: 5). These are conservative estimates with alternative assessments suggesting that up to 750,000–800,000 people nationwide were at severe risk as a result of the drought (Al-Shaib, 2010: 2). The United Nations also recognized the dire straits of many small farmers and livestock producers as a direct consequences of the drought. In September 2008, the Office for the Coordination of Humanitarian Affairs launched an appeal to raise 20 million USD in support of over 1 million Syrians affected by the drought, of which 300,000 were most vulnerable and in need of immediate support (Syria Report, 2008, 2010a, 2010c; UNO-CHA, 2008). This considerable, almost unprecedented, international call for help demonstrates the severity of the crisis, even if very little funding ever reached the neediest segments of the population.

In conclusion, the northeastern provinces were hard hit by Drought 2, causing wide-scale unemployment and significantly raising poverty in vulnerable areas. To fully leverage the HECS framework as an analytical tool, patterns of urban–rural migration must be analyzed in relation to income levels and water availability since the urban–rural divide amplified the effect of climate variation and the ensuing policy choices.

Rapid Urbanization and Unequal Urban–Rural Access to Water

The Hassake region is a critical case study of how the overall trend of increasing rural and urban poverty interacted with patterns of migration to urban centers and exacerbated inequality and insecurity during Drought 1 and Drought 2. These paragraphs will outline trends in urbanization and patterns of unequal urban–rural access to water. The next sections will address more specifically the wave of outmigration from the eastern provinces that characterized Drought 2.

Key Trends
Patterns of urban–rural migration in Syria played into existing inequalities aggravating social vulnerability in rural areas. During the 1990s and 2000s, there were clear patterns of migration from rural areas to urban centers. The pre-Drought 1 period from 1990 to 1996 saw a 1.5 percent increase in the total ratio of the urban population and a 1.9 percent decrease in the rural population; Drought 1 saw a 1.1 percent increase in urban population and a 1.2 percent decrease in rural population; and Drought 2 saw a 1.54 percent increase in the urban population and a 1.52 percent decrease in the rural population. Figure 5.12 shows this relatively linear trend using data from the ILO. The percentage of the population living in rural areas decreased from 51.07 percent in 1990 to 41.53 percent in 2017. While the absolute

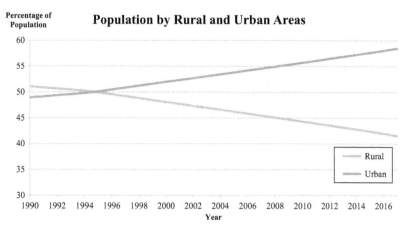

Figure 5.12 Population by rural and urban areas.
Source: Elaborated by author from the ILO, 2017

number of people living in rural areas actually increased from 1990 to 2010 as a result of population growth, the absolute numbers declined from 2010 to 2017 due to outmigration. In fact, there was an overall population decrease in the country over this period with an 18.6 percent decrease in the rural population and an 8.7 percent decrease in the urban population.

The accelerating trend of urbanization coincided with economic pressures on rural areas and the concentration of government benefits and employment opportunities in urban areas. Northeastern Syria's development had gone neglected for years by the time Drought 2 took place. Khudour (2010) outlines how regional urban centers tended to receive preferential treatment in terms of economic investment under Bashar al-Assad who courted urban businessmen more than rural peasants. Government investment in urban centers therefore ensured their economic development, which drew rural labor into cities. When the government did attempt rural or regional development projects, they largely failed because urban expansion was prioritized at the expense of agricultural land (Khudour, 2010: 5). The pre-Drought 1 period showed early trends of factionalization and gentrification of urban areas to the detriment of rural and agricultural communities who were largely left to live under conditions of accelerating poverty as a result of government policies and investment decisions (discussed in Chapter 4).

Urban–Rural Water Access

A divide between urban and rural communities' access to water is another prominent feature of structural inequality. Since 1990, the percentage of the rural population with access to improved water sources has consistently increased, whereas the percentage of the urban population with access to safe drinking water sources has steadily decreased. From 1997 to 2002 – prior to Drought 1 until the end of Drought 1 – rural access to safe drinking water went from 77.1 percent to 80.4 percent while urban access to safe drinking water went from 96 percent to 94.8 percent (FAO, 2016b). From 2007 to 2010 – the middle of Drought 2 to the end of Drought 2 – rural access increased from 83.8 percent to 87.2 percent whereas urban access dropped from 93.5 percent to 92.3 percent (FAO, 2016b). Therefore, while rural access to water substantially lagged behind urban access to safe water, rural access increased during Drought 1 and Drought 2 whereas urban access decreased.

A number of factors explain this decline in access to safe water in urban areas. For example, increased government use of wastewater in the municipal water-supply chain could have impacted urban communities' access to safe water (Khaddam, 2011: 64). Yet a more significant factor may have been increasing urbanization and the stress it placed on urban areas due to insufficient urban infrastructure development programs to accommodate urban growth. During this time, an increased share of water went to government irrigation projects away from human use both in rural and urban areas, contributing to overall stress on water resources and amplifying urban and rural poverty. For example, the government inaugurated yet another irrigation project on the Euphrates in 2010 with the objective to irrigate an additional 11,000 ha (Syria Report, 2010g). This matrix over the urban–rural divide for water access underscores the importance of the dynamic interaction between climate factors, economic and social insecurity, and the structure of equitable access and distribution established in the HECS model.

Social Vulnerability: Internal Migration, Mismanagement of Drought, and Corruption

The economic vulnerabilities outlined in the previous section including unemployment, rural poverty, and urban–rural divides interact with social vulnerabilities. This section explores social vulnerability from three key perspectives: (1) internal migration and displacement; (2) state mismanagement of environmental and economic vulnerabilities; and (3) corruption. Each of these three social elements contributed to the overall human–environmental–climate insecurity experienced by Syrians in 2011, particularly those from the rural northeastern provinces.

The Displaced: Al-Nazihin[12]

Historically, internal migration and emigration in Syria have been viewed as a consequence of lacking rural job opportunities caused by inadequate regional development plans (Seifan, 2009b; 18). In the twentieth century, when many people moved from rural areas to cities, they retained close economic ties to their place of origin. Together with high costs of living in urban areas, this contributed to a stream of people returning to rural areas in a phenomenon of "reverse migration," though internal migration trends still signaled overall urbanization (Seifan, 2009b: 19). Emigration increased throughout the twentieth century as well, and the UNDP estimates show a steady increase starting in the early 1990s at an average rate of about 14,000 persons per year (Aita, 2009: 47).

Drought 1 and Drought 2 accelerated existing migration trends. The emigration rate was 3.4 percent from 1990 to 1995, 2.5 percent from 1995 to 2000, 7.2 percent from 2000 to 2005, and 10.2 percent from 2005 to 2010. Although these intervals do not perfectly align with drought years, we clearly see very large emigration during Drought 2 whereas emigration was only high during the latter years of Drought 1. Previous bouts of emigration were due to the tendency for upwardly mobile citizens to relocate in search for higher paying jobs as previously stable industries of agriculture and manufacturing began to shrink. In fact, the bulk of migration has traditionally been one of rural youth temporarily moving to Gulf states in search of more lucrative opportunities (Al-Qadi, 2009: 65). The massive jump in emigration from 2005 to 2010 prior to the conflict has

---

[12] The migrants from the northeast have been referred to as the "displaced" populations (*al-Nazihin*) since the 2006–2010 drought.

sometimes been attributed to Drought 2, though international sources have tended to confuse the number of farmers severely impacted by the drought with the numbers of farmers actually fleeing the region.

Drought 2 also saw internal migration, especially from the eastern regions to the cities, increasing pressure on urban areas in terms of affordable housing and employment (Bakour et al., 2009: 4; Al-Hindi, 2010: 29). Drought 2, however, saw different patterns of migration: In the past, individual family members would leave a home town to find jobs elsewhere while the bulk of the family stayed behind, but with Drought 2 suddenly the exodus involved the entire extended family (Qatna 2010: 5). In particular, 37,000 families left the Jazira/Hassake governorate in just 2007 (Seifan, 2009a: 12; Al-Shaib, 2010: 2). From 2009 to 2010, an additional 40,000 to 60,000 rural families were pushed to the outskirts of major cities from Hassake (Al-Shaib, 2010: 2; Qatna, 2010: 5; Khouri and Byringiro, 2014: 110; UNOCHA, 2010: 5). The total was estimated between 370,000 and 460,000 individuals. According to the president of the Agricultural Union of Hassake, by 2010 roughly 38 percent of the population emigrated (Al-Muheissin, 2010: 4). The migration trends accelerated rapidly after the uprising so that between 2011 and 2016, and additional 30 percent of the rural population departed (FAO, 2017b: 6). The abandonment of the northeastern and eastern provinces by so many families paints a relatively dire picture of the state of affairs during Drought 2, a conclusion supported by a fact-finding mission in 2009. The mission investigated the impact of the drought as well as the cancelation of food and fuel subsidies on the region, and it notes very high levels of malnutrition and nutrition-related diseases such as anemia. Malnutrition increased by 370 percent in Hassake from 2006 to 2008 while it increased 229 percent in Deir ez-Zor over the same time period (Syria Report, 2009c). The mission's report noted other signs of the devastating social impact of the drought and mismanagement: similarly, 70 percent of students had been withdrawn from schools between 2006 and 2008 (Syria Report, 2009c). In other words, if the analysis were to apply international categorizations of environmental migrants reviewed under Chapter 2 to the Syrian case, the families of farmers displaced in Jazira at the time of the 2006–2010 drought would primarily constitute nonadaptive agents and victims.

State Mismanagement(s)

Some domestic sources felt that the government had put in place effective policies to properly address the effects of the drought although many still argued for a strengthened future response (Qatna, 2010: 6). Emergency policies included subsidized livestock feed, food aid to the poorest people in the northeast, extensions of loan periods and debt-forgiveness programs (Al-Muheissin, 2010: 5; Qatna, 2010: 6). Longer-term programs consisted of appropriating state land for poor farmers, providing grants to pastoralists to renew their herds, funding projects to encourage female employment in rural villages, and digging wells to compensate for water deficits (Al-Muheissin, 2010: 5; Al-Shaib 2010: 3). According to many experts, however, these policies came too late and were not implemented in a good way, limiting their ability to mitigate the drought's effects in the eastern provinces (Al-Shaib 2010: 3; Bakour 2009: 10; Bakour et al., 2009: 5; Nasr 2009: 9–10; Qatna 2009: 10–11; Seifan 2009a: 11). In discussion with the author, an experienced Syrian water engineer blamed the government for failing to implement sustainable policies, putting in place only 10 percent of promised infrastructure without the necessary services for delivery. This coincided with expanding soil salinity in most of the Jazira/Hassake region. Projects were not properly monitored or evaluated, and policy mistakes, like categorizing water-intensive cotton as a strategic crop, were never corrected.[13]

Concrete development plans for Hassake, Raqqa, and Deir ez-Zor were in place prior to the drought. They were part of a Five-Year Plan that allocated 523 million USD to Raqqa and Hassake for 2006–2010 (Syria Report, 2006). At the time, these regions were some of the most disadvantaged in the country, with unemployment at 26.5 percent in Hassake and illiteracy at 38.6 percent in Raqqa. The government once again proposed increasing irrigated areas as a potential solution to increase the production of wheat, cotton, and olive oil. This was accompanied by a 2008 plan in which the government proposed to invest in irrigation, targeting an additional 7.6 million ha in the northeast, although it is unclear to what degree this was implemented (Al-Hindi, 2010: 29). In 2009, the expansion of irrigated surfaces from

---

[13] Author's interview with a Syrian water expert on condition of anonymity, Beirut, December 4, 2015.

the Tigris river was reintroduced as a potential solution, this time in parallel with supplying the population with food support (Syria Report, 2009d). Beyond the pervasive recommendation to increase irrigated areas, the government had relatively few plans and suggestions, many of which were not well designed. For example, the decision to cancel fuel subsidies in 2008 hit farmers hard by increasing production costs, and while the government established an Agriculture Support Fund just three days later, it only began payments a full year later (Syria Report, 2008, 2009b).

The government's direct response to the drought was also criticized as not being well adapted to agricultural conditions on the ground and for sending contradictory signals by ending subsidies during the drought (Hidou, 2010: 1). Erian (2011) points to the inefficiency of the traditional reactive drought-management plans which were poorly coordinated and limited to ailing areas instead of extending to more comprehensive prevention and recovery mechanisms. Additionally, the government was perceived as having been totally unaware of the migration crisis until it was too late (Al-Shaib, 2010: 6).[14] By 2009, calls to reintroduce subsidies were matched by calls to expand migrant services (Qatna, 2009: 11, Soumi, 2009: 5; Soumi and Ma'an, 2010: 33–34).

Corruption

As mentioned in the previous chapter, corruption was a major obstacle to equitable and inclusive economic development in Syria. In the early 2000s, it was estimated that 200 billion lira were lost to corruption every year, amounting to 20–40 percent of GDP (Dib, 2009: 98). Seifan has already established a link between economic liberalization and the spread and intensification of corruption, and Nasr has

---

[14] In an interview with the author, a young activist involved in the Damascus mobilizations attributed the emergence of his political consciousness to when he joined youth efforts in Damascus to provide aid to displaced populations who were living parched in slums around the capital, completely neglected by government structures. According to him, the regime was so oblivious to the crisis, even though almost all the people were below the poverty line, that the United Nations distributed all the food. He also relayed a rumor circulated at the time that placed responsibility for rural displacements from the northeastern provinces on Turkey's upstream cuts of the Khabour river, in combination with the end of subsidies and the effects of climate change. Beirut, December 7, 2015.

Corruption Index

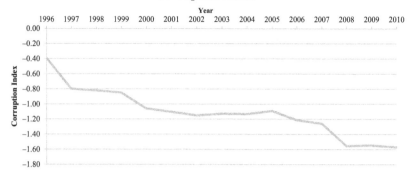

Figure 5.13 Corruption index. The corruption index reflects perceptions of the extent to which public power is exercised for private gain, including both petty and grand forms of corruption, as well as "capture" of the state by elites and private interests; Scale of +2.5 (strong governance performance, least corruption) to −2.5 (weak governance, most corruption).
Source: Elaborated by author from World Bank, 2016

extended these insights by calling for institutional reform to achieve the social objectives of the social market economy (Nasr, 2009: 13). Other economists took the view that the primary outcome of corruption is to transfer wealth from poor to rich, so any system with corruption would be disadvantaging the poor (Dib, 2009: 93).

According to a 2008 Gallup poll, Syria had the fourth lowest transparency rating in the world with only 2.1 percent of its population believing its government was transparent (al-Qadi, 2009: 62). Interestingly, al-Qadi notes that the only countries lower than Syria in this poll had already collapsed into civil war. Figure 5.13 shows public perception of the extent to which public power is exercised for private gain expressed as a corruption index. Public trust was already low in 1996 but continued to decline until 2010 with a sharp decline after 2005. This graph demonstrates the extent to which corruption was a major source of human insecurity up to 2011 and a key to social vulnerability.

Summary

This chapter applied the HECS framework to the case of Syria by analyzing sources of environmental, economic, and social vulnerability leading up to 2011 and the interaction between these factors, particularly the role of political factors such as ideology in producing social vulnerability. While parts of the international academic literature surveyed at the beginning of this chapter accepts the climate-conflict thesis, domestic sources point to another conclusion: The political context, not water scarcity, itself worsened the human security of the vulnerable populations of Syria, paving the way for the Syrian uprising. A quantitative review of key indicators clearly points to a vulnerability nexus in the northeastern and eastern regions where there was already unusually high levels of poverty and unemployment and high dependence on the agricultural sector. Combined, these circumstances created a disproportionate impact of weather-related events on rural communities in the region. While disagreement exists in the surveyed literature concerning the extent of the drought's impact on contested issues such as migration, most scholars agree that the government's water, food, and land policies did not help rural societies but rather were a driver of Syria's low climate resilience.

Syria's high environmental vulnerability is a function of its arid climate and high dependence on irrigated water, groundwater, and source water. These environmental characteristics combined with the critical role water plays in an agriculture-intensive economy such as the Syrian economy explain why Syrian communities revolted against government resource mismanagement. The trend of below-average rainfall and above-average temperatures leading to lower production outputs and yields of livestock was exacerbated by poor timing and inadequate government policies. These dynamics increased economic and social vulnerability in the form of unemployment, poverty, migration, and rising inequality.

The analytical comparison of Drought 1 and Drought 2 based on information from international academics and organizations, Syrian experts and government officials supports the claim that climate change alone was not the cause of food and water insecurity during the decades prior to the uprising. While the Syrian conflict cannot be directly and entirely linked to climate change, the region was left especially vulnerable to geographical, political, and economic threats. These catalyzed into a crisis due to mismanaged agricultural and water policies during the droughts. Throughout the chapter, however, we have seen the potential role of policy solutions in limiting the consequences of the drought on vulnerable populations (or at least of not worsening their impact for them). Particularly effective policies could consist of renewed agricultural subsidies, appropriate tax breaks, job creation, and civil-society development initiatives in rural communities, especially in the northeastern and eastern provinces.

6 | *Syria*

A (Hi)story of Vulnerability, Resistance, and Resilience

Over the past few decades, a climate–conflict nexus has emerged drawing on narratives of collapse, and it has more recently been applied to the Syrian case. According to this logic, climate change caused the 2006–2010 drought in Syria, the drought caused agricultural failure, agricultural failure caused poverty and discontent culminating in the uprising. This book questions this line of reasoning given Syria's history of climate, water, and food insecurity, arguing that government policies were at the heart of Syria's vulnerabilities in the buildup to the uprising.

Water and broader environmental conditions define Syria's historical, sociopolitical and economic development as well as its interactions with neighboring countries. I fully support the scientific consensus that climate change is happening and that global action is urgently needed. But whether climate change caused the Syrian uprising is a separate question, and, as this book demonstrates, little evidence suggests climate change in Syria sparked popular revolt in 2011, and a lot of evidence suggests it did not. While I agree climate change worsened the drought, government policies were largely responsible for turning the drought into a national crisis. In fact, even if we were to accept that climate change provoked the drought, unemployed farmers, who were the biggest casualties of the drought, did not incite the protests. Indeed, the original issues protested were wholly unrelated to the drought. Rather, the first impulse for the uprisings was a show of solidarity with the Tunisian and Egyptian revolutions. Even in the second wave of protests held in Deraa, they had no environmental basis but erupted over the torture of schoolchildren.

To evaluate the central claim that climate change caused the Syrian conflict, this book starts by introducing a new theoretical approach: Human–Environmental–Climate Security (HECS). Building on a critical environmental-security perspective, the HECS framework challenges core assumptions behind the climate-conflict hypothesis in

Syria by bringing in economic and sociopolitical factors that interact with resource variation. In doing so, I identify the ideological and policy drivers of human insecurity that impacted Syria's water and food security. Using official primary sources, debates from Syrian experts as well as interviews with Syrian experts, activists, and refugees, I explore how the policy decisions of the Syrian government under Hafez al-Assad and Bashar al-Assad significantly contributed to the vulnerability of the rural population in the decades that preceded the uprisings of 2011. The book concludes that, ultimately, political factors were more important than a climate-induced drought in the buildup to the uprising. This perspective is applicable beyond the case of climate change and human insecurity in Syria.

The book starts by exploring the securitization of climate change and engages with the scholarly debate around environmental security, human security, water and food security, and climate-induced migration. The first sections outline the broadening of traditional security studies to include non-Western perspectives and a more diverse array of potential threats, including environmental degradation, poverty, water scarcity, and climate change. Critical-security stances are essential in these debates as they examine structural inequalities of power and distribution of resources, while also considering the role of states as providers of insecurity and centering the narrative on individuals and groups that address power gaps. The discussion shows how debates on modernization and development still grapple with the concept of food security, which has evolved from a narrow focus on food availability to a more multidimensional approach that includes food availability, affordability, basic needs, entitlement programs, and sustainability. It concludes that the literature has not conclusively shown linkages between climate change, food insecurity, migration, and conflict – both globally and in Syria.

By contextualizing the evolution of Syria's water policy in the regional setting, my inquiry also further broadens the scope to understand how the management of Syria's main sources of water has been impacted by its relations with Turkey and the upstream neighbor's water projects. This chapter also carries great value for global action in showing how international understandings of human security can be harmonized with local norms. The historical assessment of water policy in Syria and the Middle East gives us insight into the ways in which the cultural and institutional norms surrounding water were put in place over the millennia. The sharing of water resources has determined the rise and fall of the great civilizations in the region as well as the development of rules and norms that have framed local practices around water-sharing. Due to Syria's arid environment and dependence on agriculture, water has been an imperative resource, subject to legislation, for as long as the country has had agriculture. Local norms were often based on Islamic legal principles and were codified until the introduction, in the late nineteenth and early twentieth centuries, of modern legislations, though these legislations themselves were often inspired by local norms. In the 1940s, the newly independent Syria drew on water legislation from Shari'a law, the Ottoman Majalla Code, and the French Water Code, and featured water-security promotion (quantity, drinkable water, water for irrigation) and environmental security (pollution, quality of groundwater resources), values that date back to the beginnings of Islam. This historical overview also explains how the norms surrounding water set up during early Islam would be treated as best practices now: Social justice, or ensuring that water was accessible to all, and sustainability, or water usage without environmental degradation, were key norms. Although these norms were picked up by later laws when Syria became independent, a shift started in the 1960s when they were no longer adhered to.

By centering the narrative on vulnerable populations in Syria, and, more broadly, in the Global South, the HECS framework provides an in-depth analysis of the human-security impact of the environment, including poverty, unemployment, marginalization, and the failure of sustainable development. In so doing, it calls for greater precision in establishing the conditions under which environmental degradation creates risks to human security more globally. Such an approach is intended to place individual human lives at the center of the narrative, making food and water insecurity a critical component of understanding how macro political, economic, and environmental trends drive individuals access to their daily sustenance.

This framework provides, therefore, a new perspective that positions vulnerability and sustainability at the center of environmental and climate risk. It sets the theoretical background for this analysis by defining climate security in human-security terms as a series of threats and vulnerabilities posed by variation in climate conditions as well as in elite decisions to human and ecological life. A crucial element is its applicability and utility in analyzing and untangling the structural, political, and economic factors of human insecurity and conflict – critical elements for understanding both the Syrian case and situations of human insecurity more broadly. It also seeks to move beyond deterministic narratives and Orientalist biases about the risks of population growth and mobility, demand-induced scarcity, resource depletion, and insecurity, which fall into patterns of core–periphery and North–South divides. Additionally, the framework draws attention to three main types of factors: structural, vulnerability, and resilience. Each of these three factors are closely examined. The first type are structural factors, including context-specific preconditions for political, social, economic, and climate vulnerability and human insecurity. The second type are vulnerability factors, which involve development conditions (water, agricultural, employment, poverty), policies (corruption, subsidies), and environmental variables (precipitation, temperature).

This approach crucially acknowledges that interacting environmental, political, and economic pressures occur in tandem with threats to water and food security and their ensuing migration and poverty, which in turn reinforce the original pressures in a recurring positive feedback loop. In this framework, vulnerability and resilience are parallel concepts that reveal how a lack of sustainability in combination with specific structural factors and inequalities threatens human life through the inability of systems to cope with unexpected change. A water-related vulnerability analysis demonstrates how specific ideological and policy choices were the guiding principles behind these disruptions. By defining the negative outcomes of such policy choices in terms of their vulnerability effects, this analysis shows how the different dimensions of threats measured in the HECS framework can be understood as interlocking and interrelated. Working in connection with the concept of vulnerability, resilience is a critical component of a community's susceptibility to climate insecurity, but in Syria this was relatively low due to poor governance and institutional weaknesses. Rural communities in the northeast have been unable to respond to and cope with risks and changes. This understanding of climate vulnerability and resilience is a critical contribution to international policy debates on the need to optimize regional and local responses in the face of global warming.

The research identifies key policy decisions taken at critical times of Syria's history. Promising food security was one way that new

Ba'athist elites of the 1960s established legitimacy in their rural constituencies, and fulfilling their promises required new agricultural and economic policies. The "Rural Contract" led to the intensification of land reclamations started in 1958, as well as the establishment of state farms and peasant cooperatives to enhance equity in land management and distribution. Under Hafez al-Assad's Ba'athist regime (1970–2000), the government tried to appease its rural base by prioritizing food security above all else, implementing agrarian reforms to collectivize agriculture. Increasing domestic food production therefore became a strategic goal for the Syrian state, in part because it allowed it greater political independence from Western countries but also in part because of fears of being able to feed a projected population of 30 million by 2025. The "peasant" became a symbol of the new ideology and a path to prosperity and legitimacy.

Agrarian reforms enhanced living conditions in the countryside. However, the improved opportunities came at the expense of sustainable water use since large-scale irrigation in rural areas depleted groundwater resources and degraded soil quality, and, ultimately, resulted in human insecurity in the form of land-tenure disputes and population displacement. Beyond the economic costs to the government's water-management approach were social costs; in particular, intensive dam construction forced local populations to relocate. Furthermore, land-reform policies that furthered Arabization, such as the "Arab Belt" policy, excluded Syrian Kurds from agricultural gains in the second half of the twentieth century. Ba'athist preferences also led to the implementation of water, food, and fuel subsidies that distorted market prices.

Decollectivization started early on under Hafez al-Assad but intensified when his son Bashar accessed power in 2000. The liberalization policies in the 1970s–1990s that aimed to increase the role of the private sector, including in the provision of welfare services, involved introducing market mechanisms; limiting the role of state intervention; offering a place in decision-making to business elites rather than trade unions and other corporations; and increasing privatization while keeping public ownership. In 2005, a major ideological shift occurred with the introduction of the social market economy, which aimed to model Syria's new economic transition on Germany's economic model after World War II. Under Bashar al-Assad's liberalizing influence, the regime tried to cater to urban businessmen and neoliberal international organizations such as the World Bank and the IMF by cutting key food and fuel subsidies and removing safety nets for farmers. While the state did follow its recommendations of subsidy reform, it did not adopt their prescriptions to undertake a gradual approach. These new policies coincided with a historically severe drought when farmers needed the support more than ever, leaving many without access to sufficient water or the ability to sell their produce. the two competing ideologies departed in the same fashion from the traditional values of social justice and water sustainability to create a unique set of vulnerabilities for rural Syria. The analytical comparison of 1998–2001 ("Drought 1") and 2006–2010 ("Drought 2") based on information from government official reports, international academics and organizations, and interviews with Syrian experts and policy-makers supports the claim that climate change alone was not the cause of food and water insecurity during the decades prior to the uprisings.

A longitudinal analysis of key indicators clearly points to a vulnerability nexus in the three governorates (Hassake, Deir ez-Zor, and Raqqa), where unusually high levels of poverty and unemployment and high dependence on the agricultural sector already existed. By the time the major drought of 2006–2010 had hit, the population exhibited high environmental, economic, and social vulnerability and low resilience, setting the stage for a crisis. Trends of below-average rainfall and above-average temperature resulted in lower production output, livestock yields, and higher food prices, exacerbated by poor timing and inadequate government policies. These dynamics increased economic and social vulnerability in the form of unemployment (particularly in agriculture) and poverty, created an urban–rural divide in water access, and triggered migration, corruption, and rising inequality. Corruption and migration were especially large sources of human insecurity up to 2011 and key to social vulnerability.

By 2010, it was clear that the neoliberal reforms had not been successful, according to renowned Syrian economists, water engineers, agricultural experts, and others involved in the SAES. In a series of exchanges and papers presented from 2005 to 2010, they evaluated the (in)effectiveness of the social market economy in terms of agricultural production, social welfare, employment, competition, crisis management, corruption, migration, and poverty, particularly during droughts. Domestic sources felt that the government had put in place effective policies to properly address the effects of the drought.

According to many Syrian experts, however, these policies came too late and were not implemented in a good way, limiting their ability to mitigate the drought's effects in the eastern provinces. Corruption was a major obstacle to equitable and inclusive economic development in Syria. In the early 2000s, it was estimated that 200 billion lira were lost to corruption every year, amounting to 20–40 percent of GDP.

While these factors might not have been sufficient to produce the Syrian uprising in 2011, the long-term structural seeds of conflict had been planted long before as a result of the government's unsustainable practices. The severe stress on water and land resources magnified inequities and produced a ticking bomb waiting to detonate. Once agricultural and fuel subsidies were removed and privatization of the economy was well under way, conflict became an increasingly likely scenario. The stress on water and agricultural resources aggravated human insecurity and became difficult to reverse. A certain path dependency had set in. In 2009, the government attempted to reinstate some of the subsidies to severely affected agricultural communities but failed because the community had already dispersed. In 2011 and 2012, faced with popular mobilization and then war, the government reversed its policy and started reinvesting in the agricultural sector (Syria Report, 2011a, 2012). The conflict, however, has increasingly decimated the sector; the situation became dramatic in 2018 with a severe shortage of farm laborers (Syria Report, 2015, 2016, 2017, 2018b). Losses in Syria's agricultural sector amounted to 16 billion USD since 2011 (Daher, 2018: 11). Syria's GDP decreased from 60.2 billion USD to 12.4 billion (Syria Report, 2018a).

Throughout the book, we have seen the potential role of policy solutions in limiting the consequences of the droughts on vulnerable populations (at least not worsening their impact on them). In other words, policy choices matter for dealing with climate change and reducing vulnerability and building resilience. In the case of Syria, particularly effective policies could consist of targeted agricultural subsidies, the elimination of corruption, job creation, and civil-society development initiatives in rural communities, especially in the northeast.

Since 2011, the Syrian Revolution has been crushed. Today, Syrians continue to mourn over one of the most tragic episodes in the country's rich history. The war intensified the patterns of human insecurity outlined for the previous decade: drastic regional disparities in the northeastern provinces, increased corruption with new networks of profit derived from war economies, entrenched political and economic domination by the military and security services, as well as business-men inside and outside the country (Daher, 2018: 19). Rather than building intrinsic resilience, the current postwar reconstruction phase is paving the way for regime resilience on the bases of structural inequalities while increasing the broader population's vulnerability, particularly the refugees who are forced to return home under unsafe conditions. This notion of resilience is critical: It shows how societies and community units respond to and cope with risks and changes.

The HECS framework could, therefore, be helpful for others moving forward. The human-security framework for the environment allows for an understanding of security that considers the deterioration of natural resources as a clear and present threat to human security; it also encourages countries to find regional and national policy solutions to environmental threats that could draw on local norms such as Islamic law and its principles of social justice and environmental sustainability. This framework seeks not only to protect but also to outline unequal power structures that cause or encourage human suffering. This perspective has significant implications for climate inse-curity – as the latter is also linked to unequal power relations between the Global North and South or a central government and its marginal-ized populations – and for how societies can improve the safety, well-being, and livelihood of their citizens, all of which are made more difficult in an insecure climate. Where environmentally deterministic narratives remove people's agency by placing it in the hands of external developments, this book gives them a voice.

References

Ababsa, M. (2013). Agrarian Counter-Reform in Syria (2000–2010). In R. Hinnebusch, A. Al-Hindi, M. Khaddam, and M. Ababsa, eds., *Agriculture and Reform in Syria*. Fife: University of St. Andrews Centre for Syrian Studies, pp. 83–108.

   (2015). The End of a World: Drought and Agrarian Transformation in Northeast Syria. In R. Hinnebusch and T. Zintl, eds., *Syria from Reform to Revolt*, vol. I. Syracuse, NY: Syracuse University Press, pp. 199–224.

Abboud, S. (2015). Locating the "Social" in the Social Market Economy. In R. Hinnebusch and T. Zintl, eds., *Syria from Reform to Revolt*, vol. I. Syracuse, NY: Syracuse University Press, pp. 45–65.

   (2016). *Syria*. Cambridge: Polity Press.

Abboud, S., Dahi, O. S., Hazbun, W., Sunday Grove, N., Pison Hindawi, C., Mouawad, J., and Hermez, S. (2018). Towards a Beirut School of Critical Security Studies. *Critical Studies on Security*, 6(3), 273–295.

Abou Zakhem, B., and Hafez, R. (2010). Climatic Factors Controlling Chemical and Isotopic Characteristics of Precipitation in Syria. *Hydrological Processes*, 24(18), 2641–2654.

Acharya, A. (2004). A Holistic Paradigm. *Security Dialogue*, 35(3), 355–356.

   (2014). Global International Relations (IR) and Regional Worlds. *International Studies Quarterly*, 58(4), 647–659.

Adams, C., Tobias, I., Barnett, J., and Detgas, A. (2018). Sampling Bias in Climate-Conflict Research. *Nature*, 8 (3), 200–203.

Adams, R. M. (1981). *Heartland of Cities: Surveys of Ancient Settlement and Land Use on the Central Floodplain of the Euphrates*. Chicago, IL: University of Chicago Press.

Adger, W. N., Pulhin, J. M., Barnett, J., Dabelko, G. D., Hovelsrud, G. K., Levy, M., Oswald Spring, Ú., and Vogel, C. H. (2014). Human Security. In C. B. Field, V. R. Barros, D. J. Dokken, K. J. Mach, M. D. Mastrandrea, T. E. Bilir, M. Chatterjee, K. L. Ebi, Y. O. Estrada, R. C. Genova, B. Girma, E. S. Kissel, A. N. Levy, S. MacCracken, P. R. Mastrandrea, and L. L. White, eds., *Climate Change 2014: Impacts, Adaptation, and Vulnerability. Part A: Global and Sectoral Aspects. Contribution of Working Group II to the Fifth Assessment Report of the Intergovernmental Panel on Climate Change*. Geneva: Intergovernmental Panel on Climate Change, pp. 755–791.

Afifi, T., Liwenga, E., and Kwezi, L. (2014). Rainfall-Induced Crop Failure, Food Insecurity and Out-Migration in Same-Kilimanjaro, Tanzania. *Climate and Development*, 6(1), 53–60.

Ahmed, S. A., Diffenbaugh, N. S., and Hertel, T. W. (2009). Climate Volatility Deepens Poverty Vulnerability in Developing Countries. *Environmental Research Letters*, 4(3), 1–8.

Aita, S. (2009). Labour Markets Performance and Migration Flows in Syria. In Labour Markets Performance and Migration Flows in Mediterranean Countries: Determinants and Effects. Fiesole, Italy: European University Institute, Robert Schuman Centre for Advanced Studies. Retrieved from www.economistes-arabes.org/Cercle_des_economistes_arabes/Samir_Aita_files/LMM%20Syria-%20Final%20version.pdf

Alatout, S. (2006). Towards a Bio-territorial Conception of Power: Territory, Population, and Environmental Narratives in Palestine and Israel. *Political Geography*, 25(6), 601–621.

Al-Hayat. (1996). Greenpeace Reveals Pollution of Waters Reaching Syria from Turkey. March 26.

Al-Hindi, A. (2010). The Agricultural Situation in the Eastern Region. Paper presented at the Syrian Economy and Future Horizons, the Twenty-Third Economic Symposium, Syrian Association of Economic Sciences. Damascus, January 26.

  (2011). Syria's Agricultural Sector: Situation, Role, Challenges, and Prospects. In R. Hinnebusch, A. Al-Hindi, M. Khaddam, and M. Ababsa, eds., *Agriculture and Reform in Syria*. Fife: University of St. Andrews Centre for Syrian Studies, pp. 15–56.

Al-Jazeera. (2016). Peter Szijjarto: "Migration Became a Security Threat." *Al-Jazeera Online*, September 24. Retrieved from www.aljazeera.com/programmes/talktojazeera/2016/09/peter-szijjarto-migration-security-threat-160923114524255.html

Alkire, S. (2004). A Vital Core That Must Be Treated with the Same Gravitas as Traditional Security Threats. *Security Dialogue*, 35(3), 359–360.

Allan, J. A. (2000). Global Systems Ameliorate Local Droughts: Water, Food, and Trade. Occasional Paper series. SOAS-KCL Water Issues Group. London: King's College. Retrieved from www.soas.ac.uk/water/publications/papers/file38354.pdf

  (2001). *The Middle East Water Question: Hydropolitics and the Global Economy*. London: I. B. Tauris.

Al-Muheissin, K. (2010). The Agricultural Situation in the Eastern Region. Paper presented at the Syrian Economy and Future Horizons, the Twenty-Third Economic Symposium, Syrian Association of Economic Sciences. Damascus, January 26.

Al-Qadi, H. (2009). Corruption and the Distribution of Wealth in Syria. Paper presented at Around the Ramifications of the Current Global Economic Crisis, the Twenty-Second Economic Symposium, Syrian Association of Economic Sciences. Damascus, February 10.

Al-Shaib, R. (2010). Social Effects of the Drought Crisis in the Eastern Region. Paper presented at the Syrian Economy and Future Horizons, the Twenty-Third Economic Symposium, Syrian Association of Economic Sciences. Damascus, January 26.

Al-Taqi, S., and Hinnebusch, R. (2013). As Seen from Damascus: The Transformation in Syrian–Turkish Relations. In R. Hinnebusch and Ö. Tür, eds., *Turkey–Syria Relations: Between Enmity and Amity*. Farnham: Ashgate, pp. 95–111.

Al-Thawra. (2005). Otri Inaugurates Several Service and Development Projects. *Al-Thawra*, November 20. Retrieved from http://archive.thawra .sy/_archive.asp?FileName=9534424982005119134612

Altunisik, M. B., and Tür, Ö. (2006). Changing Syrian–Turkish Relations. *Security Dialogue*, 37(2), 229–248.

Amery, H. A. (2001). Islam and the Environment. In N. I. Faruqui, A. K. Biswas, and M. J. Bino, eds., *Water Management in Islam*. New York: United Nations University Press, pp. 39–48.

Arab Center for Research and Policy Studies. (2013). *The Question of the Syrian Kurds: Fact, History, Myth*. Beirut: Arab Center for Research and Policy Studies.

Aras, B., and Polat, R. K. (2008). From Conflict to Cooperation: Desecuritization of Turkey's Relations and Iran. *Security Dialogue*, 39(5), 495–515.

Associated Press. (2004). Scientists Warm Up to "Day after Tomorrow." *Today*, May 4. Retrieved from www.today.com/popculture/scientists-warm-day-after-tomorrow-wbna4900768

Aw-Hassan, A., Rida, F. H., Telleria, R., and Bruggeman, A. (2014). The Impact of Food and Agricultural Policies. *Journal of Hydrology*, 513, 204–215.

Bachler, G., Klötzli V., Libiszewski, S., and Spillmann, K. (1996) *Environmental Degradation as a Cause of War: Ecological Conflicts in the Third World and Peaceful Ways of Resolving Them*. Zurich: Ruegger.

Baker, A. (2015). How Climate Change Is Behind the Surge of Migrants to Europe. *Time*, September 7. Retrieved from http://time.com/4024210/ climate-change-migrants

Bakour, Y. (1991). *Planning and Management of Water Resources in Syria.* Damascus: Arab Organization for Agricultural Development.

(1992). Planning and Management of Water Resources in Syria. In *Country Experiences with Water Resources Management: Economical, Institutional, Technological and Environment Issues,* World Bank Technical Paper No. 175, pp. 151–156.

(2009). Food Insecurity in Developing Countries: Causes and Solutions. Paper presented at Around the Ramifications of the Current Global Economic Crisis, the Twenty-Second Economic Symposium, Syrian Association of Economic Sciences. Damascus, April 28.

Bakour, Y., and Kolars, J. (1994). The Arab Mashrek: Hydrologic History, Problems and Perspectives. In P. Rogers and P. Lydon, eds., *Water in the Arab World, Perspectives and Prognoses.* Cambridge, MA: Division of Applied Sciences, Harvard University, pp. 121–146.

Baldwin, A., Methmann, C., and Rothe, D. (2014). Securitizing "Climate Refugees": The Futurology of Climate-Induced Migration. *Critical Studies on Security,* 2(2), 121–130.

Baldwin, D. A. (1997). The Concept of Security. *Review of International Studies,* 23(1), 5–26.

Balzacq, T. (2011). *Securitization Theory: How Security Problems Emerge and Dissolve.* Abingdon-on-Thames and New York: Routledge.

Barnes, J. (2009). Managing the Waters of Ba'ath Country: The Politics of Water Scarcity in Syria. *Geopolitics,* 14(3), 510–530.

(2014). *Cultivating the Nile: The Everyday Politics of Water in Egypt.* Durham, NC: Duke University Press.

Barnett, J. (2001). *The Meaning of Environmental Security.* London: Zed Books.

Barnett, J., and Adger, W. N. (2007). Climate Change, Human Security and Violent Conflict. *Political Geography,* 26(6), 639–655.

Barout, M. J. (2012). *Syria in the Last Decade: The Dialectic of Stagnation and Reform.* Doha: Arab Center for Research and Policy Studies.

Barrett, C. B. (2013). *Food Security and Sociopolitical Stability.* Oxford: Oxford University Press.

Batatu, H. (1999). *Syria's Peasantry, the Descendants of Its Lesser Rural Notables, and Their Politics.* Princeton, NJ: Princeton University Press.

Bazza, M., and Najib, R. (2003). *Towards Improved Water Demand Management in Agriculture in the Syrian Arab Republic.* The First National Symposium on Management and Rationalization of Water Resources Use in Agriculture. Rome: Food and Agriculture Organization.

Beaumont, P. (1994). The Myth of Water Wars and the Future of Irrigated Agriculture in the Middle East. *International Journal of Water Resources Development,* 10(1), 9–21.

Bernauer, T. (2002). Explaining Success and Failure in International River Management. *Aquatic Sciences, 64*(1), 1–19.

Bernauer, T., Böhmelt, T., and Koubi, V. (2012). Environmental Changes and Violent Conflict. *Environmental Research Letters, 7*(1), 1–8.

Betz, H. (1996). The German Model Reconsidered. *German Studies Review, 19*(2), 303–320.

Biermann, F., and Boas, I. (2010). Preparing for a Warmer World: Towards a Global Governance System to Protect Climate Refugees. *Global Environmental Politics, 10*(1), 60–88.

Bilgin, P. (2017). Inquiring into Others' Conceptions of the International and Security. *Political Science and Politics, 50*(3), 652–655.

Bishara, A. (2012). Revolutions, Reforms, and Democratic Transition in the Arab Homeland from the Perspective of the Tunisian Revolution. *Palestine-Israel Journal of Politics, Economics, and Culture, 18*(1), 22–25.
  (2013). *Revolution against Revolution, the Street against the People, and Counter-Revolution*. Beirut: Arab Center for Research and Policy Studies.

Biswas, A., Kolars, J., Murakami, M., Waterbury, J., and Wolf, A. (1997). *Core and Periphery: A Comprehensive Approach to Middle Eastern Water*. Oxford: Oxford University Press.

Black, R., Adger, W. N., Arnell, N. W., Dercon, S., Geddes, A., and Thomas, D. S. G. (2011). The Effect of Environmental Change on Human Migration. *Global Environmental Change, 215*(21), 53–511.

Blackaby, F. (1986). The Concept of Common Security. *Bulletin of Peace Proposals, 17* (3–4), 395–408.

Boas, I. (2015). *Climate Migration and Securitisation as a Strategy in Climate Change Politics*. Abingdon-on-Thames and New York: Routledge.

Bourgey, A. (1974). Le Barrage de Tabqa et l'aménagement du bassin de l'Euphrate en Syrie [The Taqba Dam and the Development of the Euphrates Basin in Syria]. *Revue de Géographie de Lyon, 49*(4), 343–354.

Brinkman, H. J. and Hendrix, C. S. (2011). Food Insecurity and Violent Conflict: Causes, Consequences, and Addressing the Challenges. World Food Programme Occasional Papers no. 24 (July). Retrieved from https://ucanr.edu/blogs/food2025/blogfiles/14415.pdf

Buhaug, H., Nordkvelle, J., Bernauer, T., Böhmelt, T., Brzoska, M., Busby, J. W., . . . and von Uexkull, N. (2014). One Effect to Rule Them All? A Comment on Climate and Conflict. *Climatic Change, 127*(3–4), 391–397.

Burchi, F., and De Muro, P. (2015). From Food Availability to Nutritional Capabilities: Advancing Food Security Analysis. *Food Policy, 60*, 10–19.

Burke, M., Hsiang, S. M., and Miguel, E. (2014). *Climate and Conflict.* NBER Working Paper No. 20598. Cambridge, MA: The National Bureau of Economic Research.

Buzan, B. (2004). A Reductionist, Idealistic Notion That Adds Little Analytical Value. *Security Dialogue*, *35*(3), 369–370.

 (2007). People, States, and Fear: An Agenda for International Security Studies in the Post–Cold War Era, 2nd edn. Colchester: ECPR Press.

Buzan, B., Waever, O. and de Wilde, J. (1998). *Security: A New Framework for Analysis.* Boulder, CO: Lynne Rienner Publishers.

Caponera, D. A. (1992). *Principles of Water Law and Administration, National and International.* Rotterdam: A. A. Balkema.

 (2001). Ownership and Transfer of Water and Land in Islam. In N. I. Faruqui, A. K. Biswas, and M. J. Bino, eds., *Water Management in Islam.* New York: United Nations University Press, pp. 94–102.

Central Bureau of Statistics. (2018a). مؤشرات المشتغلين حسب النشاط الاقتصادي [Employment by Sector]. Retrieved December 8, 2018, www.cbssyr.sy/indicator/mosh.htm

 (2018b). Worker's Distribution (15 years and over) by Governorate, Main Occupations, and Gender (Urban-Rural) 2006/2007/2008/2009/2010. Retrieved December 9, 2018, www.cbssyr.sy/work/2006/tab12.htm, www.cbssyr.sy/work/2007/tab10.htm, www.cbssyr.sy/work/2008/ALL-2008/tab10.htm, www.cbssyr.sy/work/2009/ALL-2009/TAB-10.htm, and www.cbssyr.sy/work/2010/ALL-2010/TAB10.htm

Chesnot, C. (1993). *La Bataille de l'eau au Proche-Orient.* Paris: Éditions L'Harmattan.

Clarke, R. (1993). *Water: The International Crisis.* Cambridge, MA: MIT Press.

Coates, J. (2013). Build It Back Better: Deconstructing Food Security for Improved Measurement and Action. *Global Food Security*, *2*(3), 188–194.

Collier, P. and Hoeffler, A. (2004). Greed and Grievance in Civil War. *Oxford Economic Papers*, *56*(4), 563–595.

 (2005). Resource Rents, Governance, and Conflict. *Journal of Conflict Resolution*, *49*(4), 625–633.

Commission on Sustainable Development. (1997). Comprehensive Assessment of the Freshwater Resources of the World. United Nations Report CN 17/1997/9. April 7–25.

Conca, K. (2006). *Governing Water: Contentious Transnational Politics and Global Institution Building.* Cambridge, MA: MIT Press.

Conca, K., and Dabelko, G. D. (2002). *Environmental Peacemaking.* Washington, DC: Woodrow Wilson Center Press.

Cook, C., and Bakker, K. (2012). Water Security: Debating an Emerging Paradigm. *Global Environmental Change, 22*(1), 95–96.

Coppens, Y. (2018). *Origines de l'homme, origines d'un homme.* Paris: Odile Jacob.

CounterCurrent. (2011). Dam Construction in Turkey and Its Impact on Economic, Cultural and Social Rights: Parallel Report in Response to the Initial Report by the Republic of Turkey on the Implementation of the International Covenant on Economic, Social and Cultural Rights. Submission to the UN Committee on Economic, Social and Cultural Rights for Its Forty-Sixth Session, May 2–20. Retrieved from www2.ohchr.org/english/bodies/cescr/docs/ngos/JointReport_Turkey46.pdf

Curtin, P. D. (1984). *Cross-Cultural Trade in World History.* Cambridge: Cambridge University Press.

Daher, J. (2018). *The Political Economic Context of Syria's Reconstruction: A Prospective in Light of a Legacy of Unequal Development.* Middle East Directions (MED), Wartime and Post-Conflict in Syria. European University Institute.

Dahi, O., and Munif, Y. (2011). Revolts in Syria: Tracking the Convergence between Authoritarianism and Neoliberalism. *Journal of Asian and African Studies, 47*(4), 323–332.

Dalby, S. (1999). Against "Globalization from Above": Critical Geopolitics and the World Order Models Project. *Environment and Planning D: Society and Space, 17*(2), 181–200.

(2002). *Environmental Security.* Minneapolis, MN: Minnesota University Press.

(2009). Scenarios of Doom: From Thomas Malthus to Ecological "Collapse." In S. Dalby, ed., *Security and Environmental Change.* Cambridge: Polity Press, pp. 13–35.

(2013). Environmental Dimensions of Human Security. In R. Floyd and R. A. Matthew, eds., *Environmental Security: Approaches and Issues.* Abingdon-on-Thames and New York: Routledge, pp. 121–138.

(2017a). Climate Change and Geopolitics. *Oxford Research Encyclopedia of Climate Science.* Online Publication.

(2017b). Anthropocene Formations: Environmental Security, Geopolitics and Disaster. *Theory, Culture & Society, 34*(2–3), 233–252.

Daoudi, R. (2001). Facing Water Resources Challenges in Syria. Paper presented at Syria: New Dawn for Business, Trade, and Investment. London, July 3–4.

Daoudy, M. (2004). Syria and Turkey in Water Diplomacy (1962–2003). In F. Zereini and W. Jaeschke, eds., *Water in the Middle East and North Africa: Resources, Protection and Management.* Heidelberg: Springer, pp. 319–332.

(2005). *Le Partage des eaux entre la Syrie, l'Irak et la Turquie: Négociation, sécurité et asymétrie des pouvoirs*. Paris: CNRS Editions.

(2008). A Missed Chance for Peace: Syria and Israel's Negotiations over the Golan Heights. *Journal of International Affairs*, 61(2), 215–234.

(2009). Asymmetric Power: Negotiating Water in the Euphrates and Tigris. *International Negotiation*, 14(2), 361–391.

(2013). Beyond Conflict? The Securitization of Water in Syrian–Turkish Relations. In R. Hinnebusch and Ö. Tür, eds., *Turkey–Syria Relations: Between Enmity and Amity*. Farnham: Ashgate, pp. 133–144.

(2016). The Structure–Identity Nexus: Syria and Turkey's Collapse (2011). *Cambridge Review of International Affairs*, 29(3), 1074–1096.

Dardari, A. (2009). The 10th Five-Year Plan: Outcomes and Challenges. Paper presented at Around the Ramifications of the Current Global Economic Crisis, the Twenty-Second Economic Symposium, Syrian Association of Economic Sciences. Damascus, February 3.

Davis, M. (2001). *Late Victorian Holocausts: El Niño Famines and the Making of the Third World*. London: Verso.

Davutoğlu, A. (2008). Turkey's Foreign Policy Vision: An Assessment of 2007. *Insight Turkey*, 10(1), 77–96.

(2013). Turkey's Mediation: Critical Reflections from the Field. *Middle East Policy*, 20(1), 83–89.

De Châtel, F. (2014). The Role of Drought and Climate Change in the Syrian Uprising: Untangling the Triggers of the Revolution. *Middle Eastern Studies*, 50(4), 521–535.

De Sherbinin, A., Levy, M., Adamo, S., Macmanus, K., Yetman, G., Mara, V., ... and Pistolesi, L. (2012). Migration and Risk: Net Migration in Marginal Ecosystems and Hazardous Areas. *Environmental Research Letters*, 7(4), 1–14.

Delvin, J. F. (1991). The Baath Party: Rise and Metamorphosis. *The American Historical Review*, 96(5), 1396–1407.

Deudney, D. H., and Matthew, R. A. (1999). *Contested Grounds: Security and Conflict in the New Environmental Politics*. New York: State University of New York Press.

Di Giovanni, J. (2016). *The Morning They Came for Us: Dispatches from Syria*. New York: Liveright.

Diamond, J. (2004). *Collapse: How Societies Choose to Fail or Succeed*. New York: Viking.

Dib, S. A. (2009). Corruption and Unequal Distribution of Wealth. Paper presented at Around the Ramifications of the Current Global Economic Crisis, the Twenty-Second Economic Symposium, Syrian Association of Economic Sciences. Damascus, February 10.

Diehl, P. F., and Gleditsch, N. P., eds. (2001). Environmental Conflict: An Anthology. *Global Environmental Politics*, 1(3). Boulder, CO: Westview Press.

Dilley, M., and Boudreau, T. (2001). Coming to Terms with Vulnerability: A Critique of the Food Security Definition. *Food Policy*, 23(3), 229–247.

Dinar, S. (2013). The Geographical Dimensions of Hydropolitics: International Freshwater in the Middle East, North Africa, and Central Asia. *Eurasian Geography and Economics*, 53(1), 115–142.

 ed. (2011). *Beyond Resource Wars: Scarcity, Environmental Degradation, and International Cooperation*. Cambridge, MA: MIT Press.

Dinshaw, F. (2015). This Is What a Climate Refugee Looks Like. *The National Observer*, September 4. Retrieved from www.nationalobserver.com/2015/09/04/news/what-climate-refugee-looks

Dohrmann, M. and Hatem, R. (2014). The Impact of Hydro-politics on the Relations of Turkey, Iraq, and Syria. *The Middle East Journal*, 68(4), 567–583.

Droubi, A. (2009). First National Communication Report: Syria to UNFCC. Paper presented at the Issam Fares Institute, American University of Beirut. Beirut, August 4.

Droubi, A., Jnad, I., Sibai, M., Ashkar, H., Mawed, K., and Hassoun, I. (2011). *Assessment of Climate Change Impact on Water Resource and Agriculture Sector in the Arab Region*. Damascus: The Arab Center for the Studies of Arid Zones and Dry Lands.

Durutan, N. (2000). Turkey: Eastern Anatolia Watershed Management. In L. A. Norsworthy, ed., *Rural Development, Natural Resources and the Environment: Lessons of Experience in Eastern Europe and Central Asia*. Washington, DC: The World Bank, pp. 112–117.

Ebner, A. (2006). The Intellectual Foundations of the Social Market Economy. *Journal of Economic Studies*, 33(3), 206–223.

Edwards, D. C., and McKee, T. B. (1997). Characteristics of 20th Century Drought in the United States at Multiple Time Scales. *Atmospheric Science Paper*, 634, 1–30.

Ehteshami, A. and Elik, S. (2011). Turkey's Growing Relations with Iran and Arab Middle East. *Turkish Studies*, 12(4), 643–662.

Eklund, L., and Thompson, D. (2017). Is Syria Really a "Climate War"? We Examined the Links between Drought, Migration and Conflict. *The Conversation*, July 21. Retrieved from http://theconversation.com/is-syria-really-a-climate-war-we-examined-the-links-between-drought-migration-and-conflict-80110

Erian, W. (2011). *Drought Vulnerability in the Arab Region: Case Study – Drought in Syria: Ten Years of Scarce Water (2000–2010)*. Damascus: The Arab Center for the Studies of Arid Zones and Dry Lands.

Falkenmark, M. (1986). Fresh Water: Time for a Modified Approach. *Ambio*, 15(4), 192–200.

(1997). Meeting Water Requirements of an Expanding World Population. *Philosophical Transactions of the Royal Society of the Biological Sciences*, 352(1356), 929–936.

(2018). Shift in Water Thinking Crucial for Realistic Planning of Sub-Saharan Future. In A. K. Biswas, C. Tortajada, and P. Rohner, eds., *Assessing Global Water Megatrends*. Singapore: Springer, pp. 147–177.

Falkenmark, M., and Molden, D. (2008). Wake Up to Realities of River Basin Closure. *International Journal of Water Resources Development*, 24 (2), 201–215.

Falkenmark, M., Berntell, A., Jagerskog, A., Lundqvist, J., Matz, M., and Tropp, H. (2007). On the Verge of a New Water Scarcity: A Call for Good Governance and Human Ingenuity. SIWI Policy Brief. Stockholm: Stockholm International Water Institute (SIWI).

Faris, S. (2007). The Real Roots of Darfur. *Atlantic Monthly*, June 16. Retrieved from www.theatlantic.com/magazine/archive/2007/04/the-real-roots-of-darfur/305701

Faruqui, N. I. (2001a). Introduction. In N. I. Faruqui, A. K. Biswas, and M. J. Bino, eds., *Water Management in Islam*. New York: United Nations University Press, pp. xiii–xix.

(2001b). Islam and Water Management: Overview and Principles. In N. I. Faruqui, A. K. Biswas, and M. J. Bino, eds., *Water Management in Islam*. New York: United Nations University Press, pp. 1–32.

Fearon, J. D. (2005). Primary Commodities and Civil War. *Journal of Conflict Resolution*, 49(4), 483–507.

Feitelson, E., and Tubi, A. (2017). A Main Driver or an Intermediate Variable? Climate Change, Water and Security in the Middle East. *Global Environmental Change*, 44, 39–48.

Femia, F. and Werrell, C. E. (2012). Syria: Climate Change, Drought and Social Unrest. *The Center for Climate and Security*, February 12. Available at: https://climateandsecurity.files.wordpress.com/2012/04/syria-climate-change-drought-and-social-unrest_briefer-11.pdf

(2015). New Research in Context: Syria, Climate Change and Conflict. *The Center for Climate and Security*. March 2. Retrieved from https://climateandsecurity.org/2015/03/02/new-research-in-context-syria-climate-change-and-conflict/

Femia, F., Slaughter, A., and Werrell, C. E. (2013). The Arab Spring and Climate Change. *Center for American Progress*. February 28. Retrieved from www.americanprogress.org/issues/security/reports/2013/02/28/ 54579/the-arab-spring-and-climate-change

Fenelon, P. (1991). *A Dictionary of Agrarian History and Geography*. Paris: Conseil International de la Langue Française.

Fischhendler, I. (2015). The Securitization of Water Discourse: Theoretical Foundations, Research Gaps and Objectives of the Special Issue. *International Environmental Agreements: Politics, Law and Economics*, 15 (3), 245–255.

Floyd, R. (2007). Towards a Consequentialist Evaluation of Security: Bringing Together the Copenhagen and the Welsh Schools of Security Studies. *Review of International Studies*, 33(2), 327–350.

  (2013). Analyst, Theory and Security: A New Framework for Understanding Environmental Security Studies. In R. Floyd and R. A. Matthew, eds., *Environmental Security: Approaches and Issues*. Abingdon-on-Thames and New York: Routledge, pp. 21–35.

Floyd, R., and Matthew, R. A. (2013). *Environmental Security: Approaches and Issues*. Abingdon-on-Thames and New York: Routledge.

Food and Agriculture Organization of the United Nations. (1996). Rome Declaration on World Food Security, World Food Summit, Rome, Food and Agriculture Organization. Retrieved from: www.fao.org/3/w3613e/ w3613e00.htm

  (1997). Aquastat: Syrian Arab Republic. Department of Natural Resources.

  (2003). The Economics of Strategic Crops. In M. Westlake, *Syrian Agriculture at the Crossroads*, FAO Agricultural Policy and Economic Development Series No. 8.

  (2008). Aquastat: Syrian Arab Republic (in Arabic). Retrieved from www.fao.org/nr/water/aquastat/countries_regions/syr/SYR-CP_ara.pdf

  (2015). Food Self-Sufficiency and International Trade: A False Dichotomy? The State of Agricultural Commodity Markets. Retrieved from www.fao.org/3/a-i5222e.pdf

  (2016a). Human Security and Food Security. Report I5522E/1/03.16. Geneva: United Nations Human Security Unit.

  (2016b). Aquastat: Syrian Arab Republic. Retrieved March 1, 2019, www.fao.org/nr/water/aquastat/data/query/results.html

  (2017a). FAOSTAT: Syria (1961–2017). Retrieved www.fao.org/faostat/ en/#country/212

  (2017b). *Counting the Cost: Agriculture in Syria after Six Years of Crisis*. Retrieved at www.fao.org/emergencies/resources/documents/resources-detail/en/c/878213/

Foy, R., and Tabeaud, M. (2012). The State Farm of Al-Assad (Euphrates) before Its Closure in 2000: Some Negative Effects of a Top-Down

Development Approach. *Journal of Mediterranean Geography, 119,* 45–55.

Frey, B. S. (1993). Does Monitoring Increase Work Effort? The Rivalry with Trust and Loyalty. *Economic Inquiry, 31*(4), 663–670.

Friedman, T. R. (2019). Climate Wars: Why This Story Needs to Be Told. *The Years Project.* Retrieved from http://theyearsproject.com/story/cli mate-wars/.

Fröhlich, C. (2016). Climate Migrants as Protestors? Dispelling Misconceptions about Global Environmental Change in Pre-revolutionary Syria. *Contemporary Levant, 1*(1), 38–50.

Furon, R. (1963). *Le Problème de l'eau dans le monde.* Paris: Payot.

Gani, J. K. (2014). *The Role of Ideology in Syrian–US Relations: Conflict and Cooperation.* Basingstoke: Palgrave Macmillan.

García, Rolando Victor (1981). *Nature Pleads Not Guilty.* Oxford: Pergamon Press.

Gartzke, E. (2012). Could Climate Change Precipitate Peace? *Journal of Peace Research, 49*(1), 177–192.

Gauthier, J. (2009). The Struggle for Unity and Relevance, 2003–2208: Has the Kurdish Question Erupted in Syria? In F. H. Lawson, ed., *Demystifying Syria.* London: Saqi, pp. 120–143.

Gemenne, F., Barnett, J., Adger, W., and Dabelko, G. (2014). Climate and Security: Evidence, Emerging Risks, and a New Agenda. *Climatic Change, 123*(1), 1–9.

Ghadban, A. (1995). *Water Resources in Syria: Current and Future Uses and Their Role in the Realisation of Water and Food Security.* Damascus: Ministry of Irrigation.

Giordano, M. F., Giordano, M. A., and Wolf, A. T. (2002). The Geography of Water Conflict and Cooperation: Internal Pressures and International Manifestations. *Geographic Journal, 168*(4), 293–312.

(2005). *International Resource Conflict and Mitigation, 42*(1), 47–65.

Glassner, J. (2002). *La Mésopotamie.* Paris: Les Belles Lettres.

Gleditsch, N. P. (1998). Armed Conflict and the Environment: A Critique of the Literature. *Journal of Peace Research, 35*(3), 363–380.

Gleditsch, N. P., and Nordås, R. (2014). Conflicting Messages? The IPCC on Conflict and Human Security. *Political Geography, 43,* 82–90.

Gleick, P. (1993). "Water." In N. Hashemi and D. Postel, eds., *Sectarianization, Mapping the New Politics of the Middle East.* Oxford: Oxford University Press.

(2006). Water and Terrorism. *Water Policy, 8*(6), 481–503.

(2014). Water, Drought, Climate Change, and Conflict in Syria. *Weather, Climate, and Society, 6*(3).

(2017). Climate, Water and Conflict: Commentary on Selby et al., 2017. *Political Geography 60*, 248–250.

Global Water Partnership. (2000). Towards Water Security: A Framework for Action. www.gwp.org/globalassets/global/toolbox/references/towards-water-security.-a-framework-for-action.-mobilising-political-will-to-act-gwp-2000.pdf

Goff, L., Zarin, H., and Goodman, S. (2012). Climate-Induced Migration from Northern Africa to Europe: Security Challenges and Opportunities. *The Brown Journal of World Affairs, 18*(2), 195–213.

Gramsci, A. (1973). *Letters from Prison.* Edited by L. Lawner. London: Harper & Row. First published 1947.

Grayson, K. (2004). A Challenge to Power over Knowledge of Traditional Security Studies. *Security Dialogue, 35*(3), 357.

Greenhill, K. M. (2010). *Weapons of Mass Migration Forced Displacement, Coercion, and Foreign Policy.* Ithaca, NY: Cornell University Press.

Haas, P. M., Keohane, R. O., and Levy, M. A. (1993). *Institutions for the Earth: Sources of Effective International Environmental Protection.* Cambridge, MA: MIT Press.

Haddad, B. (2012). *Business Networks in Syria: The Political Economy of Authoritarian Resilience.* Palo Alto, CA: Stanford University Press.

Hajer, M. A. (1995). *The Politics of Environmental Discourse: Ecological Modernization and the Policy Process.* Oxford: Oxford University Press.

Haj-Saleh, Y. (2017). *The Impossible Revolution: Making Sense of the Syrian Tragedy.* London: C. Hurst & Co.

Hannoyer, J. (1985). Grands projets hydrauliques en Syrie: La tentation orientale [Large Hydraulic Projects in Syria: The Oriental Temptation]. *Maghreb-Machrek, 109*, 24–42.

Hardt, J. N. (2012). Critical Deconstruction of Environmental Security and Human Security Concepts in the Anthropocene. In J. Scheffran, M. Brzoska, H. Brauch, P. Link, and J. Schilling, eds. *Climate Change, Human Security and Violent Conflict.* Berlin and Heidelberg: Springer, pp. 207–221.

Hashemi, N. and Postel, D., eds. (2013). *The Syria Dilemma.* Boston, MA: Review Books.

eds. (2017). *Sectarianization: Mapping the New Politics of the Middle East.* Oxford: Oxford University Press.

Hendrix, C. S. (2017). A Comment on Climate Change and the Syrian Civil War Revisited. *Political Geography, 60*, 251–252.

(2018). The Sophomore Curse: Sampling Bias and the Future of Climate-Conflict Research. *Denver Dialogues.* Retrieved from http://politicalviolenceataglance.org/2018/03/06/the-sophomore-curse-sampling-bias-and-the-future-of-climate-conflict-research/#comments

Hendrix, C. S., and Glaser, S. M. (2007). Trends and Triggers: Climate, Climate Change and Civil Conflict in Sub-Saharan Africa. *Political Geography*, 26(6), 695–715.

Hensel, P. R., McLaughlin Mitchell, S., and Sowers II, T. E. (2006). Conflict Management of Riparian Disputes. *Political Geography*, 25(4), 383–411.

Heydemann, S. (1999). *Authoritarianism in Syria: Institutions and Social Conflict, 1946–1970*. Ithaca, NY: Cornell University Press.

(2007). *Upgrading Authoritarianism in the Arab World*. Washington, DC: Brookings.

Heydemann, S. and Leenders, R., eds. (2013). *Authoritarianisms: Governance, Contestation, and Regime Resilience in Syria and Iran*. Stanford, CA: Stanford University Press.

Hidou, D. (2010). Social Effects of the Drought Crisis in the Eastern Region. Paper presented at the Syrian Economy and Future Horizons, the Twenty-Third Economic Symposium, Syrian Association of Economic Sciences. Damascus, January 26.

Hinnebusch, R. A. (1976). Local Politics in Syria: Organization and Mobilization in Four Villages. *Middle East Journal*, 30(1), 1–24.

(1982). Rural Politics in Ba'thist Syria: A Case Study in the Role of the Countryside in the Political Development of Arab Societies. *The Review of Politics*, 44(1), 110–130.

(1989). *Peasant and Bureaucracy in Ba'thist Syria: The Political Economy of Rural Development*. London: Westview Press.

(1990). *Authoritarian Power and State Formation in Ba'thist Syria: Army, Party, and Peasant*. Boulder, CO: Westview Press.

(1995). The Political Economy of Economic Liberalization in Syria. *International Journal of Middle East Studies*, 27, 305–320.

(2011). The Ba'ath Party in Post-Ba'athist Syria: President, Party and the Struggle for "Reform." *Middle East Critique*, 20(2), 109–125.

(2013). The Ba'ath's Agrarian Revolution (1963–2000). In R. Hinnebusch, A. Al-Hindi, M. Khaddam, and M. Ababsa, eds., *Agriculture and Reform in Syria*. Fife: University of St. Andrews Centre for Syrian Studies, pp. 3–14.

(2015) President and Party in Post-Ba'thist Syria: From the Struggle for "Reform" to Regime Deconstruction. In R. A. Hinnebusch and T. Zintl, eds. (2015). *Syria from Reform to Revolt*, vol. I. Syracuse, NY: Syracuse University Press, pp. 21–44.

Hinnebusch, R. A., and Zintl, T. (2015). *Syria from Reform to Revolt*, vol. I. Syracuse, NY: Syracuse University Press.

Hirsch, A. (1956). Utilization of International Rivers in the Middle East: A Study of Conventional International Law. *The American Journal of International Law*, 50, 81–100.

Hoerling, M., Eischeid, J., Perlwitz, J., Quan, X., Zhang, Z. and Pegion, P. (2012). On the Increased Frequency of Mediterranean Drought. *Journal of Climate*, 25(6), 2146–2161.

Holden, M. (2015). Climate Change Root Cause of Syrian War: Britain's Prince Charles. *Reuters*. November 23. Retrieved from www.reuters.com/article/us-climatechange-summit-charles/climate-change-root-cause-of-syrian-war-britains-prince-charles-idUSKBN0TC0NO20151123

Homer-Dixon, T. F. (1994). Environmental Scarcities and Violent Conflict: Evidence from Cases. *International Security*, 19(1), 5–40.

(1999). *Environment, Scarcity and Conflict*. Princeton, NJ: Princeton University Press.

Hough, P. (2013). *Understanding Global Security*, 3rd edn. Abingdon-on-Thames and New York: Routledge.

(2014). *Environmental Security: An Introduction*. Abingdon-on-Thames and New York: Routledge.

Hourani, A. (2002). *A History of the Arab Peoples*. London: Faber & Faber.

Hsiang, S. (2014). One Effect to Rule Them All? Our Reply to Buhaug et al.'s Climate and Conflict Commentary. *Global Food, Environment and Economic Dynamics*, October 27. Retrieved from www.g-feed.com/search?q=our+reply+to+buhaug

Hsiang, S., Burke, M., and Miguel, E. (2013). Quantifying the Influence of Climate on Human Conflict. *Science*, 341(6151), 341(6151), 1235367-1–14.

Human Rights Watch. (2002). Displaced and Disregarded: Turkey's Failing Village Return Program. October 3. Retrieved from www.hrw.org/reports/2002/10/30/displaced-and-disregarded

Huntington, E. (1945). *Mainsprings of Civilization*. New York: Mentor.

Hussein, I., and Al-Jayyousi, O. (2001). Management of Shared Waters: A Comparison of International and Islamic Law. In N. I. Faruqui, A. K. Biswas, and M. J. Bino, eds., *Water Management in Islam*. New York: United Nations University Press, pp. 128–135.

Huysman, J. (2004). Minding Exceptions: Politics of Insecurity and Liberal Democracy. *Contemporary Political Theory*, 3(3): 321–341.

Ibrahim, G. (2010). Social Dimensions of the Rent-Based Economy in Syria. Paper presented at the Syrian Economy and Future Horizons, the Twenty-Third Economic Symposium, Syrian Association of Economic Sciences. Damascus, January 26.

Ide, T. (2015). Why Do Conflicts over Scarce Renewable Resources Turn Violent? A Qualitative Comparative Analysis. *Global Environmental Change*, 33, 61–70.

Intergovernmental Panel on Climate Change. (1992). *AR1: Synthesis*. Geneva: IPCC. Retrieved from www.ipcc.ch/report/ar1/syr/

(1995). *IPCC Second Assessment: Climate Change 1995*. Geneva: IPCC. Retrieved from www.ipcc.ch/report/ar2/syr/

(2001). *TAR (Third Assessment Report) Climate Change 2001: Synthesis Report*. Edited by R. T. Watson. Geneva: IPCC. Retrieved from www.ipcc.ch/report/ar3/syr/

(2007). *AR4 Synthesis Report: Climate Change 2007– Contribution of Working Groups I, II, and II to the Fourth Assessment Report*. Edited by R. K. Pachauri and A. Reisinger. Geneva: IPCC. Retrieved from www.ipcc.ch/report/ar4/syr/

(2007). *Climate Change 2007: Impacts, Adaptation and Vulnerability*. Edited by M. L. Parry, O. F. Canziani, J. P. Palutikof, P. J. van der Linden, and C. E. Hanson. Retrieved from www.ipcc.ch/report/ar4/wg2

(2014). *AR5 Synthesis Report: Climate Change 2014– Contribution of Working Groups I, II, and III to the Fifth Assessment Report*. Edited by R. K. Pachauri and L. A. Meyer. Geneva: IPCC. Retrieved from www.ipcc.ch/report/ar5/syr/

(2018). *Global Warming of 1.5°C: Summary for Policymakers*. Edited by V. Masson-Delmotte, P. Zhai, H.-O. Pörtner, D. Roberts, J. Skea, P. R. Shukla, A. Pirani, Moufouma-Okia, C. Péan, R. Pidcock, S. Connors, J. B. R. Matthews, Y. Chen, X. Zhou, M. I. Gomis, E. Lonnoy, Maycock, M. Tignor, and T. Waterfield. Geneva: World Meteorological Association. Retrieved from www.ipcc.ch/sr15/chapter/summary-for-policy-makers

International Labour Organization (2017). Population by Rural/Urban Areas: UN Estimates and Projections (1990–2017). Retrieved April 18, 2018, www.ilo.org/ilostat/faces/ilostat-home/download?_adf .ctrlstate=13h5un2e_124&_afrLoop=295215066165322#!%40%40% 3F_adf.ctrl-state%3D13h5un2e_124

(2019). Employment in Agriculture (% of Total Employment) (1991–2014). *World Bank Indicators*. Retrieved from https://data .worldbank.org/indicator/SL.AGR.EMPL.ZS?locations=SY

International Organization for Migrants. (2007). Ninety-Fourth Session. MC/INF/288, November 1. Retrieved from www.iom.int/jahia/web dav/shared/shared/mainsite/about_iom/en/council/94/MC_INF_288.pdf

(2017). *World Migration Report 2018*. Retrieved from https:// publications.iom.int/system/files/pdf/wmr_2018_en.pdf

International Organization for Migrants. (2019a). *A Complex Nexus.* Retrieved from www.iom.int/complex-nexus#estimates

(2019b). *Definitional Issues.* Retrieved from www.iom.int/definitional-issues

Japan International Cooperation Agency and Syrian Ministry of Irrigation. (1996). *The Study of the Water Resources Development in the North-western and Central Basins in the Syrian Arab Republic.* Tokyo: Nippon Koei Co.

Jarvis, T., Giordano, M., Puri, S., Matsumoto, K., and Wolf, A. (2005). International Borders, Ground Water Flow, and Hydroschizophrenia. *Groundwater, 43*(5), 764–770.

Jones, B. T., Mattiacci, E., and Braumoeller, M. F. (2017). Food Scarcity and State Vulnerability: Unpacking the Link between Climate Variability and Violent Unrest. *Journal of Peace Research, 54*(3), 335–350.

Kadouri, M. T., Djebbar, Y., and Nehdi, M. (2001). Water Rights and Water Trade: An Islamic Perspective. In N. I. Faruqui, A. K. Biswas, and M. J. Bino, eds., *Water Management in Islam.* New York: United Nations University Press.

Kahl, C. (2006). *States, Scarcity, and Civil Strife in the Developing World.* Princeton, NJ: Princeton University Press.

(2008). *States, Scarcity, and Civil Strife in the Developing World,* 2nd edn. Princeton, NJ: Princeton University Press.

Kaplan, R. D. (1994). The Coming Anarchy. *Atlantic Monthly, 273*(2), 44–49.

Karl, T. L. (1997). *The Paradox of Plenty: Oil Booms and Petro-State.* Berkeley, CA: University of California Press.

Keane, D. (2004). The Environmental Causes and Consequences of Migration: A Search for the Meaning of "Environmental Refugees." *Georgetown International Environmental Law Review, 16*(2), 209–223.

Kelley, C., Mohtadi, S., Cane, M., Seager R., and Kushnir, Y. (2015). Climate Change in the Fertile Crescent and Implications of the Recent Syrian Drought. *Proceedings of the National Academy of Sciences, 112* (11), 3241–3246.

(2017). Commentary on the Syria Case: Climate as a Contributing Factor. *Political Geography, 60,* 245–247.

Khaddam, M. (2011). Syrian Agriculture between Reality and Potential. In R. Hinnebusch, A. Al-Hindi, M. Khaddam, and M. Ababsa, eds., *Agriculture and Reform in Syria.* Fife: University of St. Andrews Centre for Syrian Studies, pp. 57–82.

Khalifa, K. (2019). *Death Is Hard Work.* New York: Farrar, Straus & Giroux.

Khouri, J. (1990). *Arab Water Security: A Regional Strategy, Horizon 2030*. Damascus: Arab Center for the Study of Arid and Dry Areas.

Khouri, N., and Byringiro, F. (2014). Developing Food Chains. In A. Sadik, M. El-Solh, and N. Saad, eds., *Arab Environment: Food Security – Challenges and Prospects*. Beirut: Arab Forum of Environment and Development, pp. 102–129.

Khudour, R. (2010). The Failures of Regional Development in Syria. Paper presented at the Syrian Economy and Future Horizons, the Twenty-Third Economic Symposium, Syrian Association of Economic Sciences. Damascus, January 26.

Kibaroglu, A. (2013). Turkey–Syria Water Relations: Institutional Development and Political Confrontations in the Euphrates and Tigris Region. In R. Hinnebusch and Ö. Tür, eds., *Turkey–Syria Relations: Between Enmity and Amity*. Farnham: Ashgate, pp. 145–159.

Kibaroglu, A., and Scheumann, W. (2013). Evolution of Transboundary Politics in the Euphrates–Tigris River System: New Perspectives and Political Challenges. *Global Governance, 19*(2), 279–305.

Ki-Moon, Ban (2007). A Climate Culprit in Darfur, June 16. Retrieved from www.un.org/sg/en/content/sg/articles/2007-06-16/climate-culprit-darfur

King, G., Keohane, R., and Verba, S. (1994). *Designing Social Inquiry: Scientific Inference in Qualitative Research*. Princeton, NJ: Princeton University Press.

Kliot, N. (1994). *Water Resources and Conflicts in the Middle East*. London: Routledge.

Kolars, J. (2000). The Spatial Attributes of Water Negotiation, the Need for a River Ethic and River Advocacy in the Middle East. In H. A. Amery and A. T. Wolf, eds., *Water in the Middle East: A Geography of Peace*. Austin, TX: University of Texas Press.

Kolars, J. and Mitchell, W. A. (1991). *The Euphrates River and the Southeast Anatolia Development Project*. Carbondale, IL: Southern Illinois University Press.

Koubi, V., Spilker, G., Böhmelt, T., Bernauer, T., Buhaug, H., and Levy, J. (2014). Do Natural Resources Matter for Interstate and Intrastate Armed Conflict? *Journal of Peace Research, 51*(2), 227–243.

Lacoste, Y. (1993). *Dictionnaire de géopolitique*. Paris: Flammarion.

Larmour, P. (2012). Seven Types of Corruption. In *Interpreting Corruption: Culture and Politics in the Pacific Islands*. Honolulu: University of Hawaii Press, pp. 100–115.

Latour, B. (2014). Agency at the Time of the Anthropocene. *New Literary History, 45*(1), 1–18.

Lefevre, R. (2013). *Ashes of Hama: The Muslim Brotherhood in Syria*. Oxford: Oxford University Press.

Lesch, D. W. (2012). *The Fall of the Assad House.* New Haven, CT: Yale University Press.

Levy, B. S. and Sidel, V. W. (2014). Collective Violence Caused by Climate Change and How It Threatens Health and Human Rights. *Health and Human Rights, 16*(1), 32–40.

Lipschutz, R. D. and Holdren, J. P. (1990). Crossing Borders: Resource Flows, the Global Environment, and International Security. *Bulletin of Peace Proposals, 21*(2), 121–133.

Lomborg, B. (2001). *The Skeptical Environmentalist: Measuring the Real State of the World.* Cambridge: Cambridge University Press.

Lowi, M. R. (1993). *Water and Power: The Politics of a Scarce Resource in the Jordan River Basin.* Cambridge: Cambridge University Press.

Lowi, M. R., and Shaw, B., eds. (2000). *Environmental and Security: Discourses and Practices.* Basingstoke: Palgrave Macmillan.

Lynch, M. (2012). *The Arab Uprising: The Unfinished Revolutions of the Middle East.* New York: Public Affairs.

ed. (2014). *The Arab Uprising Explained: New Contentious Politics in the Middle East.* New York: Columbia University Press.

Mallat, C. (1995). The Quest for Water Use Principles: Reflections on Shari'a and Custom in the Middle East. In J. A. Allan and C. Mallat, eds., *Water in the Middle East: Legal, Political, and Commercial Implications.* London: I. B. Tauris.

Malthus, T. R., and S. Hollander. (1996). *An Essay on the Principle of Population.* London: Routledge/Thoemmes Press. First published 1798.

Marshall, S. (2009). Syria and the Financial Crisis: Prospects for Reform. *Middle East Policy, 16*(2), 106–115.

Martin, S. F., and Tirman, J. (2009). *Women, Migration, and Conflict: Breaking a Deadly Cycle.* Dordrecht: Springer.

Marzouk, N. (2013). Lost Development in Syria. In A. Ali et al., eds., *The Revolution's Background: Syrian Studies.* Doha: Arab Center for Research and Policy Studies, pp. 35–70.

Mason, M. and Mimi, Z. (2014). *Transboundary Climate Security: Climate Vulnerability and Rural Livelihood in the Jordan River Basin.* London: London School of Economics and Political Science Middle East Centre. IPCC

Matthew, R. A. (2014a). *Environmental Security,* 2 vols. London: Sage.

(2014b). Climate Change and Human Security. In J. DiMento, P. Doughman, eds., *Climate Change: What It Means for You, Your Children, and Your Grandchildren,* 2nd edn. Cambridge, MA: MIT Press, pp. 161–180.

Mathews, J. T. (1989). Redefining Security. *Foreign Affairs, 68*(2), 162–177.

McCaffrey, S. (1997). Water Scarcity: Institutional and Legal Responses. In E. H. P. Brans, E. J. de Haan, A. Nollkaemper, and J. Rinzema, eds., *The Scarcity of Water: Emerging Legal and Policy Responses, International Environmental Law and Policy Series*. London: Kluwer Law International.

  (2001). *The Law of International Watercourses: Non-navigational Uses*. Oxford: Oxford University Press.

McDonald, M. (2008). Securitization and the Construction of Security. *European Journal of International Relations, 14*(4), 563–587.

  (2013). Discourses of Climate Security. *Political Geography, 33*, 42–51.

McFarlane, N. S. (2004). A Useful Concept That Risks Losing Its Political Salience. *Security Dialogue, 35*(3), 358–359.

McLaughlin Mitchell, S., and Zawahri, N. A. (2015). The Effectiveness of Treaty Design in Addressing Water Disputes. *Journal of Peace Research, 52*(2), 187–200.

McNeill, J. R. (1992). *The Mountains of the Mediterranean World: An Environmental History*. Cambridge: Cambridge University Press.

  (2013). Eccentricity of the Middle East and North Africa. In A. Mikhail, ed., *Water on Sand, Environmental Histories of the Middle East and North Africa*. Oxford: Oxford University Press, pp. 27–50.

MacQuarrie, P. and Wolf, A. T. (2013). Understanding Water Security. In R. Floyd and R. A. Matthew, eds., *Environmental Security: Approaches and Issues*. Abingdon-on-Thames and New York: Routledge, pp. 169–186.

Medzini, A. (2001). *The Euphrates: A Shared River*. London: School of Oriental and African Studies, University of London.

Mehlum, H., Moene, K. and Torvik, R. (2006). Institutions and the Resource Curse. *Economic Journal, 116*(1), 1–20.

Meinzen-Dick, R., and Bruns, B. R., eds. (2000). *Negotiating Water Rights*. London: International Food Policy Research Institute.

Metral, F. (1980). Le Monde rural syrien à l'ère des réformes (1958–1978) [Rural Syria during the Reforms (1958–1978)]. In A. Raymond, ed., *La Syrie d'aujourd'hui [Syria Today]*. Paris: CNRS, pp. 297–326.

  (1987). Périmètre irrigué d'État sur l'Euphrate syrien: Modes de gestion et politique agricole [Irrigated State-Owned Land on the Syrian Euphrates: Management Techniques and Agricultural Politics]. *Travaux de la Maison d'Orient, 14*(1), 111–145.

Meyer, G. (1995). La Réinstallation de la population touchée par le barrage de l'Euphrate en Syrie [The Reintegration of People Impacted by the Euphrates Dam in Syria]. In F. Conac, ed., *Barrages internationaux et coopération [International Dams and Cooperation]*. Paris: Éditions Karthala, pp. 283–303.

Minot, N., and Pelijor, N. (2010). *Food Security and Food Self-Sufficiency in Bhutan*. International Food Policy Research Institute. Retrieved from http://ebrary.ifpri.org/utils/getfile/collection/p15738coll2/id/129187/file name/129398.pdf

Mirumachi, N. (2013). Securitising Shared Waters: An Analysis of the Hydropolitical Context of the Tanakpur Barrage Project between Nepal and India. *The Geographic Journal*, *179*(4), 309–319.

Mitchell, T. (2002). *Rule of Experts: Egypt, Techno-Politics, Modernity*. Berkeley, CA: University of California Press.

Morris, M. (1997). Water and Conflict in the Middle East: Threats and Opportunities. *Studies in Conflict and Terrorism*, *20*(1), 1–13.

Mualla, W. and Salman, M. (2002). Progress in Water Demand Management in Syria. Paper presented at Progress towards Water Demand Management in the Mediterranean Region, Fiugi, Italy, October.

Myers, N. (1997). Environmental Refugees. *Population and Environment*, *19*(2), 167–182.

Nasr, R. (2009). Pro-poor Economic Growth. Paper presented at Around the Ramifications of the Current Global Economic Crisis, the Twenty-Second Economic Symposium, Syrian Association of Economic Sciences. Damascus, May 26.

(2010). Structural Transformation in the Syrian Economy. Paper presented at the Syrian Economy and Future Horizons, the Twenty-Third Economic Symposium, Syrian Association of Economic Sciences. Damascus, February 23.

National Aeronautics and Space Association. (2010). How Is Today's Warming Different from the Past? *NASA Earth Observatory*, June 3. Retrieved from https://earthobservatory.nasa.gov/features/GlobalWarming/page3.php

(2019). Climate Change: How Do We Know? *NASA Global Climate Change*. Retrieved from https://climate.nasa.gov/evidence

Neep, D. (2012). Occupying Syria under French Mandate: Insurgency, Space and State Formation. Cambridge: Cambridge University Press.

Newman, E. (2004). A Normatively Attractive but Analytically Weak Concept. *Security Dialogue*, *35*(3), 358–359.

(2010). Critical Human Security Studies. *Review of International Studies*, *36*(1), 77–94.

Newman, E., and van Selm, J. (2003). *Refugees and Forced Displacement: International Security, Human Vulnerability, and the State*. Tokyo: United Nations University Press.

Null, S., and Risi, L. H. (2016). *Navigating Complexity: Climate, Migration, and Conflict in a Changing World*. Office of Conflict Management and

Mitigation Discussion Paper. Washington, DC: United States Agency for International Development.

Olson, R. (1982). *The Ba'ath and Syria, 1947–1982: The Evolution of Ideology, Party, and State*. Princeton, NJ: Kingston Press.

O'Neill, A. (2019). "The Brexodus Is Under Way": Meet the Brits Leaving the UK. *The Guardian*, March 23. Retrieved from www.theguardian.com/politics/2019/mar/23/brexodus-under-way-brits-leaving-the-uk

Oels, A. (2012). From "Securitization" of Climate Change to "Climatization" of the Security Field. In J. Scheffren, M. Brzoska, H. G. Brauch, P. M. Link, and J. Schilling, eds., *Climate Change, Human Security, and Violent Conflict*. Berlin: Springer, pp. 185–205.

Ogata, S., and Sen, A. (2003). *Human Security Now*. New York: Commission on Human Security.

Oktav, Ö. Z. (2009). Transition from Enmity to "Common Fate" Rhetoric: Water Issue in Turkish–Iraqi–Syrian Relations. *The Turkish Yearbook of International Relations*, 40, 71–90.

Olson, R. W. (1982). The Ba'th and Syria, 1947 to 1982: The Evolution of Ideology, Party, and State, from the French Mandate to the Era of Hafiz Al-Asad. Princeton, NJ: Kingston Press.

Ozis, U. (1993). South-East Anatolian Project in Turkey. *Proceedings of the International Symposium on Water Resources in the Middle East: Policy and Institutional Aspects*. Urbana, Illinois, October 24–27.

Pacific Institute. (2015). *Water Conflict Chronology*. Retrieved from www2.worldwater.org/conflict/list

Parlar Dal, E. (2012). The Transformation of Turkey's Relations with the Middle East: Illusion or Awakening? *Turkish Studies*, 13(2), 245–267.

Pearlman, W. (2017). *We Crossed a Bridge and It Trembled: Voices from Syria*. New York: Custom House.

Perthes, V. (1995). *The Political Economy of Syria under Asad*. London: I. B. Tauris.

Phillips, C. (2015). Sectarianism and Conflict in Syria. *Third World Quarterly*, 36(2), 357–376.

Pierret, T. (2013). *Religion and State in Syria: The Ulamas from Coup to Revolution*. Cambridge: Cambridge University Press.

Pinker, S. (2018). *Enlightenment Now: The Case for Reason, Science, Humanism and Progress*. New York: Penguin.

Postel, S. (1996). *Dividing the Waters: Food Security, Ecosystem Health and the New Politics of Scarcity*. Washington, DC: WorldWatch Institute.

Qatna, M. H. (2009). The Agricultural Sector: Policies and Procedures. Paper presented at Around the Ramifications of the Current Global

Economic Crisis, the Twenty-Second Economic Symposium, Syrian Association of Economic Sciences. Damascus, April 28.

(2010). Effects of the Drought on the Northeastern Region in Syria, 2008–2009. Paper presented at the Syrian Economy and Future Horizons, the Twenty-Third Economic Symposium, Syrian Association of Economic Sciences. Damascus, January 26.

Raleigh, C. (2010). Political Marginalization, Climate Change, and Conflict in African Sahel States. *International Studies Review*, 12(1), 69–86.

Raleigh, C., Choi, H. J., and Kniveton, D. (2015). The Devil Is in the Details: An Investigation of the Relationships between Conflict, Food Price and Climate across Africa. *Global Environmental Change*, 32, 187–199.

Ransan-Cooper, H., Farbotko, C., McNamara, K. E., Thornton, F., and Chevalier, E. (2015). Being(s) Framed: The Means and Ends of Framing Environmental Migrants. *Global Environmental Change*, 35(November), 106–115.

Ratzel, F. (1897). *Politische geographie*. Munich: R. Oldenbourg.

Republic of Turkey. (2002). The Turkish National Policy for Utilizing the Waters of the Euphrates-Tigris Basin (The Three-Staged Plan). Ankara: Ministry of Foreign Affairs.

(2010). Joint Statement of the Second Ministerial Meeting of the High Level Strategic Cooperation Council between the Syrian Arab Republic and the Republic of Turkey, October 2–3, Lattakia. Ankara: Ministry of Foreign Affairs. Retrieved from www.mfa.gov.tr/joint-statement-of-the-second-ministerial-meeting-of-the.en.mfa

Rijsberman, F. R. (2006). Water Scarcity: Fact or Fiction? *Agricultural Water Management*, 80(1), 5–22.

Roberts, D. (1987). *The Ba'th and the Creation of Modern Syria*. London: Croom Helm.

Romm, J. J. (1993). *Defining National Security: The Nonmilitary Aspects*. New York: Council on Foreign Relations Press.

Rose-Ackerman, S. (1999). *Corruption and Government: Causes, Consequences, and Reform*. Cambridge: Cambridge University Press.

Rousseau, D. L., and Walker, T. C. (2010). Liberalism. In M. Dunn Cavelty and Th. Balzacq, eds., *The Routledge Handbook of Security Studies*. Abingdon-on-Thames and New York: Routledge, pp. 21–33.

Sadowski, Y. M. (1987). Patronage and the Ba'ath: Corruption and Control in Contemporary Syria. *Arab Studies Quarterly*, 9(4), 442–461.

Sahner, C. (2014). *Among the Ruins: Syria's Past and Present*. Oxford: Oxford University Press.

Salamandra, C., and Stenberg, L. (2015). *Syria from Reform to Revolt*, vol. II. Syracuse, NY: Syracuse University Press.

Salloukh, B. F. (2017). The Sectarianization of Geopolitics in the Middle East. In N. Hashemi, and D. Postel, eds., *Sectarianization: Mapping the New Politics of the Middle East*. Oxford: Oxford University Press.

Sanjian, A. (1956). The Sandjak of Alexandretta (Hatay): Its Impact on Turkish–Syrian Relations. *Middle East Journal*, 10(4), 379–394.

Scheffran, J., Brzoska, M., Kominek, J., Link, P. M., and Schilling, J. (2012). Climate Change and Violent Conflict. *Science*, 336(6083), 869–871.

Schiffler, M. (2001). Review of *Water Management in Islam*, N. I. Faruqui, Biswas, A. K., and Bino, M. J. *Water International*, 26(3).

Scott, J. (2011). Four Domestications: Fire, Plants, Animals, and . . . Us. The Tanner Lectures on Human Values Delivered at Harvard University, May 4–6: 185–227. Retrieved from https://tannerlectures.utah.edu/_documents/a-to-z/s/Scott_11.pdf

  (2017). *Against the Grain: A Deep History of the Earliest States*. New Haven, CT: Yale University Press.

Seale, P. (1965). *The Struggle for Syria: A Study of Post-war Arab Politics*. Oxford: Oxford University Press.

  (1988). *Asad: The Struggle for the Middle East*. Berkeley, CA: University of California Press.

Seifan, S. (2009a). Challenges of the Syrian Economy and the Risks of Ignoring Them. Paper presented at Around the Ramifications of the Current Global Economic Crisis, the Twenty-Second Economic Symposium, Syrian Association of Economic Sciences. Damascus, June 2.

  (2009b). Social Consequences of Economic Policies. Paper presented at Syrian Association of Economic Sciences. Damascus.

  (2011). The Road to Economic Reform in Syria. In R. Hinnebusch, ed., *St. Andrews Papers on Contemporary Syria*. St. Andrews: St. Andrews Syrian Studies, School of International Relations.

Selby, J. (2018). Climate Change and the Syrian Civil War, Part II: The Jazira's Agrarian Crisis. *Geoforum*, 101, 1–15.

Selby, J. and Hoffmann, C. (2014). Beyond Scarcity: Rethinking Water, Climate Change and Conflict in the Sudans. *Global Environmental Change*, 29, 360–370.

Selby, J., Dahi, O., Fröhlich, C., and Hulme, M. (2017a). Climate Change and the Syrian Civil War Revisited. *Political Geography*, 60, 232–244.

  (2017b). Climate Change and the Syrian Civil War Revisited: A Rejoinder. *Political Geography*, 60, 253–255.

Sen, A. (1981). *Poverty Famines: An Essay on Entitlement and Deprivation*. Oxford: Clarendon Press.

  (1999). Beyond the Crisis: Development Strategies in Asia. Singapore: Institute of Southeast Asian Studies.

(2000). Why Human Security? Lecture at the International Symposium on Human Security. Tokyo. 28 July.

Servigne, P., and Stevens, R. (2015). *Comment tout peut s'effondrer*. Paris: Éditions du Seuil.

Seter, H. (2016). Connecting Climate Variability and Conflict: Implications for Empirical Testing. *Political Geography*, *53*, 1–9.

Shamout, N. (2014). Syria Faces an Imminent Food and Water Crisis. Chatham House: Expert Comment. Retrieved from www.chathamhouse.org/expert/comment/14959

Shamout, N., and Lahn, G. (2015). *The Euphrates in Crisis: Channels of Cooperation for a Threatened River*. Chatham House: Research Publications. Retrieved from www.chathamhouse.org/publication/euphrates-crisis-channels-cooperation-threatened-river#sthash.vMUxkdWt.dpuf

Sharf, K. (2009). Introduction. Paper presented at Around the Ramifications of the Current Global Economic Crisis, the Twenty-Second Economic Symposium, Syrian Association of Economic Sciences. Damascus, January 26.

Simonelli, A. (2016). *Governing Climate-Induced Migration and Displacement*. Basingstoke: Palgrave Macmillan.

Singer, M. (2009). Buying Voters with Dirty Money: The Relationship between Clientelism and Corruption. Paper presented at American Political Science Association Meeting. Toronto, August 21.

Slettebak, R. T., and Gleditsch, N. P. (2012). Don't Blame the Weather! Climate-Related Natural Disasters and Civil Conflict. *Journal of Peace Research*, *49*(1), 163–176.

Smith, P. (2015). *Climate Change as Social Drama: Global Warming in the Public Sphere*. Cambridge: Cambridge University Press.

Soumi, G. (2009). Food Security and Drought. Paper presented at Around the Ramifications of the Current Global Economic Crisis, the Twenty-Second Economic Symposium, Syrian Association of Economic Sciences. Damascus, April 28.

Soumi, G., and Ma'an, D. (2010). The Water Crisis in the Eastern Region. Paper presented at the Syrian Economy and Future Horizons, the Twenty-Third Economic Symposium, Syrian Association of Economic Sciences. Damascus, January 26.

Spector, B. I., and A. Wolf. (2000). Negotiating Security: New Goals, Changed Process. *International Negotiation*, *5*(3), 411–426.

Springborg, R. (1981). Ba'athism in Practice: Agriculture, Politics, and Political Culture in Syria and Iraq. *Middle Eastern Studies*, *17*(2), 191–209.

Starr, S. (2012). *Revolt in Syria: Eye-Witness to the Uprising*. London: C. Hurst & Co.

Steffen, W., Crutzen, P. J., and McNeill, J. R. (2007). The Anthropocene: Are Humans Now Overwhelming the Great Forces of Nature? *Ambio, 36* (8), 614–621.

Sternberg, T. (2012). Chinese Drought, Bread and the Arab Spring. *Applied Geography, 34,* 519–524.

Stritzel, H. (2007). Towards a Theory of Securitization: Copenhagen and Beyond. *European Journal of International Relations, 13*(3), 357–383.

Suleiman, H. A. (2005). The Social Market Economy: Between Concept and Implementation. Paper presented at Syrian Association of Economic Sciences. Damascus.

Swain, A., and Jägerskog, A. (2016). *Emerging Security Threats in the Middle East: The Impact of Climate Change and Globalization.* Lanham, MD: Rowman & Littlefield.

Syria Report. (2001). Miro: IMF Agrees on Syria's Development Program. *Syria Report.* January 7. Retrived from www.syria-report.com/news/finance/miro-imf-agrees-syrias-development-program

(2002). Water Brief: Miro Inaugurates Bassel Dam. *Syria Report.* April 26. Retrieved from www.syria-report.com/news/water/water-brief-miro-inaugurates-bassel-dam

(2005a). Dardari: VAT in 2008; Oil to Make Up 15% of Exports in 2010. *Syria Report.* June 15. Retrieved from www.syria-report.com/news/economy/dardari-vat-2008-oil-make-15-exports-2010

(2005b). IMF Urges Syria to Introduce a VAT System and Diversify Economic Productive Base. *Syria Report.* October 15. Retrieved from www.syria-report.com/news/economy/imf-urges-syria-introduce-vat-system-and-diversify-economic-productive-base

(2005c). Syria Faces Diesel Shortage. *Syria Report.* October 15. Retrieved from www.syria-report.com/news/economy/syria-faces-diesel-shortage

(2005d). Syria to Raise Oil Prices. *Syria Report.* November 15. Retrieved from www.syria-report.com/news/economy/syria-raise-oil-prices

(2006). IMF Commends Government Policy but Offers Set of Socially-Hurting Recommendations. *Syria Report.* June 18. Retrieved from www.syria-report.com/news/economy/imf-commends-government-policy-offers-set-socially-hurting-recommendations

(2007a). Decline in Non-Oil Budget Deficit Should Be Key Policy Objective, IMF Mission Chief Says. *Syria Report.* June 8. Retrieved from www.syria-report.com/news/economy/decline-non-oil-budget-deficit-should-be-key-policy-objective-imf-mission-chief-says

(2007b). IMF Commends Syria's 2006 Economic Performance, but Warns of Risks of Dollarization. *Syria Report.* June 25. Retrieved from www.syria-report.com/news/economy/imf-commends-syrias-2006-economic-performance-warns-risks-dollarization

(2007c). Speech of Bashar Al-Assad on the Re-election on July 17, 2007. *Syria Report*. July 17. Retrieved from www.syria-report.com/library/ assad-speeches-interviews/speech-bashar-al-assad-re-election-july-17-2007

(2007d). Government to Start Lifting Subsidies in 2008. *Syria Report*. September 3. Retrieved from www.syria-report.com/heating-oil/govern ment-start-lifting-subsidies-2008

(2008). UN Launches Appeal to Help 1 Million Drought-Affected Syrians. *Syria Report*. October 6. Retrieved from www.syria-report.com/news/ economy/un-launches-appeal-help-1-million-drought-affected-syrians

(2009a). Wheat Imports to Reach Record Level as Stocks Decline. *Syria Report*. February 7. Retrieved from www-syria-report-com/news/food-agriculture/wheat-imports-reach-record-level-stocks-decline

(2009b). Government Provides First Payment to Agricultural Fund. *Syria Report*. May 18. Retrieved from www.syria-report.com/news/food-agri culture/government-provides-first-payment-agricultural-fund

(2009c). Drought Hits Hard on Syria's North East. *Syria Report*. June 1. Retrieved from www.syria-report.com/news/economy/drought-hits-hard-syrias-north-east

(2009d). Government Announces New Measures to Support North East Region. *Syria Report*. June 8. Retrieved from www.syria-report.com/ news/food-agriculture/government-announces-new-measures-support-north-east-region

(2009e). Losses at Mahrukat Shrink as Government Prepares New Sub-sidy Scheme. *Syria Report*. October. Retrieved from www.syria-report-com/news/oil-gas-mining/losses-mahrukat-shrink-government-pre pares-new-subsidy-scheme

(2010a). Syrian Drought Response Plan. *Syria Report*. January 1. Retrieved from www.syria-report.com/news/food-agriculture/syrian-drought-response-plan

(2010b). Reclaiming of Land on Euphrates to Add 23,000 ha of Cultivable Area. *Syria Report*. March 8. Retrieved from www.syria-report.com/ news/food-agriculture/reclaiming-land-euphrates-add-23000-ha-cultiv able-area

(2010c). Lack of Funding Delays Implementation of Drought Response Plan. *Syria Report*. March 15. Retrieved from www.syria-report.com/ news/water/lack-funding-delays-implementation-drought-response-plan

(2010d). Agricultural Bank to Expand Lending. *Syria Report*. April 5. Retrieved from www.syria-report.com/news/food-agriculture/agricul tural-bank-expand-lending

(2010e). Decree to Rationalize Water Consumption in the Agricultural Sector. *Syria Report*. June 14. Retrieved from http://syria-report.com/

news/food-agriculture/decree-rationalize-water-consumption-agricul
tural-sector

(2010f). Government Provides Update on Works on the Tigris River
Project. *Syria Report*. August 30. Retrieved from www.syria-report
.com/news/water/government-provides-update-works-tigris-river-project

(2010g). Government Inaugurates New Projects in Country's Eastern
Region. *Syria Report*. September 6. Retrieved from www.syria-report
.com/news/economy/government-inaugurates-new-projects-countrys-east
ern-region

(2011a). Government Announces New Measures to Support Agricultural
Sector. *Syria Report*. April 14. Retrieved from www.syria-report.com/
news/food-agriculture/ government-announces-new-measures-support-
agricultural-sector

(2011b). Syrian President Eases Lending Restrictions on Farmers. *Syria
Report*. December 12. Retrieved from www.syria-report.com/news/
food-agriculture/syrian-president-eases-lending-restrictions-farmers

(2012). Government to Spend 13.5 Billions on Agricultural Inputs Aids.
Syria Report. February 2. Retrieved from www.syria-report.com/news/
food-agriculture/government-spend-syp-135-billion-agricultural-inputs-
aids

(2015). Syria's Agriculture Decimated by War. *Syria Report*. July 27.
Retrieved from www.syria-report.com/news/food-agriculture/syria%
E2%80%99s-agriculture-sector-decimated-war-report-finds

(2016). Syrian Government Withdraws Further from Farming Sector.
Syria Report. July 5. Retrieved from www.syria-report.com/news/
food-agriculture/syrian-government-withdraws-further-farming-sector

(2017). Syrian Businessmen Complain of Labor Shortages despite Massive
Unemployment. *Syria Report*. November 28. Retrieved from www
.syria-report.com/news/economy/syrian-businesses-complain-labour-
shortages-despite-massive-unemployment

(2018a). Government Prioritizes Spending on Core Constituency. *Syria
Report*. January 9. Retrieved from www.syria-report.com/news/econ
omy/government-prioritises-spending-core-constituency

(2018b). Report Highlights Dramatic Situation of Syrian Agricultural
Sector. *Syria Report*. October 16. Retrieved from www.syria-report
.com/news/food-agriculture/report-highlights-dramatic-situation-syrian-
agricultural-sector

Syrian Arab Republic. (1987). Protocol of 1987 on Issues Relating to Economic Cooperation between the Syrian Arab Republic and the Republic
of Turkey, July 17.

(1988). *Tableau général des projets de l'Euphrate* [*General Review of
Projects on the Euphrates*]. Damascus: Ministry of Irrigation.

(1996). *Internal Report.* Damascus: Ministry of Irrigation.

(1999). *Hydrologic Plans, 1995–1999.* Damascus: Ministry of Irrigation.

(2001). *Stratégie de travail au sein du Ministère de l'Irrigation* [*Plan for the Ministry of Irrigation*]. Damascus: Ministry of Irrigation.

(2017a). Wells and Irrigated Area by Governorate for 2000–2016 and Their Development at the Country Level. In Ministry of Agriculture and Agrarian Reform, *Statistical Abstract (2007–2016).* Retrieved April 6, 2018, from http://moaar.gov.sy/main/archives/category/%D8%A7% D9%84%D9%85%D8%AC%D9%85%D9%88%D8%B9%D8%A7% D8%AA-%D8%A7%D9%84%D8%A5%D8%AD%D8%B5%D8% A7%D8%A6%D9%8A%D8%A9

(2017b). Area, Production, and Yield of Total Wheat by Governorate for 2007–2016 and Their Development at the Country Level (2000–2016). In Ministry of Agriculture and Agrarian Reform, *Statistical Abstract (2007–2016).* Retrieved April 6, 2018, from http://moaar.gov.sy/main/ archives/category/%D8%A7%D9%84%D9%85%D8%AC%D9%85% D9%88%D8%B9%D8%A7%D8%AA-%D8%A7%D9%84%D8%A5% D8%AD%D8%B5%D8%A7%D8%A6%D9%8A%D8%A9

(2017c). Area, Production, and Yield of Barley by Governorate for 2007–2016 and Their Development at the Country Level (2000–2016). In Ministry of Agriculture and Agrarian Reform, *Statistical Abstract (2007–2016).* Retrieved April 6, 2018, from http://moaar .gov.sy/main/archives/category/%D8%A7%D9%84%D9%85%D8% AC%D9%85%D9%88%D8%B9%D8%A7%D8%AA-%D8%A7% D9%84%D8%A5%D8%AD%D8%B5%D8%A7%D8%A6%D9% 8A%D8%A9

(2017d). Production Cost Average for Irrigated and Non-irrigated Soft Wheat Crop. In Ministry of Agriculture and Agrarian Reform, *Statistical Abstract (2007–2016).* Retrieved April 8, 2018, from http://moaar .gov.sy/main/archives/category/%D8%A7%D9%84%D9%85%D8% AC%D9%85%D9%88%D8%B9%D8%A7%D8%AA-%D8%A7% D9%84%D8%A5%D8%AD%D8%B5%D8%A7%D8%A6%D9% 8A%D8%A9

(2017e). Production Cost Average for Irrigated and Non-irrigated Soft Wheat Crop. In Ministry of Agriculture and Agrarian Reform, *Statistical Abstract (2007–2016).* Retrieved April 8, 2018, from http://moaar .gov.sy/main/archives/category/%D8%A7%D9%84%D9%85%D8% AC%D9%85%D9%88%D8%B9%D8%A7%D8%AA-%D8%A7% D9%84%D8%A5%D8%AD%D8%B5%D8%A7%D8%A6%D9% 8A%D8%A9

Syrie et Monde Arabe. (1978). Étude mensuelle economique, politique et statistique: Le Barrage de l'Euphrate par l'ingénieur Sobhi Kahhaleh, ministre du barrage de l'Euphrate [The Euphrates Dam by the Engineer Sobhi Kahhaleh, Minister of the Euphrates Dam]. *25*(290), 1.

(1987). Étude mensuelle economique, politique et statistique: Les Projets d'irrigation et la sécurité alimentaire en Syrie [Monthly Economic, Political and Statistical Study: Irrigation Projects and Food Security in Syria]. *33*(400), 1–11.

Tadjbakhsh, S., and Chenoy, A. (2007). *Human Security: Concepts and Implications.* Abingdon-on-Thames and New York: Routledge.

Tejel, J. (2009). *Syria's Kurds: History, Politics and Society.* Abingdon-on-Thames and New York: Routledge.

(2014). Les Paradoxes du printemps Kurde en Syrie. *Politique étrangère,* *79*(2), 51–61.

Tertrais, B. (2011). The Climate Wars Myth. *The Washington Quarterly, 34* (3), 17–29.

Theisen, O. M. (2012). Climate Clashes? Weather Variability, Land Pressure, and Organized Violence in Kenya, 1989–2004. *Journal of Peace Research,* *49*(1), 81–96.

Theisen, O. M., Holtermann, H., and Buhaug, H. (2011). Climate Wars? Assessing the Claim That Drought Breeds Conflict. *International Security,* *36*(3), 79–106.

Tir, J., and Stinnett, D. M. (2012). Weathering Climate Change: Can Institutions Mitigate International Water Conflict? *Journal of Peace Research,* *49*(1), 211–225.

Tishrin. (2001). Syria and Iraq Concerned by Turkish use of Euphrates. *Tishrin,* November 28.

Trombetta, M. J. (2008). Environmental Security and Climate Change: Analysing the Discourse. *Cambridge Review of International Affairs,* *21*(4), 585–602.

(2011). Rethinking the Securitization of the Environment: Old Beliefs, New Insights. In T. Balzacq, ed., *Securitization Theory: How Security Problems Emerge and Dissolve.* Abingdon-on-Thames and New York: Routledge, pp. 135–149.

(2014). Linking Climate-Induced Migration and Security within the EU: Insights from the Securitization Debate. *Critical Studies on Security,* 2 (2), 131–147.

Ul-Haq, M. (1995). *Reflections on Human Development.* Oxford: Oxford University Press.

(1998). Human Rights, Security and Governance. *Peace and Policy Journal of the Toda Institute for Global Peace and Policy Research: Dialogue of Civilizations for World Citizenship,* *3*(2).

Ullman, R. H. (1983). Redefining Security. *International Security,* *8*(1), 129–153.

United Nations Development Programme. (2010). *Mapping Climate Change Vulnerability and Impact Scenarios: A Guidebook for Subnational Planners.* Retrieved from www.undp.org/content/undp/en/home/library page/environment-energy/low_emission_climateresilientdevelopment/ mapping-climate-change-vulnerability.html

United Nations Educational, Scientific, and Cultural Organization. (2018). Supporting Water Security. Retrieved from https://en.unesco.org/part nerships/partnering/supporting-water-security

United Nations General Assembly. (2012). Follow-Up to Paragraph 143 on Human Security of the 2005 World Summit Outcome (10 September 2012). A/RES/66/290. Retrieved from https://undocs.org/A/RES/66/290

United Nations High Commissioner for Refugees. (2019). Syria Regional Refugee Response. Updated March 14. Retrieved from https://data2 .unhcr.org/en/situations/syria

United Nations Office for the Coordination of Humanitarian Affairs. (2008). Syria Drought Appeal. Retrieved from www.humanitarianresponse .info/en/programme-cycle/space/document/syria-drought-appeal-2008

(2010). Syria Drought Response Plan: Mid-term Review, 2009–2010. Retrieved from https://reliefweb.int/sites/reliefweb.int/files/resources/ 20E00ADAF9F3C153852576D20068E86B-Full_Report.pdf

United Nations Population Division. (2004). *World Population to 2300.* ST/ ESA/SER.A./236. New York: United Nations. Retrieved from www .un.org/population/publications/longrange2/WorldPop2300final.pdf

United Nations. (2011). The Global Food Crises. In The Global Social Crisis: Report on the World Social Situation 2011, *ST/ESA/334.* New York: United Nations. Retrieved from www.un.org/esa/socdev/rwss/docs/ 2011/chapter4.pdf

Unver, O. (2005). Sharing Benefits from Upstream Water Storage: The Case of Euphrates-Tigris System. Paper presented at Stockholm World Water Week, Stockholm, Sweden, August 27.

Van Dam, N. (2011). *The Struggle for Power in Syria: Politics and Society under Asad and the Ba'th Party.* 4th edn. London: I. B. Tauris.

Vidal, J. (2014). Water Supply Key to Outcome of Conflicts in Iraq and Syria, Experts Warn. *The Guardian,* July 2. Retrieved from www.theguardian .com/environment/2014/jul/02/water-key-conflict-iraq-syria-isis

Vogler, J. (2013). International Relations Theory and the Environment. In G. Kütting, ed., *Global Environmental Politics, Concepts, Theories and Case Studies.* Abingdon-on-Thames and New York: Routledge, pp. 11–26.

Von Uexkull, N. (2014). Sustained Drought, Vulnerability and Civil Conflict in Sub-Saharan Africa. *Political Geography,* 43, 16–26.

Waterbury, J. (1997). Between Unilateralism and Comprehensive Accords: Modest Steps toward Cooperation in International River

Basins. *International Journal of Water Resources Development*, 13(3), 279–290.

Wedeen, L. (2013). Ideology and Humor in Dark Times: Notes from Syria. *Critical Inquiry*, *39*(4), 841–873.

  (2015). *Ambiguities of Domination: Politics, Rhetoric, and Symbols in Contemporary Syria*. Chicago, IL: The University of Chicago Press.

Weinthal, E., Zawahri, N., and Sowers, J. (2015). Securitizing Water, Climate, and Migration in Israel, Jordan, and Syria. *International Environmental Agreements: Politics, Law and Economics*, 15(3), 293–307.

Werrell, C. E., and Femia, F. (2015). Climate Change as Threat Multiplier: Understanding the Broader Nature of the Risk. *The Center for Climate and Security*, February 12. Retrieved from https://climateandsecurity .org/2015/02/12/briefer-climate-change-as-threat-multiplier-understand ing-the-broader-nature-of-the-risk

Westing, A. H., ed. (1986). *Global Resources and International Conflict*. Stockholm International Peace Research Institute. Oxford: Oxford University Press.

Wilkinson, J. C. (1990). Muslim Land and Water Law. *Journal of Islamic Studies*, *1* (1).

Williams, P. D. (2008). Security Studies: An Introduction. In P. D. Williams, ed., *Security Studies: An Introduction*. Abingdon-on-Thames and New York: Routledge, pp. 1–12.

Wisner, B., Blaikie, P., Cannon, T., and Davis, I. (2004). *At Risk: Natural Hazards, People's Vulnerability and Disasters*. 2nd edn. Abingdon-on-Thames and New York: Routledge.

Witter, S. G., and Whiteford, S. (1999). Water Security: The Issues and Policy Challenges. *International Review of Comparative Public Policy*, *11*, 1–25.

Wittfogel, K. A. (1957). *Oriental Despotism: A Comparative Study of Total Power*. New Haven, CT: Yale University Press.

Wolchover, N. (2018). "What Is a Drought?," *LiveScience.com*, September 28. Retrieved from www.livescience.com/21469-drought-definition.html.

Wolf, A. T. (1994). A Hydropolitical History of the Nile, Jordan and Euphrates River Basins. In A. K. Biswas, ed., *International Waters of the Middle East from Euphrates-Tigris to Nile*. Oxford: Oxford University Press, pp. 5–43.

  (1998). Conflict and Cooperation along International Waterways. *Water Policy*, 1(2), 251–265.

Wolf, A. T., Yoffe, S. B., and Giordano, M. (2003). International Waters: Identifying Basins at Risk. *Water Policy*, 5(1), 29–60.

Wolfers, A. (1952). "National Security" as an Ambiguous Symbol. *Political Science Quarterly*, 67(4), 481–502.

World Bank. (2008). *Agriculture in Syria: Towards the Social Market – Agriculture Sector Note and Technical Note on Agricultural Subsidies.* Sustainable Development Department, Middle East and North Africa Region, June.

(2012). *Global Monitoring Report 2012: Food Prices, Nutrition, and the Millennium Development Goals.* Washington, DC: The World Bank. Retrieved from: www.imf.org/external/pubs/ft/gmr/2012/eng/gmr.pdf

(2016). Control of Corruption, *Worldwide Governance Indicators (1996–2016).* Washington, DC: The World Bank. Retrieved April 18, 2017, from: https://info.worldbank.org/governance/wgi/#home

(2018a). Syria, Temperature, Rainfall (1991–2015). *Climate Change Knowledge Portal.* Washington, DC: The World Bank. Retrieved April 18, 2017, from: https://climateknowledgeportal.worldbank.org/download-data

(2018b). Agriculture, Value Added (% of GDP). *National Accounts Data (1985–2007).* Retrieved from: https://data.worldbank.org/indicator/NV.AGR.TOTL.ZS?locations=SY

(2019). Syrian Arabic Republic. *World Bank Poverty Database. Poverty and Equity Data Portal (1990–2015).* Retrieved from: http://povertydata.worldbank.org/poverty/country/SYR

Yassin-Kassab, R., and al-Shami, L. (2016). *Burning Country: Syrians in Revolution and War.* London: Pluto Press.

Yazbek, S. (2012). *A Woman in the Crossfire: Diaries of the Syrian Revolution.* London: Haus Publishing.

(2015). *The Crossing: My Journey to the Shattered Heart of Syria.* London: Random House.

Zala, B. (2013). The Strategic Dimensions of Water: From National Security to Sustainable Security. In B. Lankford, K. Bakker, M. Zetioun, and D. Conway, eds., *Water Security: Principles, Perspectives and Practices.* London: Routledge, pp. 273–288.

Zawahri, N. (2006). Stabilizing Iraq's Water Supply: What the Euphrates and Tigris Rivers Can Learn from the Indus. *Third World Quarterly, 27* (6), 1041–1058.

Zeitoun, M., and Mirumachi, N. (2008). Transboundary Water Interaction: Reconsidering Conflict and Cooperation. *International Environmental Agreements, 8*(4), 297–316.

Zintl, T. (2015). The Co-optation of Foreign-Educated Syrians: Between Legitimizing Strategy and Domestic Reforms. In R. A. Hinnebusch and T. Zintl, eds. (2015). *Syria from Reform to Revolt,* vol. I. Syracuse, NY: Syracuse University Press, pp. 113–132.

Index

2011 Syrian uprising. *See*: Syrian
  Revolution

Abbasid, 79
Achaemenids, 79
Adana Security Protocol, 93
adaptation, climate, 57
Agriculture, employment, country level,
  190
  employment, regional, 190–192
  share to GDP, 186
Aflaq, Michel, 106, 114
al-Assad, Bashar, 10, 94, 98, 107, 111,
  139–141, 147–149, 196, 206, 209
al-Assad, Hafez, 103–112, 115,
  138–140, 147–149, 206, 209
al-Bitar, Midhat, 114
al-Bitar, Sala-ed-Din, 114
al-maghmureen, 71, 103
al-nazihin, 71
Anthropocene, 4, 7, 163, 225, 230
Arab Belt policy, 106, 137, 209
Arab Spring, 10
Arabization, 20, 103, 106, 137, 159,
  209
Assad regime, 95
authoritarianism, 10
availability, water, 42

Ba'ath, 10, 20, 106, 108–110, 112, 114,
  131, 137, 140–141, 216, 226, 235
Ba'athism, 19–20, 89, 103, 117, 146,
  186, 237, *See* Ba'ath
Baldwin, Andrew, 28
Bitar, Salah al-Din, 106
bread protests, 62
bureaucracy, hydraulic, 81

capacity, adaptive, 21
climate change, Anthropogenic, 5

climate risk, 58
climate security, 25
climate variability, 229, 237
climate vulnerability, core components
  and definition, 58, 151
climate wars. *See* climate conflict
climate–conflict nexus, 6, 8, 56, 151,
  205
Cold War, 99, 218
collapsology, 7, 36
conflict, climate, 5–6, 65, 67, 151–152,
  156, 203, 205, 213, 225
Copenhagen School, the, 29
cornucopians, 32
Corrective Movement, 106, 139
Corruption, 188, 197–198, 201, 208,
  211–212
  Corruption Index, 202
crises, food price, 61
critical security, 25

Dalby, Simon, 18, 25, 28, 32, 49, 54
Dams, Tabqa, 127–128
  Displacements, 134, 198
Dardari, Abdullah, 144
Darwinists, Social, 4
Davutoğlu, Ahmet, 94
De-Ba'athification, 139
debt, ecological, 53
decollectivization, 209
Decree 21 of 2010, 133
demand-driven (water stress), 43
demographic and environmental stress,
  45
Deraa, 9, 13, 150
determinism, environmental, 4, 25
development, human, 52
discourses, 29
doctrine, Shia, 86
doctrine, Sunni, 87

double insecurity, 37
drought of 2006–2010, 71
drought, 44
drought, agricultural, 44
drought, hydrologic, 44
drought, meteorological, 44
drought, multi-year, 153
drought, socioeconomic, 44

ecology, political, 33
Egypt, 61–64
entitlement approach, 60, 64
environment, 28, 32
environmental migrants, 8
environmental security, 27–61
exceptionalism, politics of, 30

Falkenmark indicator, 43
flood–retreat, 80
Food and Agriculture Organization, 59
food production variability, 186
Food security, *see* security, food
French Mandate, 207

Gallup poll, 202
GDP, Syria, 211
gendered, unemployement, 191
Global South, 8
Great Acceleration, 4
Great Anatolian Project or (*Güneydogu Anadolu Projesi*), 89
greed and grievances theory, 35

Hammurabi Code, 82
HECS framework, 18, 24, 26, 48, 75, 103, 149, 195, 202, 205, 207, 212
Homer-Dixon, Thomas, 38
Human Security,
   Characteristics, 49
   Definition, 50
   Development, 51–52
   Environment, 52–53
Human security. *See*:Sen, Amartya, Ul Haq, Habib
hydraulic resources, Sunni doctrine, 85

ideology, Ba'athist, see Ba'athism
   complicity, 107
   definition, 107

as flexible principles, 108
legitimacy, 110
role, 14–16, 20, 26, 75, 99, 103–104
symbols and power, 109
tool, mobilization, 104, 107–108
infitah, 139, 147
insecuritization, 31
instability, environmental, 45
Integrated Water Resource Management, 47
Intergovernmental Panel on Climate Change, 5
International Monetary Fund (IMF), 143, 210
International Organization for Migration, 71, 228
IPCC, Fourth Assessment Report, 57, 162
   Fifth Assessment Report, 50, 57–58, 68–69, 151
Irrigation, Ministry of, 121, 123, 127, 132, 224, 229, 240–241
Islamic State of Iraq and Levant, 10

Jamal Barout, Muhamad, 143
Jazira, 157–158
Joint Technical Committee, 91–92, 96
Justice and Development Party, 91

Khabour River, 155–156
Kurdistan Regional Government, 96
Kurds in Syria, Agrarian reforms, 135, 137, 149
   Arab Belt, 106, 137, 159, 209
   Demographics, 135
   French Mandate, 135
   Jazira, 135, 181
   Kurdish question, 135

Li Ki, 83

maghmurin, 134
Majalla Code, 84, 207
Manu Code, 83
Mearsheimer, John, 28
Memorandum of Understanding with Turkey and Iraq on the Tigris waters, 96

migrants, environmental, 55, 72–73, 199, 235
migration, climate-induced, 25, 68–72, 74, 206
migration, conflict, 56, 59, 61, 68–70, 206
migration, environmental, 36, 38, 72–73
mitigation, climate, 57
migration, HECS, 16, 20
migration, internal, Syria, 65, 75, 104, 138, 144, 152, 159–161, 164, 182, 188, 195–199, 201, 210
migration, Kurds, 135
Mongol invasion, the, 79

National Rainfall Index, 166
neo-Malthusianism, 32–33, 46

Paris School, 30
Partiya Karkaren Kurdistan (PKK), 91–93, 95, 98
Persepolis, 79
policies, ethnocentric, 55
poverty, Syria, 174
power of discourses, 29
precipitations, historic rates, Syria, 165–166
    regional, 167–168
pressure, population, 41
Price Stabilization Fund, 142
Prophet Muhammad, 86

rapprochement, 94
Raqqa, 160
reforms, agrarian10–11, 106
    land, 63–64, 106, 138, 209
    liberalization, 10–11, 104, 138–139, 143–149, 159, 189, 210
refugees, environmental, 70–72
regime, Ba'athist. *See*: Ba'ath
Regional Development Plan, 90
resilience factors, HECS, 18
resilience, 208
Resolution 66/290, 49
resource conflict, 48
resource curse, 35
resource optimists, 33, 42
resource pessimists, 33, 42

riparian states, 45
risk, climate, 8, 55, 207
rural contract, 209

Saleh, Yassin Haj, 189
scarcity, environmental, 33, 38
sectarianization, 10
securitization, process of, 30
security dilemma, 29
security, comprehensive, 27–28
security, environmental, 27–28
security, food, 14, 16, 26, 59, 95, 99, 103, 112, 116, 118–120
security, food security, 14–16, 19–23, 26, 41–42, 48, 59–60, 64, 76, 91, 95, 99, 103–107, 112–113, 116–117, 166
    local understandings, 118–119
    myths, 148
    strategic crops, 120
security, human, 31
security, post-constructivist, 28
security, post-realist, 27
security, water, *see* water security
Sen, Amartya, 18, 49, 60, 64, 174
Servigne, Pablo, 7
Severity Index, Palmer Drought, 154
shafa, 86
Shalalar dam, 79
Shari'a, 84, 88, 207, 231
shirb, 86
Social Market Economy, 140–148
speech-act, security, 30
Standardized Precipitation Index, 167
Stevens, Raphaël, 7
structural factors, HECS, 17
subjects, political, 74
Sustainable Livelihoods Approach, 60
Syrian Association of Economic Sciences, 104, 151, 187, 210, 214–216, 220, 226–227, 230, 233, 236–238
Syrian Revolution, 9–10, 211

temperature variations, Syria, 163–164
threat multiplier, 6

Turkey, interactions over Euphrates, 76, 89–98, 130, 133, 169, 206
  Khabour, 201
  Syrian Kurds, 135–137, 181
  Syrian conflict, 9
threats, environmental, 19

Ul-Haq, Habib, 49
Ul-Haq, Mahbub, 18
United Nations Commission on Sustainable Development, 43
United Nations Development Program, 43
United Nations Environment Program, 43
United Nations Relief and Works Agency, 71
upgrading, authoritarian, 10–11, 148

variability, climate, 56, 58, 65–66, 74, 103
vulnerability factors, HECS, 17
vulnerability, 208
vulnerability, climate, 57–59
vulnerability, economic, Syria, 173–174
vulnerability, environmental, 203
vulnerability, social, Syria, 197–198
vulnerability, state, 65

Walt, Stephen, 28
water availability, Syria, 168–172
water availability, sustainable, 43
water crowding, 43
water deficits, 120, 162, 167, 200
water, groundwater, overpumping, 172–174
water hazards, 43
water management, international, 39
water scarcity, 14
water scarcity, climate induced, 12–14
water security,
  definition, 47–48
  themes, 42
water security, themes, 42
water war, 46–47
wells, country level, 123
  irrigated areas, 124
Whiteford, Scott, 43
Witter, Scott G., 43
Wolfers, Arnold, 27
World Bank, 43, 116, 143, 152, 163, 166, 187, 202, 210, 216, 221, 228, 245
World Health Organization, 43, 170

Lightning Source UK Ltd.
Milton Keynes UK
UKHW021225050722
405333UK00018B/331